Noise

Noise

Living and Trading in Electronic Finance

ALEX PREDA

THE UNIVERSITY OF CHICAGO PRESS   CHICAGO AND LONDON

The University of Chicago Press, Chicago 60637
The University of Chicago Press, Ltd., London
© 2017 by The University of Chicago
Published 2017.
Printed in the United States of America

26 25 24 23 22 21 20 19 18 17   1 2 3 4 5

ISBN-13: 978-0-226-42734-8 (cloth)
ISBN-13: 978-0-226-42748-5 (paper)
ISBN-13: 978-0-226-42751-5 (e-book)
DOI: 10.7208/chicago/9780226427515.001.0001

Library of Congress Cataloging-in-Publication Data

Names: Preda, Alex, 1960– author.
Title: Noise : Living and trading in electronic finance / Alex Preda.
Description: Chicago : The University of Chicago Press, 2017. | Includes bibliographical
    references and index.
Identifiers: LCCN 2016022228 | ISBN 9780226427348 (cloth : alk. paper) |
    ISBN 9780226427485 (pbk. : alk. paper) | ISBN 9780226427515 (e-book)
Subjects: LCSH: Online stockbrokers. | Electronic trading of securities. | Electronic trading
    of securities—Psychological aspects. | Investments—Decision making.
Classification: LCC HG4621 .P74 2017 | DDC 332.640285/4678—dc23 LC record available at
    https://lccn.loc.gov/2016022228

Leporello: Come forward, charming masqueraders!
Don Giovanni: My house is open to everyone. Long live liberty!

—W. A. Mozart, *Don Giovanni*, act 1, scene 20
(libretto by Lorenzo Da Ponte)

Contents

The Ethnography of Noise in Electronic Finance

This is an ethnography of noise in electronic finance. I do not mean noise as the uproar and commotion of trading pits, nor as something annoying, irrelevant, random, or incomprehensible. Neither the literal nor the mundanely metaphorical is my starting point, although both merit a closer look. Nor do I use "noise" here pejoratively. My starting point is the conceptual, the notion of noise (and its empirical manifestations) as defined in Fischer Black's 1985 presidential address to the American Finance Association: "Noise trading provides the essential missing ingredient [to the whole structure of financial markets]. . . . People who trade on noise are willing to trade even though from an objective point of view they would be better off not trading. Perhaps they think the noise they are trading on is information. Or perhaps they just like to trade" (Black 1986, 532).

It is puzzling that an essential structural ingredient of markets is predicated on a metaphor that implies lack of structure. To remember, Black's argument is that noise is the opposite of information, the imperfection intrinsic to our observations (1986, 529) but also a distinction between two categories of market actors, the informed and the noisy (531). Without the latter, the former cannot trade much (533).

Who, then, are these noise traders on whom the informed traders depend so much? While the distinction rests partly on possessing information, or relevant information, it also has to be a structural one.[1] Possessing information, or being informed, cannot be independent of the social fabric of finance. Therefore, noise trading cannot be exclusively related to some abstract, presumably less good, possession of information. Noise trading has to be linked to the arrangements, channels, and processes through which one comes into this possession. These are at the core of the present book. What is this noise trading that provides the essential missing ingredient, and what does it look like in practice? Without noise traders, there is no information; liquidity in the market is low; trading is reduced or comes to a standstill. Without noise traders, prices would not be estimates of value, but value itself (Black 1986, 534). In such an ideal state of the market, everybody would be happy but also very certain of what he or she knows and of what others know, so that there would be no trading.

This can also be read as a foundation myth of markets, something along the lines of the following: in the beginning, there were Gods and there were Mortals. Gods knew everything; they could not trade with other Gods, because all the Gods would always be on the same side of a trade. Mortals did not know much, or they only thought they knew. Hence, Gods could trade only with Mortals, and Mortals traded among themselves too. And so, markets were born.

Noise as a Sociological Problem in Finance

While noise appears to be such a crucial ingredient, it is not a disembodied one. It is not a state of the physical world (like, say, auditory noise) but a property of the social world of markets, as embodied by traders.[2] In finance, the distinction between informed and noise traders has been more often than not equated with the one between professional and retail traders.[3] So there are two codependent social categories, and the codependence itself may sound paradoxical: how could professional traders depend on retail ones? Before becoming professionals, though, traders must have been something else. Perhaps some of them have been retail traders? Or perhaps some professionals eventually become retail traders. As social translations of the conceptual link between information and noise, such questions are worth investigating. Seen from this perspective, the codependency does not seem puzzling anymore. If we are to follow this line of thinking, then we need to spell out, sociologically speaking, the conditions under which markets attract, produce, and maintain such a critical ingredient as noise traders. To think that the latter emerge randomly would be self-defeating. The production of noise cannot be a noisy process, since this would imply the possibility that suddenly, unexpectedly, noise might come to a screeching halt—and markets with it.

Therefore, the production of noise traders has to be a structural feature of markets—in Black's sense—which means it is an orderly social phenomenon. To ensure that there is enough noise (and there are enough noise traders) for markets to work, (1) markets must set in place adequate arrangements for converting nontraders into (noise) traders and for keeping them in the game; (2) trading itself must be connective enough that it can be related to other aspects of the traders' social existence (otherwise, such a conversion could not work); and (3) trading itself must be relational—that is, offer affordances for social relationships among participants (otherwise, noise could not be maintained in an orderly fashion).

These three propositions are a sociological translation—and an extension—of Fischer Black's previously quoted statement. One of their corollaries is that the more active (financial) markets become, the more effort they need to put into producing and maintaining noise traders in an orderly fashion. Another corollary is that when markets switch the medium of their core activity (i.e., the medium of trading), their orderly production of such traders will have to adapt to the new medium as well. I investigate in this book the three propositions that translate and expand Fischer Black's statements, grounded in an ethnography of contemporary electronic markets. I will discuss these two corollaries as well, especially in chapter 1, although the focus here is not historical. The focus is electronic financial markets as they were configured in the first decade of this century and the early years of the second. Methodologically, the book is an ethnography of this apparently virtual realm. Although I do occasionally use statistical data, the bulk of the empirical evidence is provided by direct observations of trading activities, by interviews with traders and brokers, and by communication among traders. This approach provides a close-up, detailed, and systematic access to the activities and the social habitats that make up noise trading. While this ethnographic investigation cannot claim to represent the entirety of noise traders, it claims to identify and represent relevant patterns of activity, acknowledged as such by those who practice them.

Again, the term *noise traders*, which I use here coextensively with *retail traders*, as so many finance studies do, has nothing pejorative to it. It points to the market-internal distinction between two fundamental categories, professionals and nonprofessionals. And while some may argue that I have succumbed to an emic category—that is, a term used by market actors as well as by finance scholars—I investigate not only the social arrangements through which this fundamental category is produced, but also the emergence of the emic concept in relationship to those arrangements.

Ethnographic work of the kind this book is based on is not only about direct observation of trading; the presentation of one's own research to different audiences and the observation of their reactions is integral to it. Of course, one key audience is the traders themselves, and I had to explain to them what I do every time I asked to be granted access, but also many times afterward. Other key audiences are academic ones, from various social science disciplines. As my research took shape, I presented its results to various academic groups from different institutions, according to the general custom in the scholarly world. Presentations, and the audiences' reactions to them, tell me—ethnographically speaking—how a topic is perceived by a particular group and how it is evaluated in relationship to other topics. In other words, What is the most important thing about an issue, as derived from a particular group's reaction to that issue? It is not only appropriate but also relevant at this point to take into consideration how various academic publics have reacted to this very ethnography during its evolution. As is often the case, it's better to start with the criticism: sometimes, reactions of incomprehension involuntarily produce crisis experiments, revealing better the established schemes framing particular issues, schemes that my audiences expected me to follow. The neglect of those schemes, willful or not, is akin to a crisis experiment in which the failure to act according to expectations can provoke irritation and calls to "get your act together." At the same time, such reactions reveal issues that are critical to understanding the phenomenon at hand and which in their turn provide the ethnographer with challenges. In this sense, the critical reactions of audiences can be invaluable pointers to conceptual puzzles. It is with genuine gratefulness that I discuss three such pointers:

Scene one. I am giving a talk to sociology colleagues at a university in the Midwest, about how electronic traders link trading goals with their broader social lives. One member of the audience, who has announced himself from the start as both an academic and a trader, raises his voice in an irritated question: "But you have not mentioned the most important thing: traders are there to make money!"

Scene two. I am giving an expanded and improved version (or so I hoped) of the same talk at a Continental European business school, before an audience of finance scholars. A voice from the public interrupts my talk with an impatient remark: "But what is relevant about them? Can they move markets?" The rest of the audience nods approvingly.

Scene three. I am presenting the same talk at another business school, this time in the United Kingdom, to an audience including both sociologists and finance scholars. At the end of the talk, a colleague and friend asks me: "But don't you have here a sample bias? You have looked at traders who stay in the market. What about those who quit the market forever?"

Moments like these revealed not only what audiences had expected from my talk and how they defined the relevance of noise traders as a topic of discussion. These ways of seeing are informed not only by the perceptions and experiences of a particular group, but also by what counts as a track record of community-relevant issues. They also revealed three genuine puzzles, which I had to confront.

I was being offered precious insights into relevant conceptual schemes about traders. The first scheme is that of means-ends adequacy, where the end is assumed to be the profit ("make money"). The scheme of means-ends adequacy justifies the activity with respect to attaining a specified goal and implies that if the goal isn't realized, the activity will become unjustified, participants will fail, and the activity will have to cease. It is different from the assumption that an activity can be justified as an activity-to-an-end, without the end necessarily being realized, or being realized only occasionally. Amateur fishing, for instance, has "catching fish" as its goal; yet, amateur fishermen can remain fully committed to it even if they catch fish only on very rare occasions. "Catching fish" is intrinsic to the practical definition of the activity of amateur fishing but not an external goal that, if not realized, will make amateur fishing completely cease. In other words, while goals are intrinsic to the definition of activities, sporadic practical accomplishments of the goal will not change the character of the activity or diminish the participants' commitment to it or define participants as failing.[4]

In the means-ends adequacy scheme, trading is a means to the external goal of "making money" or profit. Since trading is an economic activity, it has to be kept apart from interferences coming from the "social" (relationships, family, and so on). Traders are there to make money! There is no relationship between trading strictly speaking and the traders' social lives. This scheme rests on two assumptions: first, an assumption of disconnectedness (the economic and the social are separated—but see Granovetter 1985; Krippner and Alvarez 2007); second, an organizational assumption that work is separated from private lives, one that has come increasingly under scrutiny.[5] Industrial and office work is nine to five and is strictly separated from other domains of life. But trading is not nine to five; trading is around the clock. Trading is not always and not necessarily office work. For a whole series of reasons, it cannot be separated from other aspects of life. Moreover, this conceptual scheme replicates a distinction between market transactions as the site of the "rational" (maximizing utility, making choices based on expected utility, etc.) and other social activities as much less rational (family commitments, relationships, moral obligations among friends, etc.). Traders are there to make money! Electronic trading is a means of making money! Is it? After so many years of ethnographic observations, I thought the jury was still out on that, but some people definitely had fewer doubts.

The real puzzle is that if traders are there "to make money," then we should expect all those traders who lose money to exit markets sooner rather than later and to stay away from them. This would resonate with the third question my audiences raised, regarding a sample bias against failure. Later in my research, I found out that only a small minority of retail traders make money in any consistent fashion. I also learned that the odds of making money were skewed against them, simply because trading is not a cost-free activity. This was not a closely guarded secret. There is a well-established body of finance literature documenting it.[6] It is known among traders and has been confirmed to me by brokers as well. If traders are trading to make money (as an external goal with respect to the practical activity of trading), and if they know only a small minority are making any significant money (in some situations, 1.3%), why don't they quit? What makes them continue trading, not only as they fail to make money with any consistency, but as they know this, together with the fact that only a tiny fraction are making money? Needless to say, this tiny fraction does not mean that one and the same cohort of traders is making money time after time: individual traders can be in and out of luck all the time, yet the tiny fraction of the overall population of traders stays more or less constant. Even during the crisis of 2009–

2010, the number of retail traders did not recede in any significant fashion. Were they there to do something other than making money, at least some of them?

Therefore, a first topic to be dealt with responds directly to this first challenge I was confronted with: why are traders in the market under the given circumstances? We could argue that traders are persuaded or manipulated into engaging in transactions. This would imply not only that we face a formidable persuasion machine, capable of working equally well under various circumstances and in different settings, but also that trading as an activity that by definition implies agency is actually nothing but a very passive yielding to persuasion efforts. What is more, if such a persuasion machine is so formidable, why doesn't it engulf everybody? If that were to happen, the advantages to financial markets would be enormous.

The puzzle is not "Why study noise?" The real puzzle is, "Why is there sustained, long-term noise?" One would expect noise—that is, the presence of retail traders—to subside after a while, when said traders have realized that they cannot make money. One would expect financial markets, the efficiency of which has been praised so many times, to weed out noise, at least in the long run. However, if noise is an essential ingredient in markets, not only will it not be weeded out; it will be produced more or less regularly in an orderly fashion. Not only is there persistent, long-term noise in finance, but, with the advent of electronic markets, this noise appears to grow. Financial economics explains noise persistence in functionalist terms—that is, it says retail traders contribute to liquidity pools (e.g., Greene and Smart 1999; Bloomfield, O'Hara, and Saar 2009). However, contribution to liquidity is a consequence, not a cause, of noise in the markets, nor is it a mechanism for generating noise. The persistent, long-term presence of retail trading should be explained in terms different from its post hoc functionality. Nor can we easily argue that this persistent, long-term presence is the exclusive outcome of persuasion tricks used by brokers and dealers. Statistics about the (lack of) profitability of trading are known among traders, and it is implausible that even the most persuasive advertising could be the sole cause of this persistence. Rather, we need to look into the activity of trading itself to find the reasons for its persistence.

One could say that only the uninformed (weak, impressionable, etc.) engage in trading, while the informed (strong, knowledgeable, etc.) stay out of it. This sort of argument simply reproduces the standard distinction between informed and noise traders; it does not explain anything about how noise is produced in an orderly fashion. The argument that "traders are there to make money," while not grounded in any empirical evidence, actually reproduces assumptions about institutional traders. Indeed, the latter are there to make money, in the sense of being formally expected by their employers to make a profit on the trading capital allocated to them, and are paid a salary (and potential bonuses) for this activity if successful. It would be unwarranted, however, to extend this assumption to all traders.

Instead of assuming that all traders are there exclusively to make money, I will follow the motivations, life circumstances, and projects that bring potential traders to electronic markets. Instead of assuming that how you get into markets is irrelevant with respect to what you are doing there, I will follow the paths leading incipient or potential traders to electronic trading. Instead of assuming a separation between trading and social lives, I will follow the ways in which the two intertwine.

The second challenge, presented to me by colleagues from finance, revealed a different, no less relevant, way of seeing things. Traders, you are worth studying only if you can move markets. "Moving markets" meant in this context "being able to influence the price" of a particular financial instrument. From this perspective, it was definitely not worth studying retail traders, since they do not have at their disposal the gazillions of money that professional traders usually have (or are supposed to have). Later on, when I read about the London Whale, the J. P. Morgan trader who lost $6.2 billion (though nobody knew for sure how much exactly), I could understand better (see Santoro 2013). Everybody likes to go whale watching, but who has ever heard of sardine watching? Majestic size is there to be enjoyed, even if (or perhaps especially because) it can sink billions of other people's money with one flip of the tail (or one bad trade). Noise traders, ordinary people who put their (sometimes meager) savings into a trading account, are no whales. As a research topic, this apparently is the epitome of uncool, guaranteed inattention at every postconference drinks reception.

The fascination with "big" traders stems perhaps not only from the (not infrequent) reports we read in the media about individuals losing billions. Capacity for incurring huge losses is taken as a sure sign of organizational and social importance. It also stems from the assumption that in finance, the phenomena worth studying, the significant ones, are those that make an impact on price movements and hence register in a data set that can be later analyzed by academics. The presence of a transaction as an entry in a data set (to which academics can have access on a subscription basis) is taken as an indicator of its significance. Retail traders rarely fill the bill. Of course, their transactions can be retrieved from the databases of retail brokers, but this is proprietary information not offered to academics on a subscription basis. Otherwise, their transactions are aggregated and transmitted further by electronic brokers, thus getting lost in the continuous stream of data that makes up electronic trading.

The absence of retail traders as a distinct blip in the data sets broadly available to academics is not the only reason for dismissing retail transactions, though: it is widely accepted that institutional traders, who work on behalf of investment banks or hedge funds, have more money, more information, more technology, more knowledge—in a word, more everything—when compared with retail traders. That should make retail trading uninteresting from an academic point of view: while institutional trading is "signals" (that is, meaningful), retail trading is "noise" (to put it euphemistically, less meaningful). Such a distinction has found its way into the vocabulary of financial economics, which has come up with a distinction between signals and noise much replicated nowadays in the talk of brokers and analysts.[7]

If noise is crucial to finance, then taking a closer look at its structure might teach us something about how contemporary markets work. With noise and signal being understood as complementary, we can learn something about the latter by looking at the former. We can learn, for instance, how noise and signal become distinct not only on trading screens, but as career and activity paths in finance. We have no grounds for assuming that the two are separated, just like that. We should rather ask how they are made separate, not only as an institutional process of separating retail brokerages from institutional trading, but also as a process of separating those who become institutional traders from those who become retail traders. What is more, it may well be that within the institutions of finance, institutional and retail traders are not completely separated but meet with and influence each other in more than one way. If so, it is important to investigate how they shape each other's strategies. This should add to our reasons for taking noise as a conceptual avenue into (electronic) finance.

The theoretical assumption of a fundamental (and formal) distinction between the two categories of traders cannot be translated into the representation of a unique empirical setting (the "market") where the two categories are seen as entirely separate. There are actually no conceptual or methodological grounds for jumping from a purely theoretical distinction (overwhelmingly used for modeling purposes) to an empirical assumption. If we abandon the notion of "the market" in favor of the more realistic one—the interconnected trading populations and communities, each with their own characteristics—then we can inquire whether within communities of noise traders some can indeed move prices. This, however, requires departing from a monolithic view of markets in favor of groups and communities with particular social organizations. As a key ingredient of markets, noise has to be socially organized, and I examine this organization in the present book.

The third challenge reveals yet another set of expectations with respect to how electronic finance works: that there will always be exemplary failures, traders who lose their money and are weeded out of the market. Failure should then change attitudes with respect to trading. Failed traders are not expected to return to the market. They have learned a lesson. Thus, markets contain the seeds of their own defeat. Over time, failures will accumulate. Stories of failure will spread. Fewer and fewer people will be willing to engage in trading. The argument works well as long as we equate "failure" with "losing money in the market." This assumption is actually situated within the same conceptual distinction ("informed" versus "noisy") that we encounter in financial scholarship and within the scheme of means-ends adequacy. It is relevant to note here that informed (aka institutional traders) do not quit when they lose (vast sums of) money. They get fired. They get prosecuted. What if the traders' definition of "failure" is a different one? There are always different ways in which one might fail, and losing money isn't necessarily the only one. What if in some situations losing money isn't seen as the main failing at all?

When my friend and colleague asked this question about failure in the market, I almost panicked. In all the years of ethnographic observation, I hadn't discovered any failures! I had met traders who had lost their money, sure, and not just a few. However, I had encountered traders who lost money and came back after a while. I had talked to brokers who told me that on average, a foreign exchange trader stays in the market for three months. Yes, I had not encountered failed traders, in the sense of participants who viewed their experiences as a personal failure. I had not seen the kind of epiphany that teaches a moral lesson about trading. Combine this with the fact discussed before, that only a very small proportion of traders make money from trading over a longer period of time, such as one year. According to this fact, there should be plenty of failures, and I should have seen some epiphanies. Yet, observations told me otherwise.

Perhaps our more narrow understanding of failure does not exactly overlap with the participants' understanding of failure. Perhaps the very activity of trading produces particular understandings of success and failure, understandings that are not reducible to making money. Electronic markets have found ways to reproduce noise, even though the vast majority of participants do not make money consistently over time. So what is success and what is failure from the viewpoint of participants?

After having talked about my research to academic audiences time and again, I was left with a number of puzzles. (Electronic) markets seem to have sustained, long-term noise. Why are retail traders in the market, if a majority of them do not make money consistently? What understandings of success and failure crystallize within trading activities? I decided then to bundle these questions and try to answer them in a book. I know these are not the only questions one can ask about financial markets. They are, however, fundamental issues about how markets work. They address directly the institutional setup through which markets produce and maintain noise, the links between trading and the broader social lives of traders, and social relationships within trading. Taken together, these questions address a key expectation of academic publics, one that has been formulated in many interventions after my talks: that supposedly uninformed, less knowledgeable retail traders should not trade at all. I have been told this many times, not only as a theoretically motivated expectation, but also as a normative and ethical expectation. Retail traders should not trade. And yet they do. What is the secret? How do markets manage to keep them trading?

Talking to and about Traders

On one occasion during my fieldwork, I discovered that I was not the only social scientist investigating retail traders. I met my competition at a trade show. As I was patiently sitting in the audience and taking notes on the speakers telling us how to be good, successful traders, I suddenly noticed that the person taking the pulpit was an academic whose name

I knew. Sure enough, the speaker came from a different discipline, yet one that was not far away from mine. I knew some of the speaker's published work, which addressed academic publics. This time, however, the colleague in question was talking to a group of traders (including one ethnographer) about how to become better traders. The first image projected for our benefit was that of a lion crouching among the tall grasses of the African savannah, supposedly stalking his prey. The analogy was not hard to decipher. We were told from the start that we should take that lion as an example and wait patiently for the prey (read: the profitable trade) to come closer. More images like this followed, and the feeling we had—being compared to lions—was supposed to be a positive one. Not every speaker I have witnessed has compared retail traders with big cats! After the presentation, the speaker invited us all to sign up for a research experiment; this was organized by a firm that specialized in data collection for research projects, and the firm had set up a desk in the foyer of the conference venue. (To be honest, I counted the people in the room and then went to see how many had signed up.)

It later occurred to me that using the image of a predator stalking the prey essentially told the audience that markets are a force of nature, devoid of ethics and consisting of predators and prey. Other presenters at trade shows—usually not academics—sometimes use similar language, resorting to war imagery. I once heard the president of a trading club compare himself with "a battle manager, an RAF fighter controller." He said, "Beneath the gentle soft exterior beats the heart of a natural born killer" whose mission was to "help you find out who you are as a trader." Such a view is questionable, even more so perhaps when coming from corners of academia. In the particular situation, though, I was suddenly made aware that I was not the only one trying to observe and investigate trading and traders. Not only that, but I was not the only one trying to tell traders, and others as well, what they were really like. I had just witnessed an attempt to tell traders that they were like crouching lions, lying low in the grass and waiting for the prey. This made me think of what anthropologists had been discussing for quite a while under the banner of "the problem of representation" (Marcus 1980; Marcus and Cushman 1982; Clifford 1983; Clifford and Marcus 1986). Simply put, this means that social scientists assume the authority and the expertise to tell various publics (including here said subjects) the real nature of the subjects they study, or what their nature should be. Both text and images are used to these ends. Social scientists also employ text and images to put a distance between them and the subjects they study, as a way of displaying objectivity and, in some cases, to assert superiority as well.

The photograph of the crouching lion in the savannah, evoking an exotic, unfamiliar landscape, made me think of all the images anthropologists had used earlier to present their subjects as exotic and far away: photographs of unfamiliar masks, ritual dances, painted bodies, and the like. In the photograph we had all seen, supposedly advanced electronic financial markets were reduced to something as simple and primitive as a predator waiting patiently for the prey. This reduction enabled the social scientist in question to distance himself from the audience (the potential subjects of his studies), while at the same time inducing a sense of superiority (they were predators) and predefining trading for everyone's benefit.

When I realized that I was not the only social scientist observing retail traders and trying to tell them about themselves, I started thinking, Who else might be doing a similar thing? We have not just one mode of representing our traders, but several: not only books and academic articles, but also photographs, diagrams, Power Point slides, and media interviews (social scientists love them, too), to name but a few. And we are addressing not just one kind of public, but several: we address our academic peers, but also broader informed publics and the traders themselves. When I mentioned to traders that I was writing a book about them, they showed interest and were eager to learn about (other) traders. They were trusting me, a stranger, to describe other people doing similar things. And we social scientists were not the only ones trying to tell traders who they were. We were just a small group among many.

I will therefore need to try to systematize a little when talking about those who talk both about traders and in the name of traders. Why not start with my own tribe of social scientists? There are several academic families among them, the most prestigious of whom are probably economists and psychologists (although the latter are sometimes seen as belonging to the natural sciences). I have witnessed firsthand at some of my talks how economists think about and represent retail traders: as lacking financial resources (and hence the information, the know-how, and the technology) required to move markets. Retail traders should not be there at all. I have also witnessed how some psychologists represented traders: as incapable of mastering their own emotions and therefore not capable of making a kill. By implication (and by opposition as well), professional traders were considered to have both resources and the sang froid necessary to make (ideally) large and consistent profits. During my research, however, I also attended the presentation of a law firm that included a list of the 10 biggest losses made by professional traders over the past two decades. When I added them up, the sum was bigger than the GDP of many countries. I wasn't that convinced anymore that professional traders were so much better than retail traders.

More relevant, perhaps, is to ask this question: based on what kind of evidence, and what assumptions, and for which publics do academic tribes talk about noise traders? A first audience is, of course, their own and other related academic communities. A second audience is practitioners from the financial industries; and a third is what we call the "general public," usually imagined as the readership of newspaper and magazine articles, blogs, and interviews.

While genres can vary according to audiences—ranging from academic articles and books to consultancy papers, talks, and interviews—we can usually distinguish at least three types of evidence and three types of problems that are usually present in talks to academic audiences. A first type of evidence is provided by the traces left by traders—price and volume data of their past transactions, mostly—which have been recorded in data sets. Such sets can be bought or subscribed to; they can also be proprietary (belonging to a brokerage, for instance, which will agree to make them available to a researcher). Since most, if not all, data about noise traders is proprietary, a good number of studies using trading data have focused on institutional traders, the transactions of which are captured in, for instance, the data sets of the New York Stock Exchange, the London Stock Exchange, or the Chicago Mercantile Exchange. (Such data are either publicly available or sold to researchers by data providers.) Studies of noise traders based on quantitative data are relatively few and recent.[8] Since researchers need considerable computing power to process such data (making the analysis more costly), often only a reduced subset (e.g., based on fewer traders or over a shorter period, or both) will be examined.

A second type of evidence is experimental or survey-based. Data can include profits made and losses sustained during the duration of the experiment, neurophysiological data, and also opinions and attitudes expressed in a questionnaire.[9] Since it is easier to find institutional traders in situ for a quasi-naturalistic experiment (one only has to get access to a trading floor), existing trading experiments have been performed mostly on institutional traders or on students (e.g., Bloomfield, Taylor, and Zhou 2009). Experimental data come from much smaller groups than those included in large sets of transaction data (usually up to 100 participants, while a large data set can easily include millions of transactions). A third type of data—different in nature from the first two—consists of direct observations and interviews with traders and other financial workers, necessarily conducted in a limited number of local settings.[10] Forcefully, the bulk of this information comes from institutional traders, and, though it is very valuable, its production and extraction are molded on the template of a few ethnographic loci.

One of the first things to be noticed here is that the vast majority of data—whether quantitative or qualitative—is from institutional traders, which leaves "noise" mostly in the shadows. We should either treat the noise as irrelevant—which runs counter to a major theoretical assumption—or, if not, as similar to informed trading, about which we know more. If we cast the two as similar, we run into conceptual and methodological difficulties, since informed traders should be different from noise traders. At the same time, these three kinds of data serve different theoretical aims and assumptions. Quantitative data about price, volume, and types of transactions can be used to analyze the internal structure and dynamics of trading (e.g., the structure of the order flow), from which behavioral aspects can be inferred, based on the assumption that behavioral patterns are identifiable from their decisional outcomes. Experimental data serve more to link patterns of decision making with underlying neurological mechanisms or to analyze the former as individual cognitive processes. Observational and interview data allow studying social relationships, processes, and rationalizations thereof as present in trading activities, though not always in direct connection to particular acts of trading. Relevant here, however, is that noise traders have an ambiguous position: empirically, for a host of reasons, they are treated as derivative, or at best as similar to institutional traders. Theoretically, though, this doesn't lead to a reconceptualization where noise does not have to be substantially different anymore. In the end, we are left with a tension between the available empirical evidence, on the one hand, and theoretical assumptions, on the other hand.

Academics, however, are not the only ones telling noise traders how they should be. Whole armies of education providers take the pulpit at trade fairs, rent stalls or broadband capacity, and seem dedicated to telling retail traders how they can improve in what they are doing. The fact that we don't see this happening with institutional traders should already tell us that some significant differences might be at work here. More often directly than just by implication, these "educators" also tell traders what they actually are like. It is not very difficult to guess what the evaluation is: far, far from perfection. While using different rhetorical styles and different, more or less friendly ways of addressing their audiences, education providers offer seminars, coaching hours, and lectures dedicated to the betterment of traders. If there is so much room for improvement, traders must be assumed to be uneducated. During my ethnographic observations, I have witnessed self-styled educators shouting at, praising, insulting, cajoling, and flattering traders, but all without exception told the traders that they needed a proper trading education (I am going to talk more about this later in the book).

Another category of people telling traders what they are like and what they need is salespeople, of course. Education providers sell seminars and coaching hours; salespeople sell trading software and trading accounts. Of course they have to tell potential clients how buying their software or opening an account with this or that brokerage will make said traders much better off. While talking to salespeople at trade fairs or investigating the websites of electronic brokerages, I have often left my name, e-mail address, and telephone number. Sure enough, for a while I was being telephoned every workday, at least once a day, by salespeople trying to persuade me to open an account with them. Even when I told them that the suggested transactions seemed pretty risky to me, or that I was skeptical about the possibility of making a great deal of money, they insisted with their pitch (which, I must say, is different from that of educators). The implication was that retail traders were either in constant need of money or very greedy indeed.

These experiences showed that various groups with different agendas were engaged in telling traders about themselves. Whether with the aim of selling them something, of recruiting them for the purposes of a study, or with a (genuine?) intention of contributing to their betterment, these groups insisted that they knew better.

And here I am, with an ethnographic book telling publics what trading and traders are like. I have tried to understand what trading means by asking traders about what they do, but also by observing them in action and by trying to replicate these actions myself over several months. I have let traders use their own voice, while fictionalizing all proper names. I have made an exception here with Joe Ricketts, the founder of Ameritrade, because of the unique character (and hence easy recognizability) of the technological developments he talks about. I reproduce, sometimes copiously, from the conversations traders had with me. Even if I ask a good number of conceptual questions, I don't intend here to confront traders with any normative model about who they should be and what they should do. I do not make judgments about whether they move markets or about their supposedly not being knowledgeable enough. I have no images of crouching tigers or dragons to offer, and no medicine, image-based or otherwise. Mine is a scaffolding made of conversations, observations, and direct experiences, a scaffolding that I hope offers a different vantage point from which to view the puzzles at the core of this book.

The Ethnography of Noise

I have tried to take a close-up look at what traders and brokers really do by sitting next to them and observing their on-screen trading activities, for hours at a time, and by talking to them in a systematic fashion. I was lucky enough to be able to start these observations in Edinburgh, where I was based at the beginning of this research in October 2005. After a while, I thought that was not enough: I should talk more to traders. I went out to find retail traders; I talked about my research with those I found and persuaded many of them to talk more extensively about what they were doing. This took me mostly to London, New York, and Chicago, where I conducted many of my interviews. But on occasion, while traveling in eastern Europe, I encountered brokers and retail traders willing to tell me more about their trading, and I seized these occasions as well.

Eventually I realized that interviewing traders, though very useful, was not enough. I thought I should try trading myself. I had been to numerous classes and presentations organized by brokerages, and I had attended webinars and demonstrations as well. I thought I should give it a try, and so, in the fall of 2009 and then again in 2010, I signed up with two electronic platforms and traded for three months and two weeks, respectively, while keeping a detailed, minute-by-minute journal of what I was doing. I should warn readers that this book is not about how to trade successfully. I wasn't a particularly good trader; I did it only to gain firsthand experience of how electronic trading works. Nevertheless, in the process I learned a few things that helped me not only understand the logic of trading but also communicate better with other traders.

When I was well advanced into interviewing traders, I thought I should interview institutional traders and analysts also, so that I could understand better where the differences between the two lie. This took me back to New York and to Chicago, two of the major centers where financial technology companies are based (the third being London). I went to the trading pits of Chicago, only to discover that they have been affected by technology too, and that different groups of traders viewed each other with various degrees of technology-related suspicion. I interviewed institutional traders and analysts. During a longer stay in Chicago, I started looking into how electronic trading had developed from the 1970s to our days. This took me to the issue of how electronic trading platforms work and how trades are executed. I sought out and talked to electronic brokerage houses and software developers.

Institutions like brokerage houses and technology companies have regular conventions, so I attended those as well. Not only did I learn from presentations about issues and developments within electronic trading; I also met professionals who were willing to help me with my research. Soon enough, I noticed that there were shows dedicated to retail traders. I went to these too, from California to New York to London. These were great occasions not only for meeting traders and learning about trading technologies, but also for understanding how the whole industry works.

On some occasions, while attending professional conferences, I also encountered protests and protesters against the world of finance. This was the autumn of 2011, when movements like Occupy Wall Street were at their zenith. While I encountered protesters outside conference halls, I only once witnessed one individual criticism in the conference room after a presentation. I observed and talked to protesters as well, trying to see how critics of finance understood what was going on within the world they protested against. And, as I already said, I gave several talks before colleagues from the academy, where I was confronted with how scholars of finance understood what was going on in the world they were studying. Interestingly enough, during this process I also talked to brokers who had social scientists for clients, so I got a glimpse into how the world of finance perceives academics when they become traders.

During these trips, notebooks filled up and documents accumulated from conferences, as well as from reading trade publications about computer technologies in finance. Audio files stacked up from interviews, together with some video recordings of trading activities. After several years of research, I have a hard drive overflowing with audio files, interview transcripts, and electronic documents, stacks of paper documents, envelopes stuffed with business cards from the conferences I attended, and eight thick field notebooks. (I also became particularly picky about and fond of the notebooks I use.) All these notebooks, files, and documents contain the substance of my ethnographic investigation of electronic markets, of the journey undertaken as an answer to the question, What does it mean for ordinary people to be traders, and how are they made into traders?

Some might say that this scaffolding and the vantage points it offers do not necessarily allow a big, panoramic view, for instance on financialization, or on markets, understood as broad, encompassing diagnoses of how the economic world has changed and the implications thereof. Topics like financialization have been understood mostly as institutional changes affecting, among other things, the ways corporations operate, the growing importance of financial operations as centers of profit for the corporations, or the centrality of the financial services sector in developed economies (e.g., Krippner 2005; Lapavitsas 2011; van Treeck 2009). As far as I can see, little has been said about financialization seen from below, about how financial markets and trading activities affect the lives of ordinary people who engage with them (but see Martin 2002). Similarly, more often than not, social scientists like to look at financial markets as a more or less encompassing institutional landscape that should include almost everything possible. In a manner akin to that of eighteenth-century panoramic landscape painting, one can see all the paths, buildings, roads, bridges, canals, vessels, and carriages, but one cannot see the people very well, because they appear as little dark dots.

The vantage point I take here is that of trading as social action—its situational character, its relationality, its affordances,[11] and its consequences. This is no less meaningful for understanding what markets are and how they work. Having traveled along with traders, I will ask readers to undertake the journey with me and the traders I have met. I have not spent time with all the hundreds of thousands of retail traders who have accounts with brokerage houses.[12] While I do not make claims about the generalizability of the actions I discuss here for all the traders who are out there, I make claims about their typicality. I do not aim to show readers what a majority or a minority of traders do in electronic markets, but what traders typically do in markets. Hence, this is neither a mere travelogue, nor an account of past actions, nor a statistical description of what particular percentages would do on average. It is an account of the ways of doing things in electronic markets, ways that appear to be typical to those who follow them. And it is told together with those who have followed and are following these ways.

What Does It Mean to Observe Electronic Finance?

When I began my research in October 2005, I was fascinated by the trading screens: their flickering, colored numbers, continuously moving up and down, were a brave new world in itself. It was flat and shiny and apparently so much smoother than the real world of face-to-face interactions, with all its edges and uneven surfaces. Forget the shouts in the trading pits, the sweat, the eye contacts, the hand signs, the sharp elbows, the paper strips littering the floor. . . . Everything was shiny, smooth, and flickering. Dealing with the smooth, the shiny, and the flickering has come to represent what is usually called virtual ethnography or netnography.[13]

The growing awareness that Internet activities and their interaction formats are not quite like face-to-face activities has led many social scientists to look for ways of doing ethnography that do justice to the novelty of the Internet phenomenon. In a way similar to that of classical ethnographers, who spent longer periods of time in rather isolated, remote, and unfamiliar communities, virtual ethnographers recommend becoming immersed in the world of online communication, within networks of "friends," blogs, and tweets, to work out their particularities (e.g., Beneito-Montagut 2011).

Such immersion is predicated on the assumption that, like the villages studied by classical ethnographers, online communities are remote and isolated from face-to-face communication. They are remote in the sense that online communication bears little resemblance to mundane conversations anchored in physical copresence, and they are isolated in that there is little by way of exchanges or flows between online and face-to-face communication (e.g., Wenhong 2013; Gulbrandsen and Just 2011; Boellstorff 2009). It is much more difficult to credibly perform an assumed identity in a face-to-face encounter than in a virtual one, for instance. Yet, this is not impossible: we can find many instances of impersonation in face-to-face interactions as well. A more important point, perhaps, is that online communication formats such as instant messaging have a different structure from natural—that is, oral—conversations (Menchik and Tian 2008; Welser et al. 2007). Talk does not flow in the same way in a mundane, face-to-face chat and in a chat room. Face-to-face gossip, for instance, places more severe constraints on communication by (for one thing) a stricter allocation of speaking rights in the form of turns.

These differences, together with some others, can give the impression that online communication is not only remote from its face-to-face counterpart, but isolated as well. Face-to-face identities are carefully kept apart from online identities, and, in many instances, activity formats, interests, and occupations are kept separate. An example here is provided by role-playing fantasy games, which are an overwhelmingly online activity bearing little connection with the face-to-face occupations, professions, and social situations of participants.

It would seem, then, that online worlds require virtual ethnographies, understood as participative immersions in electronic communication formats, to the near exclusion of face-to-face participant observation. The ethnographer should go online and participate in chat forums and messaging systems, inventory the array of screen names and chat topics available on the net, record the types of photographs and information posted on social networking sites, and decode e-mails and tweets as new communicative genres. When I started observing traders in their activities, I soon discovered that there were a great number of chat forums dedicated to trading; trading journals posted on the net; and opinions, commentaries, traders blogging and tweeting under assumed screen names. I could have filled all those years to the brim with just reading the posts in trading chat forums.

I definitely spent time reading the posts and reading trading journals, and yes, I subscribed to traders' tweets. To do be able to do that, I had to set up my own tweeting account, from which I never tweeted. I also quickly discovered that many people were following my nonexistent tweets. Chat forums, tweets, journals, and the like contained valuable information. And yet, a few questions kept arising time and again: In what ways are all these activities consequential with respect to trading? Is that all there is to electronic trading? In other words, trading, electronic or not, implies making decisions and taking actions, with very concrete consequences. I was observing a particular type of actions, namely chats. My ultimate interest, however, was a different type of actions, the screen clicks by which buy and sell orders were sent from a computer terminal to a remote server. How could I reconstitute the link, if any, between forum posts and buy and sell orders?

If I looked only at forum posts and tweets, I was going to have some difficulties with following this link. In addition, there were a few other questions that I deemed important but which could not be answered so easily if I spent my time only in chat forums. For instance, How does one become a trader? Are there any set paths or ways to achieve this? How does the whole technological setup of trading work? With whom are traders actually trading? And many more questions of these sorts. There must be something outside and beyond chat forums and tweets, something that supports all this.

In trying to find answers to these questions, I started interviewing traders and brokers and software developers, and their answers pointed to phenomena and modes of interaction that were not virtual at all, but continued to keep the old-fashioned format of face-to-face encounters. My ethnographic observations became less and less virtual as I started attending various meetings, conferences, and trade shows (and sometimes protest meetings as well) that stubbornly continued to require participants to meet in person, sometimes traveling considerable distances. At the same time, I began attending more and more webinars, interaction formats that differed substantially from chat rooms and in which participants interacted through speech and visual displays. Some of the webinars were informational, and some were live trading sessions, in which audiences connected in real time with a remote trader and observed his transactions, while being able to ask questions. I started observing real-time chats among traders too, and discovered that these were far more important with respect to trading decisions than forum posts.

All in all, my ethnographic journey took me across a rich variety of communication and interaction formats that were relevant for and constitutive with respect to electronic markets. Yes, these latter were not strictly virtual: some substantial activities took place face-to-face, and there were few if any signs that they were going to be replaced with anything else. Becoming a trader, for instance, is still dependent on particular institutional arrangements (I am going to talk more about these) that rely on face-to-face interactions.

Was my virtual ethnography regressing to a more classical format?

Well, for starters, I had never planned to label it in any particular way. My aim was to analytically understand how electronic markets work, not to affix a label on a particular set of methods. Yet, during this participative work, it became clear to me that electronic markets do not exist simply on shiny computer screens and that it is not nearly enough to go into chat forums to understand what is going on. It also became clear that electronic markets are socially very rich: they are not arrangements that sweep out social life and interactions in favor of uber-anonymous, hyperrational, and ultraefficient exchanges.

If anything, the opposite is true: electronic financial markets have more social life than one might think. This life, however, is not "virtual" as opposed to a real one; it is a mix of various communication formats using different tools and anchored in specific institutional arrangements. Some parts are indeed located on shiny computer screens, but some very important parts are not. What characterizes the social life of electronic markets is not its virtuality, but much more the differentiation and specialization of various communication formats within which specific transaction-relevant activities are performed. In dealing with the challenges presented by online activities to how we think about basic notions such as human interactions and situations, Karin Knorr Cetina (2009, 63) has suggested the notion of synthetic situation. It designates the environments constituted mainly (though not exclusively) by on-screen projections to which participants respond. Synthetic situations are interaction formats characterized by temporal coordination and by the response presence of participants. Another notion put forward for the characterization of online realms has been that of synthetic worlds (Castronova 2005, 4), which emphasizes consequentiality. Synthetic worlds may exist on computer screens and server hard drives, but actions undertaken within these worlds have consequences outside these narrow boundaries. The consequences of actions within synthetic worlds are not entirely self-contained (e.g., playing online games can have consequences outside the world of the game). Thus, we have at least two criteria by which to evaluate action: the interaction format within which it unfolds and the consequentiality of this action.

Seen this way, electronic finance can be characterized as synthetic, in that it comprises online and off-line activities and institutional formats geared toward producing not only a particular type of copresence, but also transactional activities, the consequences of which lie outside the realm of temporally coordinated copresences.

If we compare the ethnography of online markets with the ethnography of classical, floor-based ones, perhaps the main differences can be summarized in this way: more often than not, ethnographies of classical financial markets implied getting access to an organization—that is, being allowed to spend time in a trading room or on a trading floor for a few months, to talk to the employees and, if one was lucky enough, perhaps to do (more or less demanding) clerical jobs as well. (In rare instances, one could advance to being a trader, too.) In the trading room or on the trading floor, people shouted, ran around, exchanged glances, communicated through hand signs, and so on. Everything was in one place, where the dominant mode of communication was face-to-face. Such a hard-to-access place was connected to other hard-to-access places, which were run similarly or, in any case, in a fashion recognizable as such by participants.

The ethnography of electronic markets cannot be limited to (hard-to-get) access to a single organization operating a trading floor, pit, or room (see also Marcus 1995; Falzon 2009). Nor does it imply observing face-to-face communication as the unique or the dominant mode. The ethnography of electronic markets requires getting access to various interconnected organizations, ranging from trading groups to electronic brokerage houses to software developers to data warehouse operators to upgraded trading pits to exchange platforms. These organizations are mostly spread around the (economically developed) world. None of them concentrate all relevant activities, but each of them includes substantially relevant activities. Face-to-face communication is not dominant everywhere, but it is still substantially relevant. Along with it, there are other relevant modes of communication, including both written and verbal interactions conducted online. Ethnographers do not, perhaps, need to spend an equal amount of time in each organization, but they need to spend time with each of them and allocate the bulk of observational time according to the questions they investigate.

Perhaps a good analogy would be with the loci of classical ethnographies: trading rooms, floors, or pits are akin to a traditional village situated in a clearing in the rain forest, where buildings are huddled together, so that the ethnographer can go from one building to the next while staying within the cleared patch in the forest. Electronic markets are like villages scattered throughout the rain forest; the ethnographer has to find his way through the thicket, from one building to the next (which might be a few miles away), knowing that they all host relevant activities. Some villagers know some paths, while some others know some other paths. With their help, the ethnographer will hopefully find as many paths as possible, but he will spend different amounts of time on them. The paths may look different from one another, and so do the various parts of the rain forest they cut through. Nevertheless, they have to be traveled; I had to learn how these sites link together and how and where they cross each other. I had to try to understand how they are organized and what makes them tick.

For instance, I had to understand how electronic brokerages work in order to understand how they respond to the transactions placed by traders. Such a brokerage, which may be incorporated in the Caribbean (for a variety of legal and procedural purposes, including but not limited to tax advantages), headquartered on Mediterranean shores, with the chief programmer residing on (and working from) the Pacific Rim, with its financial backers on the East Coast and in the northern parts of the European continent, with its trading data on the Amazon cloud, and with its traders spread across 12 to 14 time zones, epitomizes the synthetic character of the market: all coordination has to be temporal (though not all interactions are online), and the consequences of action undertaken along different paths constantly ripple outside the brokerage's world.

Once I understood what happened with the transactions placed by traders, things became much clearer. I had to do all this to grasp consequentiality—that is, how certain actions undertaken on specific paths and at specific sites within a brokerage have consequences with respect to what will happen next within and outside it. I also had to understand the logic of action at specific sites—what it means, for instance, to calculate a trade from the numbers on-screen—and what kinds of communication can support it. I had to understand the very real constraints under which traders operate, but also the ways in which they try to avoid such constraints, or make them work to their advantage.

Seeing my task this way, I could not be limited to observing the screen in my ethnography of electronic markets. During the fieldwork, I went back many times to rereading Erving Goffman, to remind myself to look for "where the action is." For Goffman (1967, 194), action is "wherever the individual knowingly takes consequential chances perceived as avoidable." The locus of action would be the trading screen, because it is there that consequential chances are taken. We should perhaps introduce here a distinction between participation and engagement in action, understood in this sense. Traders engage in action; the software engineers, salespeople, lawyers, and venture capitalists who make possible the organizational setup of trading participate in but do not engage in action. They participate in it because they have to make sure that trading platforms are functional, that orders are registered in the order book and queued up, that spreads are in place (and that they are the right spreads), that the software works, and so on—a myriad of mundane aspects without which engagement in action would not be possible. Meeting fate in action is mostly a carefully orchestrated date, not a random encounter.

An Overview of the Book

In the first chapter, I examine the history and institutional development of retail trading from the 1960s until our days, paying special attention both to the technological developments that marked the transition to electronic trading in the mid to late 1990s and to the place of retail brokerages within the institutional structure of financial markets. The focus is on institutional developments in the United Kingdom and the United States, and I look more closely at three kinds of processes: the evolution and diversification of retail brokerages in relationship to trading technologies; regulatory regimes and changes after the crisis of 2008; and the evolution of the client structure of retail brokerages in relationship to online trading. I argue that in the 1980s retail brokerages introduced or adopted technological innovations meant to increase the frequency with which their customer base was trading, since theirs were clients different from the typical, more affluent, buy-and-hold investor. This technological trend continued in the 1990s, when the first online trading platforms emerged. Technological innovation combined with product innovation, often supported by firms from the gambling industry crossing over into financial services. The creation of financial products tailored to retail traders and to more frequent trading was accompanied by a regulatory regime that also encouraged trading frequently (e.g., via a favorable taxation regime and high leverage). Between 2000 and 2010, the demographic structure of retail trading populations began to shift toward younger age groups, while income spreads grew larger.

Chapter 2 examines the links between noise and institutional trading from the viewpoint of each one's capacity to morph into the other. While noise and institutional trading are usually regarded as conceptually separate, I show here that there are practical circumstances in which they mutually support and reproduce each other. I show, for instance, how financial institutions encourage noise trading as a recruiting ground and how former institutional traders and finance professionals craft second careers for themselves in retail brokerages and advisory firms. Overall, my argument is that from an institutional point of view, noise and institutional trading are not completely separate and that transitions from one domain into the other regularly take place.

Chapter 3 looks at an aspect deemed to be crucial with respect to market transactions: trading competitions. Yet, while this textbook definition is often predicated upon market activities, in practice it is exercised mostly in a carefully managed, staged way. I investigate here trading competitions as a regular feature of trading shows and conventions (including professional ones) and ask why they are so significant as dramatic displays, when in the practice of trading, we rarely (if ever) encounter purely competitive moments, simply because the institutional setup does not allow competition. I argue that competitions as dramatic displays are organized to solve moral issues related to trading.

Chapter 4 examines the act of online trading itself—what it means, from the viewpoint of the trader, to use an online technology to conduct financial transactions. I describe in this chapter what happens when traders place orders on their screens, both how that order is handled within the institutional and technological infrastructure of electronic brokerages and how traders perceive their activities. While the orders placed by traders are not always matched against each other, the trading screen is geared toward producing a necessary illusion of relationality— that is, of relating to other traders. I investigate how various experiences of using the trading screen are articulated and how social hierarchies are produced in this process. I highlight forms of observation and action that are not necessarily egalitarian. I examine the types of actions that constitute trading and the ways in which they are shaped by the inherent relationality of the trading screen.

Chapter 5 investigates forms of collaborative activities in online trading. While a common image of trading in electronic markets is that of relentless, individualized, and atomistic competition, retail traders constantly collaborate with each other in trading. They communicate while trading, and they build groups in order to solve specific, trading-related issues. I examine here communication among traders and their group activities, arguing that both the institutional setup and the format of electronic trading make such collaborations necessary. Online collaborations enable observation and the formation of shared pools of experience as the basis of decision making.

Chapter 6 asks: What does it mean for traders to have a trading strategy? The trading strategy is predicated as a major component of decision making in trading, and every trader is supposed to have or develop one. Strategies are the object of much online communication; they are seen more as transient prescriptions than stable principles of action. I investigate in this chapter to what degree traders really stick with or follow particular strategies, how they understand strategies, and why strategies are not kept secret but are revealed to others. Continuing a line of argument initiated in chapter 4, I look at the ritualization of strategies and the ways in which they are used to consolidate hierarchies among traders. While chapter 5 deals with collaborative communication among traders, chapter 6 shows how strategies are used as tools and tropes of individualization, to produce (the illusion of) autonomous, individualized decision makers in trading.

Chapter 7 leaves the realm of trading strictly speaking and returns to the broader context in which it takes place. While the introductory chapters examined the institutional context of noise trading, I discuss here the place this activity occupies in the broader social lives of traders. How is noise trading integrated with the traders' family life and friendships? What do traders aim to achieve by trading, socially speaking? Has trading changed them in any way as persons? What motivates them to trade? In the ways traders talk about what they are doing, surprisingly little pertains to utilitarian motives, and there is a constant preoccupation to relate this activity—admittedly not a very usual one—to their broader social lives. What does this relationship look like?

The conclusion takes up one more time the conceptual question of noise trading as a key ingredient of markets. Why do financial markets need noise? Is it all about creating pools of liquidity? The liquidity produced by noise trading, while significant, is not necessarily indispensable to markets. Noise trading is far from random; it is socially organized, institutionally maintained, and reproduced in ways that do not fit the carefully promoted view of a competitive spirit. Its puzzle is social rather than simply a matter of reproducing capital, especially since noise traders make sense of what they do in nonutilitarian terms. In the conclusion I try to solve the double puzzle of why markets need noise trading and why people willingly and continuously engage in this not-very-usual activity.

As I stated in the opening of this introduction, my aim is to translate a finance puzzle sociologically—both in theoretical and in empirical terms. I hope that the following chapters will persuade readers that such a translation is productive.

CHAPTER ONE

Noise in Financial Markets

During my ethnographic journey, I heard a good number of academics say that noise trading is to a large extent tied to the "day trader" phenomenon of the late 1990s, which in its turn was conjoined at the hip with the "dotcom bubble" and the "Internet mania" from about 15 years ago. Often, when I presented my research to academic audiences in the years 2005 to 2010, whether the scholars were from sociology, from accounting, or from finance, one of the first reactions was "Oh, you are dealing with day traders!" Among colleagues from finance, this comment had a slightly dismissive undertone, which could also be attributed to the perceived ephemeral and superficial character of the "day trader." For most of the decade beginning in 2000, day traders were considered to have been buried under the ruins left behind by the "Internet mania." Overall, this might have been a temporary and mildly interesting phenomenon in the late 1990s, but it was gone for good—or, if still present, it was completely insignificant.

Closer to 2010, newspaper reports were signaling with some degree of surprise "the comeback of the day trader." Within a little more than a year, from March 2008 to July 2009, stories published in Canada, Australia, the United Kingdom, and Kenya were reporting individual traders who wanted not just to trade, but to make a living out of trading (see also Yenkey 2015, 565).[1] This was much more ambitious than just earning a few dollars of additional income. Although there is no official definition, making a living from trading implies earning consistently, and earning an amount of money that should be at least equal to the minimum (if not the average) income of a trader's country.

At least as relevant is that such an assumption implies not only regular but very frequent trading, as well. It is difficult to imagine "making a living from trading" for somebody who, say, buys or sells every year just a few financial instruments. This distinguishes trading from activities like investing, which may be singular, irregular, or regular, but not frequent. The notion of investor implies a low frequency of participation in transactions, while that of trader implies both regularity and high frequency.

The prominent trope in the public discourse was thus that day trading (and now retail trading) is new *and* surprising (many were expecting it to die off when the Internet bubble burst). Another, closely related, trope was that it is inextricably tied to the Internet as the main if not the only explanatory factor. This is akin to a Big Bang theory: the advent of the Internet triggers the emergence and the spread of noise in the financial system. This theoretical necessity does not square with the trope of novelty or with that of the Internet as the sole (or the dominant) causal factor. If noise (aka day or retail) traders are a theoretical necessity, it means that, empirically, the conditions of their sustained presence and maintenance in the financial system should be created by the system itself. In turn, this means that we should look first and foremost at those institutional developments (including technological but also regulatory ones) that not only provide retail traders with affordances for being what they are and for doing what they are doing,[2] but also create the very position of "noise." In other words, this latter is not a (more or less desirable) by-product of general technological developments but is intrinsic to financial institutions.

This does not necessarily mean that only financial institutions create affordances for retail traders and that the latter are completely devoid of agency. If we look at technological developments, for instance, and especially at how trading platforms emerge, we see that there is a great deal of initiative on the part of individual traders-cum-developers and that the financial services industry is initially somewhat slow to respond, but when it does, such developments are absorbed into the technological infrastructure of trading. Nor does this mean that these affordances are created according to a blueprint. In some instances, institutional changes intended to deal with issues of global institutional competition have spillover effects for retail trading. In other instances, the technological infrastructure created for institutional trading needs to adapt to ongoing developments and challenges by including provisions for retail traders as well, or by attempting to define the boundaries between retail and institutional trading.

I have said above that the financial system creates affordances for retail traders. I have purposely avoided using the notion of opportunity, which can be understood as merely a convenient occasion for action, a convenience that can be transformed into something more systematic. Viewing the Internet as the cause of day trading would mean it was something of an opportunity. As I use it here, the term *affordance* denotes a match between opportunities (provided by financial institutions and technological setups) and abilities (of the publics such opportunities address). The public's abilities are attuned to particular constraints and paths of action provided by financial institutions, while the latter adapt themselves to the abilities of the publics they address (Greeno 1994, 338). This process includes the public's unplanned and unforeseen appropriation and modification of tools and resources created by financial institutions, and it is consistent with my previous argument that noise trading is not a "natural" product but an institutional outcome: as such, it cannot be produced overnight.

Affordances rarely, if ever, emerge spontaneously. In examining them, we need to go beyond the Internet enthusiasm of the late 1990s. I will discuss here at least two types of closely interrelated affordances, which are essential: affordances of access and affordances of action. They shape the integration of retail traders into the regulatory system of financial markets. The first type answers a simple question: how do diverse individuals access trading, based on what they've got at hand? Where do they go? What do they need to know? What do they need to do? What do they need to use? The emphasis here is on "based on what they've got at hand"—that is, based on their abilities and on the particular situations they are in. Seen in this sense, the affordances of access for retail traders are different from those for institutional traders. The networks of information-rich relationships, the capacity of calling on favors from other traders (Knorr Cetina and Bruegger 2002), the willingness of others to answer one's calls, and so forth, are not benefits that can be afforded outside the relatively narrow confines of investment banks and funds.

The second type of affordances answers an equally simple set of questions: what do noise traders need in order to participate in action? What types of knowledge and skills are implied by the action of trading? How does this trading relate to other kinds of action present in financial markets?

Roughly speaking, we can distinguish three phases in the evolution of trading institutions addressing publics made of individuals: before 1960, well-to-do individual investors were dominant in slower-paced financial markets (e.g., Kynaston 2012; Michie 1999; Geisst 1997; Traflet 2013). Then came a phase from the 1960s to the mid-1980s, when institutions such as mutual funds became dominant. Toward the end of this phase, discount brokerages introduced technical setups allowing for an intensified pace of trading. Access means not only attracting more individual money into the system, but also increasing the speed with which individual money can enter it. Finally, in a phase extending from the mid-1980s to our days, institutions came to specialize in absorbing and recycling individual money into markets at great speed. This specialization includes not only tailored products, dedicated access ways, and dedicated technologies, but also regulatory provisions (including taxation) specific to retail trading.

Access

What did a person have to do to transact financial instruments in an individual, not an institutional, capacity? Before the 1960s, the person would have had to know a broker—a member of one of the firms associated with one of the exchanges on the East Coast or in Chicago, mainly. The person would have had to have a significant chunk of disposable income (in other words, to be at least well-to-do). The person would have had to have a good deal of disposable time to spend reading publications like *Barron's* and to be regularly on the phone with her broker or at the post office sending telegrams. These requirements entailed relatively high costs, not only in terms of commission fees but also in terms of time—and only investors with money and leisure time could afford them.

A broker on the NYSE recalled how he had started trading as an individual in the late 1950s:

GEORGE: I was working in Washington DC in a position there for a few years, and I met a friend of mine. We were going into the National Guard for a 6 month service and he was telling me about his cousin who was a stockbroker and whatever, and all you had to do was buy a stock at 33 and you would sell it at 39. And then it would go back to 33, you'd buy it again, and you would sell it at 39. So I said, really? That's all there is to it, I mean, and

he said, yes, that's it. So I, and this . . . the company's name was American Marietta at the time, which has now become Martin Marietta, and
I said, okay, so I waited, and the stock went to, to 33, and I bought a few
shares, and it went to 39! And I sold it. [*laugh*] The guy's right, I quit my
job, and [my wife] and I, we took off about 6 months and we just traveled
around and, and during the time I was gone, I had bought 100 shares of a
company called International Bank of Washington, which because, and I
said, I bought it, like, at 25, and, what did I know, I said, sell it at 55. Then
I went away. And I get a . . . we were in [country] at the time, and I got a
telegram . . . sold your 100 shares of International Bank of Washington at
58. It went up too fast, I couldn't sell it at 55. Now, that wouldn't happen
in this current day and age, but it gives you a sense that the way the markets worked and that, it was wide markets and, and so forth. . . . Well, this
was 1959, actually.

In this period, one needed to somehow know a broker ("It was much
more of the buddy system in those days than it is now"). One also needed
to have substantial disposable income (a few thousand dollars that could
be put into shares—but we are talking here about 1959, when the average
income of an individual in the United States was $2,600).[3] And above all,
one needed to have disposable time. Yet, according to the same broker,
financial markets were not held in particularly high regard:

GEORGE: I would think, for the most part, and I'm representative, I didn't
    know anything about a stock. I never knew until I was 25 years of age that
    you could buy and sell stocks and make money or whatever. We were all
    coming out of the war, I was at . . . college, and then graduate school, and
    I never even thought of the stock market as a career opportunity. Now,
    and so people were not educated in the opportunities of the market. We
    had come through difficult times and the markets were just building and I
    would say that there was a benign neglect towards the stock market. Most
    people didn't know about it, and it was not a very important part of the
    American scene at the time. It wasn't, you know, it had its role, but it's
    not like it is now, where the enormous advances in retirement accounts,
    401(k)s, IRAs and so forth, where just about everybody—and then with
    the whole stock options for employees. It's now come into the forefront of
    our thinking. In those days it wasn't. I mean, you were going to, I was, you
    were a teacher, you worked for the government, you . . . business was not,
    business schools were not significant at that time. You, it . . . You would

go to business school, you were thought to be, boy, you're not so smart, you couldn't get into, you couldn't become an engineer or you couldn't do something.

The 1960s brought the expansion of the mutual funds industry (Useem 1996; Fink 2008), but also the reemergence of discount brokerages,[4] a process that has been less investigated. (Concomitantly, business schools were improving their public perception, to the point of becoming fashionable; see Khurana 2007, 288). While the mutual fund industry created new, more affordable (in money terms) products (by pooling together financial securities and selling shares in these pools) geared to (middle-class) individuals, they did not change much else in terms of access: somebody wanting to put his money in a mutual fund still had to walk into an office, make an appointment with an adviser, call the adviser on the phone, wait to receive the certificates in the mail, read the prospect, read *Barron's*, read the *Wall Street Journal*, and so on. The relatively long time it took to get access was geared to the horizon of the activity itself: one would have expected that mutual fund shares, similar to the shares of a corporation, would be held for a long time. At the same time, the creation of associations of individual investors such as the American Association of Individual Investors in 1978, with regional chapters, regular face-to-face meetings, and publications, supplemented the provision of data, notions, advice, expert recommendations, and other paraphernalia of "informed access." When I attended a chapter meeting in 2009 in the Midwest, I (as a middle aged man) was clearly the youngest person in the room, and if the outfits were any indication, the least affluent, too. The discussion, during which the audience knowledgeably (and sometimes furiously) grilled a local mutual fund manager, made it clear that at stake was an "investment" process during which financial securities were held for one year and more.

Discount brokerages, however, were different in some respects. They did not provide new products (that is, pools of shares) and stood in tension with the more established, full service houses of New York City and Chicago, which, to a large extent, were based on close-knit family networks (see also MacKenzie and Millo 2003). Many operated in the so-called third market, meaning they listed shares that were traded over the counter. In 1975, when the Securities and Exchange Commission (SEC) finalized the introduction of negotiated commissions (meaning that customers could shop around for the cheapest full service broker), this third market became attractive for many brokers: over-the-counter trading meant it was much more difficult and time-consuming for clients to find a standardized price, and therefore it was more difficult to negotiate commissions as well.

Wealthy individual investors had always had the possibility of accessing stock market data straight from their homes. Even in the 1970s and the early 1980s, technology companies were leasing stock tickers and data services to individual investors. Prices, however, were prohibitive. In 1983, for instance, a private stock ticker cost $1,350 and the monthly service fee was $85 ("Brokers and Others" 1983, 58). When personal computers became more widespread and modems were introduced too, at around the same time, brokerages started selling data services to individual investors over the computer and over radio transmitters, and even providing execution services over the computer. True, the latter were initially offered only by one discount broker on the West Coast, while data services were offered by established houses such as Dean Witter and E. F. Hutton. Subscription prices were high, though: for instance, one service called QuoteDial had a monthly minimum charge of $50 and an additional charge of 10–38 cents per minute (58). In June 1983, the American Association of Microcomputer Investors was formed. While personal computers were seen early on as a channel for financial data transmission and even for order transmission and execution, only those who could afford the high costs used them.

A reduction in costs came initially not from this corner, but from novel usages of a well established technology: the telephone. To keep costs down, discount brokers based in the Midwest started taking orders mainly by phone, offering clients toll free numbers as an incentive. They also bought line capacity in bulk from phone operators; some brokers, based near communication hubs, got deeper discounts on line capacity. In the mid-1980s, a consequential innovation, the touch tone system, was spreading out:

JOE RICKETTS, FOUNDER OF AMERITRADE (HENCEFORTH JR): So moving on to the middle 1980s we had gotten to the point where the larger business also brought the same amount of costs, so we were doing more business but we were not improving our profits. So I was looking for something that would allow me to grow the business and keep my costs lower. At that time, Alex, the touch tone system was becoming popular. So I asked my technology person if he could develop a order entry and quote system off of the touch tone telephone and he indicated yes. I asked him how long it would take, he said it'd take about six months. I said how much money, he said a little under a million dollar[s]. . . . And but it took two years and it took about five million. [. . .] Because we were doing things that had never been done before and these people really didn't know. So they were cutting new ground with technology and were guessing the best they could. When I finally had the system in place I was . . . I had a focus group as the business schools tell you. . . . So I went out to my customers through our agents and I asked them if they would use the touch tone system, and the overwhelming response was no, why would I, as a customer, want to use a touch phone system when I can talk directly to a broker? So I was fearful that my cost was a lot higher than what I anticipated and that I would lose money, so I put the prices of the commission very low if people would use the automated touch phone system. In fact we put it down to three cents a share. [*clears throat*] It had . . . a retail brokerage that had never been advertised before that way and so we, you know, we just showed a palm of a hand with three pennies and the system started to . . . started to grow.

Lowering commission fees was not the outcome of a better technology, but a measure to encourage more usage of an unexpectedly costly and initially not very popular order-placing technology. What was being offered as an opportunity matched the possibilities of users who were not as affluent as the customer base of full service brokerages. These users, however, didn't take the introduction of the touch tone order system passively, but improved on it. They started programming their trades on the touch tone phone, which would contribute to increasing both the frequency and the rapidity of trades:

JR: So you didn't have to talk to the broker about the weather, the football game last weekend, how their family . . . you could just touch . . . you could just watch the tape on the television and put in your trades. And some of the people's trades went in so fast, Alex, that I couldn't understand how they could punch those numbers fast enough. So I called them, I asked how do you put your touch tone orders in so fast. They said well, we use an automatic dialler. So we preprogram buy 200 shares of General Motors at the market.

AP: You just press "one." [*laughs*]

JR: And just press "one," that's right and it goes "trrutt." And so it was very, very popular. We really started to expand and to grow. Now that was from '85 up until the middle 90s.

This excerpt illustrates well the notion of affordance, which isn't merely creating a new opportunity for action. Users take an opportunity tailored to their resources and constraints—an opportunity designed to recoup some investment costs rather than merely increase convenience— and modify and adapt this opportunity by transplanting routines of daily life (preprogramming phone numbers) onto it. Customers of discount brokerages can not only afford to place orders more quickly, but they can also afford to circumvent social rituals like small talk before placing an order. A trader who had been active in the 1980s told me that, being of a working-class background, he preferred a more impersonal order-placing system because he didn't trust brokers:

LOU: For many people, day traders, a broker was an intimidating decision. If you are . . . many people, especially, I came from a blue collar, my parents were industrial workers. Anybody who is giving you advice on using your money is not trusted. They are trying to steal something, they are trying . . . they are having a vested interest in getting you to spending your money in a certain way. I mean it's true. So, many people, even of my generation but certainly the prior generation, if they weren't big investors they looked upon brokers with a little bit of distrust. The broker is trying to get you [to] do something that's good for him not for you. That's not necessarily the case, mind you.

The distrust of full service brokers didn't necessarily mean that execution-only, discount brokers would be distrusted in the same way: after all, in this latter case customers retained the notion that trading decisions, whether good or bad, were entirely theirs. In terms of access affordances, then, the factors that appear to have been decisive with respect to the creation of noise trading from the late 1980s to the mid-1990s were the existence of securities out of the control of the established stock exchanges (and hence of full service brokerage houses, with their higher transaction costs and higher lots) and the primitive automation of order-placing through tone dial, initiated by users.[5] This last element was important because, as I argue in the next section, from the middle to the late 1990s, users also played a significant role in developing electronic ways to gain access to financial transactions. Access affordances had emerged for investors who, while less well-to-do than the traditional investors of the 1950s, still had disposable income to invest in financial securities. With the new lower fees for automated access, investors could increase the frequency of their trading without incurring substantial additional transaction costs. For anybody who wanted to trade more frequently during the day, fees of three cents per share, as in the example above, were not a big deterrent. In this case, technological innovation did not occur through intra-institutional changes in which heterogeneous professional groups competed for informational jurisdiction (Pardo-Guerra 2010). It occurred through repurposing existing technologies (such as the tone dial telephone line) by providers (brokerages), as well as by users (investors). This repurposing changed the interaction format between brokers and customers (from a personal to an impersonal one) but also allowed brokers to gain a price advantage and thus to attract new types of clients.

In parallel, consequential developments within the institutional segment of trading were started in the 1980s. In the wake of deregulation, but also of external competitive pressures, and relying on regulatory blueprints established in the United States in the early 1960s, stock exchanges started inputting trading data (price and volume) in electronic formats. These data could be accessed now directly on terminal screens or from the memory of servers. The move to inputting and recording data electronically was triggered partially by the fact that in the mid-1980s overseas stock exchanges (especially from Asia) started listing US financial instruments, thus creating opportunities for arbitrage. Owing to the considerable difference in time zones, stock exchange brokers either had to work in shifts (which proved impractical) or had to record trading data on computers. They resorted to the latter. This transition to electronically recording price and volume of transactions, though intended for the benefit of institutional traders, proved to have unintended consequences in the 1990s. First, data stored in computer memories could be accessed from the outside, for instance by individual traders who also had hacking skills. Second, when computerization went into swing in the financial services industry, floor and pit workers had to adapt or were laid off. They tried to adapt to the new environment by using their skills elsewhere. Chris, who had worked for a brokerage house in Chicago, quit in the early 1990s partly because pit trading was becoming physically too demanding and partly because he saw the writing on the wall—that is, what computerization was bringing about. Becoming an independent trader was not a sudden process but a slower adjustment.

CHRIS: Oh, I left, I stepped out trading on the floor in about 1990. I just didn't . . . it was hard for me physically. And I just didn't like it. And then I decided I wanted to be more quantitative, and then I started doing research. And I started becoming more interested in computing, because one of my fortes was always that I could do pricing and so forth, so I wanted to . . . and the other thing was, after Globex[6] came about, I started seeing the writing on the wall, and I thought to myself, well, I don't want to be left behind in this revolution. I think the floor's gonna close down some day and that [is] why I started making the switch and then I started coming back to it once I became more saddled in what I was doing with respect to computing and with respect to . . . when I came back to it. I started trading totally off the floor, but again once it became available, but the other thing was that it was just too costly for me for a while to do it off the floor, yeah these terminals and getting e-signal and all that kind of stuff was very very expensive for a long time, thousands of dollars for something like that, just couldn't afford it, it didn't make economic sense for me. And the calls were so bad too. But once it became more . . . it made more and more sense and I started trading some options off the floor and some futures. The[n] eventually I got involved in the forex market and then I started becoming interested in that. Which sort of, you know, I've gone a big circle because this is actually where I started out, at least as far as trading is concerned.

Internet trading for individuals, though, was still an expensive affair. In 1996 the London-based broker Currency Management Corporation introduced foreign exchange trading over the Internet, requiring minimum deposits of $20,000 (Tomasula 1997, 38). Internet trading was advertised as offering an advantage of up to 10 seconds compared with placing orders over the phone. Anybody who wanted to trade several times per day and take advantage of the changes in price for a particular security would have to have low-cost access to intraday price variations. One solution to this problem was to hack into the computer systems of brokerage houses. Around 1997, some savvy programmers (based in New York City) with a background in game programming developed a system to trawl the brokerage databases for price and volume data in real time (a process called scrapping). Initially developed for personal usage, this scrapping program (called QuoteTracker) proved popular with other traders and was sold to them as well. A code writer who participated in the creation of the QuoteTracker describes it this way:

> CHARLIE: Every one of these trading companies like Ameritrade and Day-Tech and God, whatever they had, 30 or 40 of these online brokerage[s] that offered online access to your portfolio. He [another code writer] and his brother would actually spoof a browser, that is, pretend to be a browser going through http getting . . . acting like a browser or acting like the application and asking for this information right. Logging this person in if a client bought the [name] quote trader product they would enter in preferences whatever brokerage whatever companies they actually got accounts with and it would log on to each one of those and get whatever information it could and then, you know, keep the channel open and continue, so it was like this very interactive relationship. It was much faster and more robust than a browser relationship where you click one thing then click another . . . no! This thing would in a batch, you know, get the quotes, go and say bang! This person has a window open for like an intraday chart or candlestick or something like that, get that information dynamically, update it every 10 seconds. [. . .] Well mimicking a combination of the browser's facility and the user's constant update, so he was getting a lot more information, he was asking for a lot more information, a lot more systematic way than sluggish here click on IBM then you go to the IBM screen and it shows you this chart.

This is another instance of how affordances of access, and not mere opportunities, are created. Users take available resources and adapt them according to their abilities. The response of brokerage houses was threefold: to change their code, to sue in court, and to buy the software created by such developers. While changing the code didn't prove very successful, court battles and buying up trading software were more so: some developers were deterred, and the products of some others were incorporated by discount brokers.

Overall, speeding up the rhythm of transactions gave brokers the possibility to consolidate, diversify, and expand their client base. Since this client base was not as well-to-do as the old-fashioned investors, discount brokers in some cases had to absorb customer losses and get used to a new type of customer, whom they were eager to acquire nonetheless. This was a customer who perhaps had fewer financial resources, transacted much more frequently, and was at a higher risk of losing money too. This shift, which was initiated with the touch tone system, continued with the advent of online trading:

> JR: When we went to the system in the late '70s and the early '80s the trad-
> ers started to develop, they understood the power that they had with pay-
> ing the lower commission, so they would call us on the telephone on the
> 800 number and they would increase their trades. That was relatively new
> and that developed slowly but again it was the same customer. Predom-
> inantly male, middle aged, usually their own business man or an attor-
> ney or somebody that had extra funds. [. . .] The system of the touch
> tone, they wanted trades back immediately 'cause they knew that as soon
> as they punched that button it went and they wanted to have a response
> right away, so we got reports of our executions down within seconds. And
> that accelerated the type of trading that people were doing so that peo-
> ple became very active in trading. Some people might trade you know 5,
> 10 times a day. Prior to that it would . . . people never did that. And it was
> a bull market, so the trades were usually profitable, so what it inspired was
> people quitting their jobs just to go trade the market. They thought they
> could make a living trading the market. And they did. Until the bad mar-
> ket came along. And then they lost all their money. [laughs] And this was
> a younger, lot of times they were not as well educated, a lot of times they
> didn't have the same amount of money but it was the, it was the gambling
> spirit that drew it to them as well, as well as the investing part of it. So
> there were huge numbers of people that came to us to be traders. When
> the bad market came along in 1988 they almost all disappeared. They
> did . . . you know they lost their money 'cause they didn't have a lot and the
> market went down very fast. They didn't have a chance to get out so they
> went away. In fact at Ameritrade which was at that time called First Na-
> tional Brokerage we lost a lot of money because customers went into their
> margin requirement and they didn't get us the money and so we had to sell
> them out, but then we sold them out at losses. The customers didn't have
> the money to pay us so we have to absorb those losses.

This points to several aspects: first, that there is a shift both in composition of traders and in aspirations; second, that this shift is not so recent
but had started happening already in the mid to late 1980s; and third,
that technological changes introduced as a means of attracting new customers put various institutional pressures on the firms themselves (not

all of which were foreseen). Increasing ease of access does not simply make it easier for old-type customers (moneyed, prudent, knowledgeable, expecting a steady return over a long time, etc.) to place orders. New affordances bring in new types of customers with new aspirations (less moneyed, from diverse backgrounds, expecting more substantial and speedier returns, but also ready to trade more frequently).

Brokerages had to adapt their organization to the new challenges (especially when faced with programmers scrapping their data): they had to hire more IT workers and train them in the business of brokeraging. Initial orders placed via the Internet were little more than just e-mails.[7] The QuoteTracker discussed above visualized price data on a chart with a delay of seconds. How could brokers compete with this if they weren't retraining their workforce, both in the front office and in the back office?

JR: There was two parts to the technology. The first is what's normally called the front end, which is the order entry system, and then the backend, which is your accounting system. We really struggled originally with the backend system, the accounting system. We used a system where one of our clerks would type in all of the activity for the day into a perforated tape and then we would dial a computer in Pittsburgh and put the phone into a receiver that would send that information. They would print out all of our reports that night and send them by overnight so we had them the next morning. The system did not work very well. So we were looking to . . . as our business continued to grow we were looking to improve it. One of the people that was my partner at that time was very bright. He was an accountant and he wanted to build the computer that would do our back office, so he explored that and we went with him. I mean we were so naive we had no idea what kind of decisions we were making, but he did build the back office system and then when he understood what it took to make the back office accounting system work, then he could adapt some of that technology to the front end. Using that information, using that experience, then we started hiring technologists. But hiring people that were good at the kind of work we wanted to do was very, very difficult. [. . .] There were a lot of software writers, but they didn't understand brokerage, so we were in an agricultural area [Nebraska—AP], not in a technology area and so it was very difficult for us to find the right people. So we hired a number of people that didn't work, that didn't work out well. We wasted money on building systems that never did work. [*clears throat*] Eventually I hired a CEO that was a technology person who was able to bring in the engineers that really knew what to do, and so that was the first time that we could move into a big robust reliable system, and that was in the '96, '97 era.

In discussing the automation of the London Stock Exchange, Juan Pablo Pardo-Guerra (2012, 575) emphasizes the importance of social status in speeding up this process. Typists in the back office did not have the same clout as brokers, so it was easier to overcome their resistance than that of the brokers. In the case of brokerages, though, the automation of the back office provides the experience required for undertaking the automation of the front office. Automating trading procedures—with a view to attracting more clients—required a novel type of experience and novel sets of skills for brokers, both difficult to acquire. Computerization was brought forward when brokers could afford it—that is, when the opportunities for technological change matched their possibilities, both in terms of experience and in terms of skills.

Within institutional trading, increased automation posed some challenges to the job security of employees. On the trading floor, being well connected was also necessary if one was to stay in business as an institutional trader. Not all traders, however, had an equal gift for making friends. The difference in sociability and networking skills, together with the challenges presented by computerized trading, made the transition to retailing attractive for some institutional traders: "Sometimes you want to be an entrepreneur," managers explained to me. The uncertainty and job insecurity triggered by market automation in institutional settings pushed some former traders toward becoming entrepreneurs, and—as the same managers explained—trading is available, cheap, and accessible.

Chris, who had been an institutional trader in Chicago, recalled that in the 1980s getting a job in the financial industry was very easy, especially if you were an economics graduate. One would get hired on one's first job application and start working one's way up from phone clerk to trader, reaching this latter stage in a few years. Then with the help of a loan, one could buy a seat and start trading options and futures. In the early 1990s, however, things started to change.

CHRIS: And then people started leaving because I mean markets started getting much more tight, and then people competing for like a quarter of a tick, and then there was no point to it because no, you make an error . . .

you know you have to make 10 good trades to make up for that one. It would not make any sense.

With this sort of pressure brought upon institutional traders, a job loss is rationalized as an entrepreneurial opportunity, as freedom, and as a new chance (see also Bröckling 2007, 169). Chris switched to being an educational entrepreneur in the mid-1990s, teaching about trading in different parts of the world:

> CHRIS: So that increases opportunity tremendously. It also has increased opportunities in that I met people I would never had met, I traveled pretty much all over the world as a result . . . I've introduced technology. You know I've always been on the side of introducing technology to people as opposed to being on the other side and saying, "This is a bad thing." One of the things that I did that was so interesting was that I went over and I would do seminars. I would do financial engineering seminars and teach people about, you know, what I knew about finance and about options and so forth. Yes, I did. And I found that was fascinating to do. So people were switching over because this was the thing to do. You know, financial engineering was sort of like a trend . . . what's the word I'm looking for? [ethnographer suggests the word "in"] Yeah, was in like the disco in the seventies. That [1996] was the explosion of those markets and markets started going overseas. [. . .] They were also fascinated to hear me because I would put on my old trading jacket with my badge and everything and they thought that was really great, so . .

At the start of our conversation, Chris had said "All I wanted to do was to be on my own, I don't like working in corporations, I'm sort of a loner." Yet, the narrative he unfolded after this opening—the pressure of the trading floor, the status hierarchies, the constant need to be well connected in order to get valuable information, the institutional changes, the job loss—seemed to undermine this stated motivation. It looks more as if after all this, one has to want to be a loner—this is the only option left. This narrative points to the fact that interest in or perhaps even passion for trading does not occur spontaneously but is nurtured by an industry that at least in part seems to have emerged from the transformations institutional exchanges went through since the early 1990s: one has to dust off and put on one's old trading jacket and the badge and travel around the world giving talks about trading. This pattern has become institutionalized nowadays in the regular "money shows" and "traders expos" that take place around the globe, where the rhetoric of freedom is regularly preached.

The retechnologization of brokerages had among its consequences that some of the existing employees were laid off. They may not have had a lot of technological knowledge, but they were familiar with aspects of the trading business and had to reorient themselves. One way of doing so was to start "educational" businesses targeting individual traders, by offering seminars, trading lessons, coaching, and the like. These contributed to generating an additional market for support services, including publications, counseling sessions, retreats, trading clubs. Such new service businesses were accepted by the industry as a way of bringing in and stabilizing customers. Chris, whom I have quoted above, left the pits of Chicago in the early 1990s. The transition to independent trader was a longer process of adaptation, which included, among others, phases as a financial educator. The financial globalization of the mid-1990s helped: overseas, many were interested in learning more about how options markets worked:

AP: Tell me, when you did these seminars in South Africa, were you sent, did you do them on behalf of a firm, or were you self-employed, like a freelancer?

CHRIS: I was self-employed, but I did it in partnership with a firm. And I did my standard options, I did you know talk . . . about futures, options and different options strategies and so forth, that['s] pretty much what I did. That was, let's see, '94 through '96. Because I did one in London, did another one in Brussels, I did a bunch in South Africa. That was right after the Safex opened, the South African options exchange. And that was, that's why everybody became interested in it, because everybody wanted, they all wanted markets like Chicago had at the time.

Vince, who had worked in London in the trading room of a corporation, encountered difficulties in the early 1990s too:

VINCE: I finished my corporate life in 1990. I was in IT for several years as a consultant. . . . Because of the change of tax regime, they brought in 1990, they brought in a new tax code called IR35 . . . Ah okay, well it crippled IT consultants because of course we paid hardly any tax up til then and then we had to start paying tax, so I got out of that business. I was also getting a bit long in tooth for it, a bit too old, and I wanted to do something else, and my last contract I worked in the trading room at [oil corporation], the oil company. I used to look after the infrastructure in the trading room and having got to talking to a lot of traders during my time there, I just got interested in trading. I knew nothing about it before. Just kind of picked it up. Yeah. And so I'm self-taught. I've done the [technical analyst] examination but I haven't done a course or anything. Everything I know I'm self-taught.

He decided to found a trading club on the model of a professional society, because he had noticed that retail traders could benefit from similar opportunities for socializing:

VINCE: And I started going there [meetings of an analyst society] and I met a few other mainly people who go to the [analyst society] or typically from the financial services industry. They tend to be analysts who work for banks and so forth and very few prop traders—proprietary traders. And I bumped into two other, three other guys who were doing the same thing as I was. We used to go to the pub afterwards and socialize and really the idea of the [trading club] really came around because we were just discussing one evening, you know, how there really should be something like the [analyst society] but geared towards proprietary traders, i.e. people who trade their own money as opposed to trading other people's money, which is pretty much the situation at the [analyst society]. . . . So then we spoke about doing it as a partnership and they lost interest and so I just did it on my own. . . . I mean what I did I booked a hotel for . . . I started off by doing it twice a month and I found a hotel which was that one [name] and I booked six months, so twelve evenings in the club, eh sorry, in the hotel and what I did I phoned up people like [bank], several of the brokers and I said oh I've got this great club going, I've got lots of people, lots of investors coming. Will you come down and give us presentations? And so that's what happened. So really people used to come down from the business.

Chris and Vince had to find new opportunities to match their experience and skills. This type of reverse affordance leads to becoming engaged in or even initiating domains of action that, while apparently on the periphery of markets, contribute to spreading out established institutional models. The practices of Chicago markets are enacted on various continents; the model of professional, trading-relevant societies morphs into an amateur club. This process signals the emergence of an educational-cum-advertising industry that expands spatially, as well as socially (from professionals to laymen).

Being a broker-entrepreneur or an educator-entrepreneur catering to retail traders (or a combination of the two) means that new ways of trading have to be encouraged, different from the "buy and hold forever your favorite stocks"—a style I had witnessed at a meeting of old-school investors in the Midwest. Retail brokers and educators could not hope to make much income by promoting a buy-and-hold way of trading, or by limiting themselves to offering only stocks. They had to promote continuous trading, as well as to diversify "over the counter products to entice customers." A diversification in products being offered could only go hand in hand with educators-entrepreneurs promoting a variety of trading "styles" or "strategies."

Action

If affordances of access were substantially changed by the emergence of discount brokers and technological innovations, what about affordances of action? Assuming somebody got enough money saved and could access a broker to open an account, what came next? What did that person have to do in order to buy or sell the securities of her choice? How was that choice made in the first place? What kind of choice was it? In the previous discussion, I have already hinted at some of the requirements: up to even the mid-1990s, making a choice meant primarily reading the business pages of newspapers and other specialized publications (*Barron's*, the *Wall Street Journal*, *Investor's Chronicle*, and the like) in search of information about stocks and about options on stocks mainly. Then that person would have to call her broker or send a fax or use a tone dial phone, or send an e-mail giving instructions. The order would be routed, filled (more or less accurately), and then processed in the back office at some point during the day (or during the next days). The investor never knew how her orders were executed: was it a counterpart in the market (i.e., a third party with whom the broker matched the order), or was it the broker himself taking the counterpart? Often, the back office wasn't even in the same location as the front office, so that processing orders took some time:

AP: Now about this touch tone technology. So say if I'm a trader, an investor, and I've preprogrammed my phone, and I press "one" for buy or sell, say, General Motors. What happens afterwards at your end . . . what happened at your end when I press the button?

JR: We . . . when you press that button, we have that electronic message already going into our computer which communicated directly to the exchange, so it got there immediately. And then what the exchange did was built systems that automatically gave you an execution and just reported back. So it was very very fast. We . . . it didn't print out anywhere. Now the first Internet order we received, that printed out. It was an e-mail message that printed on a machine. [*laughs*] It [printed] on a piece of paper and we had to take that and call. But by the time that we had started to use the Internet, we put the Internet order entry system that the customers had into automatic on our routing system that we had from the telephone, so that the customers' orders could flow right into it and go onto the exchange and get a report back right away.

Trading actions were intermediated several times, in a way that was invisible to the initiators: they could not see what happened with these actions and had to wait to hear back about them. Moreover, the search for data (about price and volume) was separate from the analysis of the data and from trading decisions proper: traders had to find information in places or through channels different from those used to place orders, and they had to analyze the data separately from the finding process. The automated tone dial orders did not change this. What individual software developers did in the late 1990s, though, was to produce visual interfaces that integrated price and volume information with analytical displays (in the form of charts), which made possible the analysis of information as it was delivered on the screen. As they were scrapping price data from brokerages, they grafted the scraps onto visual displays charting the evolution of the price. End users now had an interface (the Quote Tracker) that showed them not only updated prices, but also their evolution. The fact that developers opened the product to user input facilitated reciprocal adaptation:

CHARLIE (CODE WRITER): It was the problem with [developer of Quote-Tracker] is that he was he was bloat . . . it was bloated the first day it was on the market. It was bloated with what everybody wanted. He had a very interactive, he had a highly active user base that would say we love

QuoteTracker, we want . . . hey you think you could do this? Can we get? And unlike Microsoft, where you ask something like this and it takes focus groups and marketing department and, you know, some sort of sifting process that takes 1,200 this is [name] and his brother kind of going through the blog and oh this guy wants this to be a little screen to do this and the next day it's there, okay. I mean he was indiscriminate about what he would . . . he would code. He was a very fast programmer, could do almost anything, you know, when I said this button I said that's gonna be hard to get a pointer to be able to look . . . no, there . . . no problem. The problem was that he was insensitive to the bloat.

These products, bought later by brokerage houses, formed the backbone of trading interfaces allowing traders to place orders directly onto visual displays of data. The creation of MetaTrader4 a few years after 2000 took the integration a step further, allowing the integration of various asset classes into the same visual display. A scopic system (Knorr Cetina 2003; Knorr Cetina and Preda 2007) was thus created, which integrated observation with action. On the institutional side, broker dealers catering to individual traders were integrated into electronic communication networks (ECNs). These were electronic trading platforms that bypassed the National Association of Securities Dealers Automated Quotation system (Nasdaq) and were owned by broker dealers, as well as by information providers such as Reuters and Bloomberg (Louis 1999; Fink, Fink, and Weston 2006).[8] In 1996 Island was founded as an electronic platform for trading orders of fewer than 500 shares among member brokers. It initially addressed retail traders, though it later grew to attract more and more institutional traders as well ("Island ECN" 2015; MacKenzie and Pardo-Guerra 2014).

At the start of the new millennium in the United States, 6 brokers processed 70% of all daily online trades; 150 brokers processed the rest. Of all trades, 37% were made online, but only 5% of total assets were used in online transactions (Wells 2000, 66). These statistics indicate institutional consolidation but also the fact that online traders had relatively modest assets; this isn't surprising if we recall that the traders' profile was different from that of the more traditional investors. Besides the relatively modest financial power, the character of financial products as well as margin limits made it relatively difficult for small accounts to engage in trading. The price of shares was in some cases high for somebody with limited resources, and while options trading was cheaper, opportunities for individuals to trade options were still limited. Other products such as currencies were out of reach, because the size of contracts (lots of 100,000) was too large for individuals and because they implied physical delivery: who could have separate accounts for the US dollar, the pound sterling, the Canadian dollar, the Japanese yen, the Australian dollar, the New Zealand dollar (USD, GBP, CAD, JPY, AUD, NZD), and so forth? Currency trading over the Internet was offered for the first time in 1996 for wealthy investors and small firms by the Currency Management Corporation.

Leveraging possibilities for individual traders were limited in the 1990s too. Until 2006, traders could do portfolio margining (that is, adjust their margin requirements—how much money they were required to keep in their accounts—to the overall risk of their portfolio) only if they had at least $5 million in account equity. In December 2006 the SEC eliminated this requirement, and in the next year Options Xpress, a brokerage addressing individual traders, introduced real time portfolio margining for accounts of $100,000 or more, which meant that the leverage traders could afford was adjusted to their trading situation ("OptionsXpress" 2007, 1). Individual traders could leverage their trades up to 1:200 (for every dollar in a trading account, up to $200 of transactions could be executed), although this changed in 2010 with the new regulations introduced by the Commodities and Futures Trading Commission (CFTC), which reduced leveraging to 1:50 (the initial proposal was 1:10). Outside of US jurisdiction, though, leverage remained unchanged (up to 1:400).

In parallel with the expansion of leveraging possibilities, new products tailored to individual traders were introduced in the period 2000–2010, together with an attractive taxation regime and with incentives such as air miles on trading accounts. First, new types of foreign exchange contracts were introduced, which did not require physical delivery but were continuously rolled over to the next day and settled for the difference. This change contributed to a rapid expansion of individual trading in forex, so that around 2010 retail traders made 8% of a worldwide, $4 trillion daily market (Paz 2011; King, Osler, and Dagfinn 2011). Contracts such as spread betting—an innovation from the gambling industry— and contracts for difference (CFDs; see Norman 2009) were introduced around 2005;[9] they represented essentially bets on a future outcome such as the value of a stock or an index going up or down with respect to a given value at the time the bet was placed. The attractiveness for individual traders was, among other things, that they could avoid owning any underlying instrument and any delivery obligations, as well as that CFDs were relatively simple (compared with options). A few years later, exchange traded funds (ETFs) were widely traded in retail markets: these were instruments tracking baskets of financial assets (such as stocks) traded daily like stocks on electronic platforms. They were cheaper than shares, had low administrative costs, and were easily accessible to lower budgets. ETFs became so popular that in January 2016 in the United States alone, they incorporated assets of $2.006. trillion.[10]

On the taxation side, profits from trading had always been taxed at least partly as capital gains, at a rate lower than income tax. Some of the new products emerging in the 2000–2010 decade, such as spread bets, were entirely tax free (available in the United Kingdom, but not in the United States). Other products, such as the CFDs, offered tax relief on losses. This regime tended to increase their attractiveness compared with more traditional instruments such as shares, and, perhaps as important, it created the impression of a special domain for the "small trader," who was treated differently and more favorably than institutional investors.

Overall, the introduction of new graphic interfaces, together with new products tailored exclusively for individual traders, the relaxation of leverage rules, and a favorable tax regime, contributed to providing individuals with affordances of action that were much larger than previous ones. Some of the products discussed here were not so new: ETFs, for instance, had been around since the late 1980s, but they really took off when they were marketed to individual audiences. Some products (such as spread betting) were imported or adapted from the gambling industry—but more in Europe than in the United States. When we look at the forces that created these affordances of access, we can see that they mostly came from within the financial services industry. Software developers were quickly acquired by brokerage houses; banks and full service brokerages had to react to the pressure coming from discount brokerages (and, in the United Kingdom, from a rapidly expanding gambling industry). An industry segment that was initially rather marginal—discount brokerages—was fully incorporated into the financial services industry.

Legitimacy

Expanding the domain of individual trading activities beyond the sphere of the well-to-do, while changing the pace of trading activities (from "buy and hold" to repeated "buy and sell and buy and sell") required in the end integrating the new types of participants into the system of finance in a formalized way, including regulatory definitions. The medium of trading has changed from visits to the broker and phone calls to computer clicks and websites. New products tailored for retail traders have been introduced. Matching opportunities and possibilities for action and access, respectively, has to be accompanied by formally defining the identity and activities of new entrants. Some of the relevant issues here were not new, just reformulated in a new context—the binding character of trading orders as contracts, for instance. The redefinition of spread bets as financial transactions was not dissimilar to debates around the legitimacy of short selling or around options contracts as gambling, which had occurred more than a century earlier.[11]

There are at least two mechanisms through which legitimacy is created in this case: one is provided by regulatory tools. The other, related to the former, is provided by institutional arrangements for the public display of trading activities as acceptable, and for knowing these activities. With respect to the former, a crucial moment was provided by the SEC definition of day trading in 2001, together with establishing minimum equity requirements and margin utilization rules by approving amendments to National Association of Securities Dealers (NASD) rule 2520 (SEC 2001; NASD 2001). Before 2001, the major definition concerning individual investors was that of the "accredited investor" (Rule 501 of SEC Regulation D) as a high-net-worth individual who acquires the shares of the company. The 2001 definition keeps worth as a criterion, though at a much lower level (the equity requirement is $25,000), but the emphasis shifts on the frequency of trading (four trades or more within five working days). In 2010 the CFTC defined a retail customer in forex as an individual with less than $10 million in total assets, or less than $5 million in total assets if entering into a transaction to manage risk, and who is not registered as a professional. Nonfinancial companies with total assets of $10 million or less than $1 million net worth are included in the definition (CFTC 2010).

Making the retail trader the object of a definition (and of regulation) makes it much easier to design legitimate products targeted at that trader, someone who has at least that amount of equity, who trades about that often (and hence will like low transaction costs). It also becomes much easier to design tax advantages around specific products. Interestingly enough, this regulatory definition also does not prevent one from changing one's status from an individual to an institution: in September 2010 the CFTC introduced a requirement that all counterparties to off-exchange retail forex transactions had to be registered with the commission (meaning that within a year US traders holding accounts with foreign brokers had to shift them to US-registered entities).[12] A good number of discussions among retail traders focused on how to incorporate a firm in Panama and transfer the trading account in the name of that firm.

In parallel with the introduction of these definitions, we see a concerted effort on the part of the industry to change the name "day trader" to "retail trader," since the latter was not associated with the Internet bubble of the late 1990s and was more neutral. The initial regulatory definition retained the name "day trader." The newer ones use predominantly "retail trader." "Discount broker" was abandoned in favor of "execution-only" or forgotten altogether. Around 2009 a new category emerged, that of "social trader," directly related to Facebook-like trading platforms where traders can communicate with each other while trading. The integration of "retail" into the regulatory system of trading and the multiplication of individual trading categories—with "social" as a subdivision of "retail"—make further regulatory moves with respect to subdivisions necessary. For instance, one category of trades popular with social traders, copy trades, is not regulated at all, although it replicates the business model of hedge fund managers.

The regulatory integration of "retail trader" means neither that it happens everywhere in the world, nor that it becomes a homogeneous financial category. It is accompanied by a diversification of brokerages, according to whether they are licensed for regulated jurisdictions.[13] The integration means that it is possible now to regularly organize public displays of trading activities for retail traders: since about 2005, trade fairs (such as the Money Show and the Trade Show) have been taking place several times every year, bringing together traders, brokers, and providers of additional services. Additionally, trading clubs (which attend such fairs too) regularly meet as forums for swapping ideas and strategies, hearing invited speakers, and socializing. These events help make trading into a legitimate activity that connects to and integrates into the broader social lives of participants. (A few years ago I witnessed a meeting in a mid-Manhattan Starbucks where young mothers, babies in tow, were learning how to trade.)

The Conceptual Evolution of "Noise"

Does this newly won legitimacy resonate in any way with the academic interest about "noise"? Since the concept is so central with respect to theory, one would expect academics (and journals) to be interested in investigating its dimensions—in other words, one would expect a sustained program of research on what it means to be an "uninformed trader" (or to "trade on liquidity").

We can look at the evolution of academic papers published on these topics from several angles: first, we can see whether papers published in finance journals preceded in significant numbers these institutional and technological changes. Then we can look more closely at whether the meanings of notions such as noise, being uninformed, or being a day trader have stayed more or less the same across a longer period of time in academic papers. While the popular notion of day traders emerges in the media in the late 1990s in conjunction with a particular phenomenon (the Internet) and evolves later into retail traders, it is not a concept. This notion acquires institutional significance only when it is formalized into a regulatory definition.

Over almost 40 years (1976–2014), 82 articles were published in academic finance journals on the topics of day traders, liquidity, noise, or uninformed traders.[14] Of these articles, 73% were published in the period 2000–2014; 19.5% in the period 1990–1999; 4.5% in the period 1980–1989, and 3% in 1976. Almost 93% of all academic papers published in finance journals on these topics overlap with the period of the institutional and technological changes outlined above.

What about the meanings of these notions, then? Have they stayed constant over time? Among the aspects to be noticed here is that the notion of day traders used in the few papers published in the 1980s (before the concept was popularized by the media) is much more neutral than its contemporary understanding: a day trader is somebody "interested in outperforming the 'market portfolio' through the use of daily stock market forecasts generated from an aggregate technical indicator

model" (Van Landingham 1980, 342). The crucial distinction is that between fundamental and technical analysis, and it does not assume differences in knowledge or information. Another paper published in 1976
on the topic of uninformed traders does not assume a substantive distinction between informed and uninformed, either: the starting point is
that information will arrive not all at once, but sequentially. Each information sequence will affect the trader's decisions (Copeland 1976, 1150).

Yet another 1976 paper distinguishes indeed between informed and
uninformed traders, explaining the latter as those who prefer to "invest
no resources in collecting information, but they know that current prices
reflect the information of informed traders" (Grossman 1976, 573). In
the end, being uninformed is more efficient, since the equilibrium price
incorporates better-quality information: "A trader who invests nothing
in information and observes the market price can achieve a utility as
high as traders who pay for the information" (574). Grossman's paper,
which also uses the concept of noise, does not make a qualitative distinction among types of traders (who is more knowledgeable and who is
less), but one based on the willingness to spend money on acquiring information. (We assume that all traders can spend that money, but some
choose not to.) A distinction among socially different kinds of traders
can hardly be found in the very few academic papers published up to the
mid-1980s. At the end of the 1980s, however, we already encounter some
social attributes (e.g., young versus rational) characterizing noise traders
as compared to rational investors (DeLong et al. 1989, 683).

Overall, concepts such as noise or uninformed traders have a particular career within the finance literature. Their period of glory and attention stretches over the past 15 years, coinciding with the transition
of markets to an electronic format, but also with institutional transformations geared toward attracting individuals into trading. At the same
time, the notion of uninformed or noisy trader had a change in meaning in the 1990s and the following decade, from being efficient and rational to being a particular social category of traders, a transformation
that is in line with broader institutional shifts within the industry. Both
quantitatively and qualitatively, the academic concept of informed versus uninformed traders appears to have a career linked to these shifts.
Many times, though, the notion of uninformed trader remains a purely
formal position in a system of distinctions based on metrics such as the
frequency of profitable versus unprofitable trades. Besides some proprietary surveys conducted by consulting firms, there is little investigation, if

any, of the social attributes that characterize an uninformed trader. The underlying assumption, though, is that uninformed or noise traders are overwhelmingly situated outside the institutional domain, in the sphere of retail trading. (Otherwise the implication would be that investment banks, hedge funds, or brokerage houses employ a substantial number of uninformed traders. This would undermine the very idea of professional trading.)

The Numbers

If academic interest in noise, liquidity, uninformed, or day traders rose during 2000–2010, have such traders' numbers increased as well? What is their gender composition? Their educational status? Being a trader is different from being an investor, and data on stock ownership do not necessarily say much about trading. First, owning stock does not necessarily mean trading stock. Second, trading activities are not restricted to trading stock. For instance, direct ownership of publicly traded stocks in 2010 in the United States was 15.1% (the peak was 21.3% in 2007), but it is not evenly distributed across income quintiles. High- and very-high-income families own much more publicly traded stock than low-income families do, and the latter tend to own stock only related to an increase in their income (FRS 2012, 34). Stock trading would be a subset of this category, but trading in other financial instruments, such as derivatives, is statistically captured together with royalties, lawsuit settlements, and other items (40). Brokerage accounts are lumped together with checking, savings, and money market accounts. Of all transaction accounts, call accounts (which include brokerage accounts) were held by only 2% of US households, while 50.5% of these households had savings accounts (28). These numbers indicate that only a small fraction of the population engages in financial transactions in the markets.[15] (Absolute numbers can be considerable, though, owing to the large size of the population.)

Using records from Finland for 1998–2000, Linnainmaa (2003, 3) identifies 7,686 traders (1.85%) who made a complete roundtrip trade per week, out of 413,645 households who at some point during the period executed at least a transaction on the Helsinki Stock Exchange. An industry report published in the United Kingdom (Mintel 2008, 55–56) forecast that the number of online investors would rise to 1.438 million in 2013, while predicting at the same time a reduction in the individual investors' overall market share. Private client trades were 17 million in 2000 and only 10 million in 2007, meaning that trading activity was much more intense before the dotcom crash. At the same time, spread betting, introduced in 2002, was reaching 1.2 million transactions in 2007. The number of online investors (including active as well as less active traders) had risen from 510,000 to 940,000 in 2007 (56). This estimate, however was made before the crisis of 2008 broke out, and it does not distinguish between active and less active traders. While the market share of execution-only brokers had fallen in revenue terms, execution-only trades represented 26.7% of all individual transactions in 2007 (59), indicating a fall in the fees of online brokerages (which, in turn, encourages more frequent trading).

Foreign exchange markets are a case apart, because here the distinction between active traders (four or more transactions within five working days) and infrequent traders does not make much sense. The nature of the contracts (no physical delivery, rolling from one day to the next) and the costs incurred by keeping positions open overnight means that traders cannot just buy, say, a US dollars (USD) lot in pound sterling (GBP) and keep it for days. You're either active or you are not trading at all. One can, however, just open an account without funding it (or fund it with $1), and then one will count as a trader. We need to make a distinction, then, between how many individuals open accounts (it costs next to nothing) and how many truly trade. Newer industry studies on retail forex offer the following estimates compiled from brokers: the retail forex market is divided into the visible (aka regulated) one, the Japanese one, and the undercounted (or unregulated) one. Data for 2012 indicate 1.5 million active traders in the regulated market, with a monthly trading volume of $2.73 billion (QIR3 2013, 22).

More reliable data about the number of retail forex traders come from the United States and are recent. From October 18, 2010, all US forex brokers have been required by the CFTC to disclose quarterly the number of nondiscretionary active accounts they hold, as well as their account profitability. The latter means the percentage of accounts that were profitable over a quarter—but not necessarily that the said accounts were consistently profitable (making a profit one or two times would count as profitable). For the largest US retail brokerage houses, the data show that the number of forex traders with active accounts peaked in the first quarter of 2010 at above 126,000, after which it declined. In the third quarter of 2015, there were a little above 94,000 forex retail trading ac-

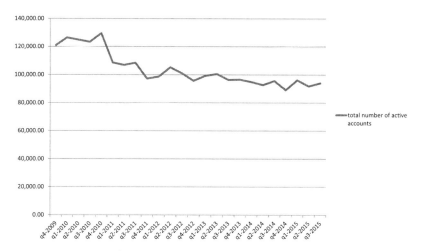

FIGURE 1. Active trading accounts reported to the CFTC by the largest retail forex broker-ages, 2009–2014. *Source*: Forex Magnates quarterly reports, compiled by the author.

counts registered with the largest firms, on an upward trend (fig. 1). The profitability of accounts bottomed at 25% in the second quarter of 2011, after which it rose to 31% in the third quarter of 2015. Concomitantly, a consolidation took place in the industry, with the number of retail brokerage firms (again, only for forex) declining by 60% between early 2012 and late 2015 (fig. 2). Overall, the picture in late 2015 was that trading accounts were divided among a smaller number of firms, while the percentage of profitable accounts did not improve at all compared with the start of the decade (from 31% in the last quarter of 2009 to 31% in the third quarter of 2015).

Industry reports suggest that traders in stocks have higher incomes than forex populations: in the United States, for instance, 58% of stock traders have annual household incomes above $75,000, as compared with 35% of forex traders. In the European Union, though, only 37% of stock traders have annual household incomes above 55,000 Euros (Paz 2011, 22). In terms of gender, in the United States 32% of forex traders are female, compared to 26% of stock traders (21). Other data from a global population of traders suggest, though, that only 8% of forex traders are female, with an average age of 24 years (males have an average age of 25 years) (Zamboglou 2016). In light of my own work, this latter is a much more plausible gender ratio, and it suggests that in foreign currency markets, the population is younger (and therefore less affluent). There are,

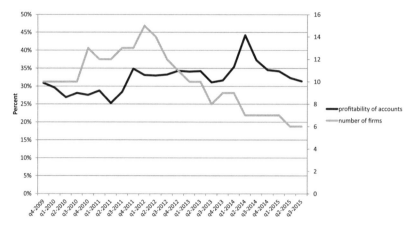

FIGURE 2. Profitability of nondiscretionary accounts and number of retail brokerage firms, 2009–2014. *Source*: Forex Magnates quarterly reports, compiled by the author.

however, considerable variations: a few traders can have account deposits up to $10 million, which runs counter to the usual assumptions about the modest funds of retail traders. I could not find any statistical data on the education profile of traders for any population.

The conversations I had with heads of brokerage houses (who have their own estimates) suggest that it is rather misleading to talk about "the population of retail traders." It is more accurate to talk about "populations," not population, simply because the traders are highly differentiated not only with respect to jurisdictions (regulated versus unregulated), but also with respect to financial instruments, the frequency of trading, the size of their assets, and trading forms. Thus, the retail forex population does not overlap with the shares population or with the ETF population (or at best they overlap partially); and trading populations in regulated jurisdictions (e.g., trading through a licensed broker in the United States or the United Kingdom) do not overlap with populations from unregulated jurisdictions. Populations on social trading platforms are a part of retail trading populations only. In addition to this, within most populations there appears to be a small hard core of very frequent and stable traders and an outer ring of less frequent, more fluctuating traders.

Conversations conducted in 2010 with London-based heads of brokerage houses have given the following estimate: only 20% of online traders are active traders, and within that percentage only a few hundred are highly skilled and conduct a high number of transactions daily. If we take 20% of all online traders as being active in the sense of the SEC definition (four or more trades over five business days), this gives us about 188,000 active traders for the whole of the United Kingdom in 2007. If we take a more conservative estimate of only 10% active traders, the number becomes 94,000.

However, the field of retail traders appears to be highly differentiated and dynamic:

JAMES [HEAD OF BROKERAGE 1]: You know the super active 10,000 per country with three, four, five hundred of them being able to do hundreds of trades a day each and been able to be 5%, 6% of the volume of the local exchange, 300 people, so the distribution is very, you know, the home people, the home security and they do a transaction a year, many are the real traders even in the US I think it is estimated to be in the tens of thousands.

AP: But these smaller communities are highly specialized and I understand from you, and I have seen from some of them, that they are also very skilled. You said they are almost like professionals.

JOHN [HEAD OF BROKERAGE 2]: Yah.

JAMES: I think it's probably almost half and half. Some people are very very skilled and they do that for a living and they have done so before, some of them, and they worked for a broker etc. and now they trade for themselves. Some of them are gamblers and they lose a lot of money, so there's active traders and a number of people that come and go and that burn themselves and then disappear because, you know, anyone which is an investor and catches the right trend and says now it's time to buy and the stock exchange grows 30%, everyone makes money and then they keep on buying, buying, buying, and then at some point they burn everything. But they don't do hundred[s] of transactions a day, but those that trade a lot, they tend to, you know, those that are skilled stay, those that are not can go and there's a lot of stoical memory, you know, people forget and then they come back again and they do it again and so I would say almost half of them are people that come and go and half of them are people that actually know what they're doing and they make profit. And this is in line with the comments that you hear from the brokerage community of those that service the kind of community.

I will discuss in the next chapter one of the issues that is hinted at here, namely the fuzzy boundaries between institutional and retail traders. For the time being, the aspects I want to point at are these: even heads of brokerages had to rely on estimates and did not know the exact numbers; the numbers of active traders per country are in the low hundreds or, more often, in the tens of thousands; there is a "hard core" of active traders who are at least more resilient, if not more skilled; and while the rate of losses appears to be very high, the return rate of burned traders is thought to be high too.

All in all, what do we know about the statistics of "noise"? Based on the above, we should not even talk about noise, but about noises. These traders can be highly differentiated, and all available indicators point to the fact that they are structured—therefore, based only on these scarce data, one could argue that the term is a misnomer. "Noises" have dynamics: they evolve in time, and they appear to have been fostered by particular institutional and technological developments. Furthermore, a lot of systematic work needs to be done on the structures of these noises, much more extensive work than this book will allow. Nevertheless, I will continue examining them here from the inside: How do they work in practice? What is their organization, and what are the effects of such organization upon trading? And perhaps the first key question is: How does one become a trader?

CHAPTER TWO

How Does One Become a Trader?

During my observations, I met traders of different ages, who had started trading at different moments during their lifetimes. I met some who had started while they were in middle school (using their parents' accounts) and some who had started in midlife, not to mention all those who had started in their twenties. The variability indicates that there is no single or dominant way of becoming a trader, no single path similar to the career paths we encounter in the professions, for instance. Becoming a lawyer or a doctor is closely associated with a specific and carefully laid out educational path. But becoming a retail trader? Listening to the career stories of older professional traders, I learned that some had begun on the lower rungs of the ladder and had worked their way up to buying a (very expensive) place in the pit. Some had been recruited by banks and brokerages straight from college and over several years had gained a seat at the trading desk. Both education and social networks are not atypical as gate openers for a career in the financial services industry. The mix may vary from place to place (see Hernandez 2014; Ho 2009), in the sense that in some situations relationships weigh more heavily, while in others education status matters more. Nevertheless, these are at least two gate openers for the industry. The notion of gate opener implies both that those aspiring to trading careers should possess attributes such as educational status and relationships *and* that they are willing to enter a recruitment process—an orderly, systematic way of transforming nontraders into (future) traders.

The financial services industry, though, includes many professional occupations (e.g., accountants, economists) for which there are established educational paths. If we look closely, there are no similar educational paths for becoming a trader. One can graduate in accounting or in economics, for instance, but (with perhaps a handful of exceptions) there are no graduate or undergraduate programs focusing solely on financial trading.[1] Certification as an institutional trader is part of an on-the-job training process, meaning that prospective professional traders will first be hired by financial firms and then become professionally certified at the end of the training process. How, then, do banks or brokerage firms identify potential trading professionality? How can they see which ordinary people have the potential to become professional traders? And how is such potential professionality established in the recruitment process? If the financial industry makes use of recruitment processes (which may include formal as well as informal elements) in order to gain, time and time again, future professional traders, what about retail traders? Are they subjected to similar processes? Do educational status and social relationships matter for them too? If recruitment processes exist, do they overlap with the ones for professional traders, or are they completely different?

One possibility here would be to consider the transformation of ordinary people into (retail) traders as a random process. Is it just boredom, or the desire to make some additional income? Can so many people, hundreds of thousands of them, become retail traders just like that, randomly? Or does one become a trader by the sole force of advertising undertaken by brokers? How could a supposedly random process be reproduced again and again? Or how can advertising be so forceful? Is the mere existence of discount brokerages, ETFs, CFDs, and the like, discussed in chapter 1, sufficient to explain how ordinary people become traders? If the transformation of ordinary people into traders is more or less random, it means that noise comes into markets from the outside. Is the recruitment of professional traders a random process as well? While opportunities for such inflows may be created by market institutions, those institutions, in such a case, would be more or less passive receptacles. Another possibility is to consider noise as being created in an active, organized fashion by these very institutions. Then we would have to look for (more or less systematic and well organized) recruitment processes and, if they exist, to determine whether they are completely different from the recruitment of professional traders.

Studies of recruitment into (elite) professions have stressed the complex character of the hiring process, in which the skills and the cultural practices of applicants are matched with the practices and the self-perception of the organization (Rivera 2012, 2011; Cottingham 2014). Formal recruitment processes are iterative, including several rounds of interviews, screening, and a résumé tailored to signal in multiple ways the elite status of the applicant: having attended the right schools and having been involved in the right extracurricular activities (Rivera 2015, 18). Recruitment processes, however, are not always entirely formal and do not always take place exclusively in preset steps, such as "read ad—send résumé—go to an interview." Some forms of recruitment can involve quasi-formal or negotiated activities preceding the more formal ones, significant with respect to building a pool of potential applicants for a particular type of professional activities (see also Tan 2015). These activities can require active involvement from those wanting to be seen as particularly suitable candidates. They can include the transformation of an ordinary person into somebody who is not yet a professional—such as a professional trader—but who is not a layperson anymore. For instance, an ordinary person might want to become a retail trader as a step toward possibly entering the world of professional trading.

The first major argument of this chapter is that becoming a trader is not a random process, with market institutions simply offering quasi-passive opportunities or mere incentives. And becoming a trader cannot be simply ascribed to advertising, no matter how aggressive or sophisticated it may be. This is not to say that serendipity is completely excluded from the picture. But if this process were random, then traders should be scattered around not only geographically, but socially as well. We should expect to find them in all kinds of places and situations, with different levels of education, in different professions, and having different hobbies. More significantly, we should expect all sorts of events to play roles in the transformation from nontrader to trader, and we should expect the transformation itself to be irregular. Accessing and observing traders would then be a very difficult enterprise indeed. If, however, the intervention of market institutions in making traders is more than just advertising, we need to find the regular and stable ways in which this transformation occurs. Ethnographically speaking, finding these ways also means finding a way to gain access to traders and being able to observe the transformation processes themselves.

The second major argument is that these ways—and they do exist—are not completely and strictly separated from the processes through which professional traders are created. Noise and information—to put it this way—are not separate from the start but are made separate within the transformation. We expect professional and retail trading to be two distinct and separate activities, characterizing two distinct groups. In fact, such a clear-cut distinction is not encountered in practice. Financial institutions intervene actively in making traders, and to a significant extent they make both types at once: professional and retail, the separation of whom occurs only in a longer and somewhat arduous process. One key social arrangement used by financial institutions to generate both types of traders at once is student trading clubs. Other significant arrangements are nonstudent trading clubs (different from investment clubs; see also Harrington 2008), Internet trading groups, and trading fairs. To a lesser extent, restructuring processes in the financial services industry produce retail traders as well, in the sense that some laid-off staff will move on either to become retail traders themselves or to provide auxiliary services such as education, coaching, or advising for retail traders.

With that, I come to my third major argument: all too often, when we talk about market institutions, we mean regulatory bodies, organized exchanges, brokerages, funds, and other forms of hierarchical organization directly, regularly, and quasi-exclusively implied in transactional activities. And when we talk about recruitment into (elite) professions, we tend to focus upon formal processes of recruitment, such as job interviews, assembling glossy résumés, and writing the "right" letters of application. We mostly leave out a variety of quasi-formal and informal ways of recruitment. We leave out quasi-formal social activities around market transactions, which are neither entirely nor exclusively economic. We also leave out activities that are not arranged in the major key of "serious" trading—that is, activities such as exercises, rehearsals, or mock-ups, which appear to be either peripheral or inconsequential, or both, with respect to trading.[2] These ways play a significant role in reproducing essential aspects of market activities (for instance, traders), and they should be counted among market institutions as well (Fine 2012; Fine and Harrington 2004). Minor keys play a significant role in recruitment processes, especially when combined with informal or quasi-formal ways of organizing social activities in small groups. The transformation of ordinary young men and women into traders occurs first in such minor keys, and in small groups.

Morphing into a Trader

While physical trading clubs (i.e., clubs that meet face-to-face) and Internet groups can include a broader mix of ages and professions, student trading clubs are tailored to a specific age and education bracket that is of particular interest to banks and hedge funds. Among their student societies or unions, many universities in the United Kingdom (and in the United States as well) have student trading clubs. I spent extensive time with three of them: one at a university offering a broad spectrum of educational programs, and two at academic institutions with more specialized ranges within the sciences. I also interviewed the president and vice president of a fourth student trading club, from another UK university, which was not as high up in the rankings as the other three. Internet searches and e-mail exchanges with club presidents revealed a similar situation at many Ivy League universities in the United States: investment and trading clubs autonomously operated by students were present there as well. In parallel, I soon discovered—almost serendipitously—that financial institutions (at least in the United Kingdom) heavily recruit graduates of science programs. (European higher education programs are specialized not only at the graduate level, but at the undergraduate level as well.) As I attended undergraduate open days in science departments during one summer, I noticed that a central sales pitch made by presenters was the number of science graduates hired by the financial services industry from their departments. One brochure stated that about 40% of the graduates of that particular science program went not into the lab, but straight into the investment bank.

This made me think that there must be some arrangement in place, encouraged or at least (partly) supported by financial institutions. Such an arrangement could help recruit graduates into the financial services, and particularly into trading and the related activities (analysis, for instance). That arrangement, I came to understand, is the student trading club! Club membership does not, of course, guarantee a trading career, but it is the way to go for students interested in one. All the presidents of the three trading clubs I observed during my fieldwork are now employed by global banks as traders or as trading-related analysts. Quite a few club members I talked to also found trading-related positions within investment banks after graduation. (Usually, recruitment happens during the last year of study, but it's a longer and thorny process.)

The student clubs I observed had between 300 members and 60 members each; undergraduate students dominated in one club. Only between 30% and 15% of club members were female students. In one case, members were scattered across the entire spectrum of academic disciplines. In the other two cases, owing to the nature of the institutions, membership was heavily tilted in a particular direction (science, including the social sciences), and graduate students played a significant role. Female students were a minority, although in one case I observed, they were part of the club leadership. The clubs were organized into groups specializing in trading a particular class of securities: categories of stocks, foreign exchange, or options (in some rare cases). At one institution, though, there were groups specialized in producing and testing trading algorithms (this also had to do with the heavy presence of scientific expertise there).

Within each club, dedicated groups had allocated trading accounts (with a share of the overall club funds) from which they traded weekly. Each group (or sector, as they called themselves) had a steering committee meeting weekly to discuss the evolution of accounts and make trading recommendations, which were presented to the group in question. While trading decisions were made collectively, trading itself was done individually by one member of the group entrusted with placing transactions online from the trading account. The steering committee of each group met first for an hour or two (mostly in the evening, after lectures; in one case, on weekends as well). Immediately afterward, the groups met; after the groups met, there was a general assembly of the club, often followed by a round of drinks. Then orders were placed from the trading accounts. This struck me as a highly organized process, rekeying to some extent, albeit in a different temporal rhythm, the meetings of trading teams in investment banks (e.g., Beunza and Stark 2004; Gibson 2005).

Trading clubs rekeyed not only the hierarchical structure of financial institutions (with presidents, vice presidents, sector heads, committees, etc.) but also the very processes of recruitment in a bank. They rekeyed the major mode of formal recruitment into something more playful, though not entirely so. At one club I observed, one of the tasks of the incoming president (elected for the duration of one academic year) was to select candidates for committee positions. My expectation was that personal friendships would play a significant role here. What I encountered instead was a process based on the evaluation of CVs and on interviews with the candidates:

PAUL (ELECTED CLUB PRESIDENT, MATHEMATICS UNDERGRADUATE): Yeah, yeah, sure, so obviously, this is my committee for next year and those are basically the positions that I am recruiting in, and to what extent that influences my personal experience of trading is that obviously I can now make more of the strategic decisions. So what happens here is that those Account Directors will be managing subfunds of our larger funds and the Vice President will be sort of the Executive, then you have a Treasurer, which is kind of like the controlling department, and our Secretary in information, which is kind of like marketing, and the events which I've sort of outsourced from the marketing because I want them to look very specifically for the welfare of the people that are in the club. Then we have something that's for Project Teams, so those are the out of the box thinkers if you like. They are in a box now but they are supposed to be going outside of the box and the [name] is a new concept that we've started as a trading education certificate, so we are trying to implement that and . . . I've talked to a couple of banks already who are very interested, the banks are very interested and . . . so that might be something really useful, so we have educational modules right now which we want to, which we want to sort of make more structured and make more, yeah, make certified by a bank.

The trading club was entirely self-organized as a voluntary student activity. Its undertakings were not part of the university curriculum. They were not entirely informal either. The club was part of the student union, an umbrella organization that included many other clubs (the opera society, the badminton club, the gaming society, etc.). And yet, the club rekeyed the organizational chart and positions within a bank, adapting them to an activity format lacking the status, the formality, and the character of a bank. Paul adopted the organizational language too, and positioned himself "as if" he were the CEO of the enterprise (that is, he rekeyed his identity). He saw himself as able to make decisions but also took care to have some "out of the box" thinkers.

The entire process of running a student trading club was explicitly seen as an avenue leading to a financial career, as providing advantages in this respect, but also as a group enterprise where formal education (this was a science and technology school) had to be supplemented by the club's own courses. The notion of the trading club offering a trading certificate recognized by banks was meant to confer an edge to the school's graduates in their future careers:

AP: So you, you are setting up here an educational program?
PAUL: Right.
AP: Which people will have to go through in order to get this certificate?
PAUL: Absolutely.
AP: So this certificate will be in the end some piece of paper?

PAUL: Absolutely.

AP: It will be some sort of written . . .

PAUL: Yes.

AP: . . . confirmation . . .

PAUL: Yes.

AP: It's not just a name?

PAUL: No. There will be a written . . . I mean at least that's the optimum right? We're in the beginning phases. We are working out the concept right now, we are approaching the banks that are interested. I don't know exactly, I can't make any promise, but if it were my vision of it, my vision of it is yes, that the people, they spend one maybe even two years in here, they learn everything, fundamental, maybe even technical financial risk etc. and then get a certificate and something that they can . . .

AP: . . . Irrespective of their program of study, although they are studying here Physics or Chemistry or . . .

PAUL: Absolutely independently of what they study.

This indicates that at least some student trading clubs are more than just another distraction, or just a way of getting to know new people. They are systematic, well-organized settings for providing ordinary people with affordances for becoming retail traders and then for transforming some of these into professional traders. In other words, student trading clubs work as settings that transition ordinary people into traders.

The clubs were not only busy with trading; they also invited speakers from various financial institutions and organized trading competitions, job interviews, and internship opportunities. Every week during a school term, there was somebody giving a talk about a substantial topic, about the person's own trading experiences, or about career paths in financial institutions. While banks recruit from trading clubs, the latter also recruit banks into their efforts to create traders and to signal potential professionality. The rekeying of organizational hierarchies as formal structures grafted onto entirely voluntary activities helps the participants acquire formats of organizational behavior before they actually join an organization. One playfully learns to be an account director or an executive before entering a career path on which one might actually become a real account director. Such behavioral formats are exercised first in minor keys before being deployed in a major one.

This brings me to one essential question: where did the money come from, that these clubs traded with? To some extent, in the case of one club, it came from the members' own pockets; quite a few students traded on their own as well, but membership in the club was associated with a nonexclusionary investment of £300 (about $470, a modest sum, unless you are a student). The investment could be withdrawn after one year, together with any accruals; the club kept statistics on the returns on investment. There was a smaller group of traders within the club who had invested £2,500 (about $4,000) each. Failure to come up with this investment did not prevent membership, though. Many clubs also received donations from banks. The donations varied from £10,000 to £30,000 (about $15,700–$47,000). One exception here, I must say, was the trading club (with 85 members) of a different university, which recruited overwhelmingly students from disadvantaged backgrounds. Most members of this club traded on demo accounts, and very few of them traded with their own money. However, they too saw their activities in the club as a gateway to a career in the financial services industry:

> AP: So do you do another . . . I understand that another plan of yours is to go and work in investment banking.
>
> TIM: Yeah.
>
> AP: And do you see your activity, like your trading, as being related to this?
>
> TIM: Yes, another reason why I set up is to . . . obviously extracurricular activities is seen as an extremely positive attribute to any application you do, and this is directly related to the job applications in the banking industry, so it can only be seen as a positive aspect.
>
> AP: But on the other hand if you're going into the banking . . . the banking industry, then probably you know that you probably have to stop.
>
> TIM: Yep. No. Yep. That's fully accepted though. If you're a private trader, trade privately, you get a job it's against the law, you stop, so you close your positions, you know, and then you're trading for them. Whether you're a prop trader, an investment banker, or you know.

In at least two cases, trading performance was regularly communicated to club members; this feedback, together with set performance benchmarks, was seen as a way of teaching newcomers about trading, as signaling skills to the outside world, and as fostering competition among groups within the club:

> AP: Do you set any benchmarks for them, any performance benchmarks?
>
> PAUL: Definitely, every two weeks there is a pnl [profit and loss] published on

the website so, for everyone to see, even outside people, so even the students, whoever wants to check it out, and I do not necessarily want to fos-
ter that sort of competitive environment, because I do think, I do want
people to have fun, and these directors will have teams under them, right?
So there will be teams of fresh people, new people, some of them have
never even touched finance, and they are going to be in the same group
with these guys, and they will have teach them and manage that group as
well, so obviously their performance is not only measured with their personal performance but also with the performance and the quality of the
team members that they have, but, obviously there will be competitive,
competitiveness between them, to the extent that we are thinking about
a bonus system as well, yeah, we are still working that out, how the bonus
system could exactly work but yeah. [. . .] Yeah, yeah, I mean I am leaving them free, obviously within our risk management framework, but they
can, if they want to do commodities they can do commodities, if they like
currencies, if the[y] like equities, and they are supposed to do that, because . . . see, if a student comes to us with £300, right? If we make 30%
over the five months, then he earns 90 pounds. He might as well go work
in a bar for two days and he earns more money than that, right? So, this
is not about the return, this is really about the learning and about giving
people the feeling of actually being on the market and learning about the
markets, and that is something new. By the way that is the first year that
we've actually implemented it, this year is one group only, so we have only
[one] group which manages the 20,000. The splitting up is a new idea for
next year.

Based on Paul's statements, what does it mean to transform ordinary
people into traders? It doesn't necessarily mean making money, because,
as Paul said, one can earn more from bar tips. It means the "feeling of
being on the market" as expressed by competition, and although competition is not necessarily wanted, it is presented as a sort of necessary
evil. (It is another story, though, whether club members wanted to compete against each other. I discuss this in the next chapter.) It is also about
rekeying as much as possible the incentive system of an institutional environment (introducing a bonus system); it is about creating a network
of social relationships, but it is also about providing participants with "a
story to tell"—the story of their own accomplishments and experiences as
amateur traders, a story that can be useful when students are transition-

ing to professional trader status (see also Rivera 2015, 157). It is a documentable story of potential professionality. This rekeying is not mere mimicry: Paul's club didn't strive to simply imitate the formal institutional arrangements of an investment bank, such as the much reviled bonus agreements. Rekeying is not institutional isomorphism, since the latter implies imitating (consciously or not) arrangements across equivalent institutions in the same major key. In other words, institutional isomorphism is serious. The rekeying of competitiveness and of the bonus system as learning activities and as "fun" is significant with respect to facilitating the social transformation of young men and women into traders. Such rekeyings produce "stories" as means of social differentiation at the same time, with a view of deepening this differentiation in the future:

PAUL: Ok, so I am very fascinated about this group, where you will be able to build a community to the extent that people are emotionally attached. That is my big aim, to get these people to a community where they feel like they are really part of it. Not only a society. So, I want to create a real community, and that is the big advantage that I am giving these directors, is that they will be part of this community and they will begin to build a network which will last them into their professional careers, and this is something that I can be really tangible with and advertise with now but that I will make them feel, right. I will tell them, you are part of the elite, you are part of the guys that will definitely have good careers and the guys sitting left and right of you are exactly the same. So, I really want to create a sense of elitism and a sense of that, and I think that is partly what is attractive for that position and also, you know, you can write that you are a member of the investment club, but the real difference is if you are, if you write that you are a director and you have a story to tell, it's much nicer to have on your CV, than just yeah, I was a member of the Investment Club and I went to a couple of meetings. That doesn't impress anyone, but to tell the story that, yes, I was £7,000 and I had all of these people and proposals etc., and so it's a story to tell.

Paul was not the only one who used the word *elite*. As I discovered talking to another member of the same club, a small group had created a subdivision within the trading club, called "Global Investments Partnership," so that they could trade more quickly, with more money than the standard club share, and without involving all members of the club:

MARK (TALKING ABOUT THE GROUP WITHIN THE CLUB): Sure, three of us met through [club] and we do very similar things to [club] but everything is quicker, it's snappier, it's trading without the burden of carrying 60 people, the money of 60 people. It's trading knowing that every other individual has a certain level of knowledge. We all have a certain level of financial markets and experience, and it's getting things done faster and taking quicker action, and it's essentially very similar to [club] but with a more experienced group and with a sort of more elite, small group of people if you like, and of course there is less discrepancies, everything is just done faster, and we quite often send e-mails around in the morning. One person could propose to take a position on, I don't know, the Sterling, [the] Yen, and by midday we would all have agreed and done our research on it and it would go through, so it's much quicker, whereas in [club] it may take up to a week for the stock to be executed.

Being a student at a prestigious university (Paul and Mark's was widely regarded as being one) is not enough to be elite (see also Armstrong and Hamilton 2013, 216). One needs to be and do more than that. One needs to be more than a member of the trading club. One needs to already be a director if one is to aspire to becoming a director one day (although this is not the ultimate career goal). Trading clubs appear as arrangements for signaling potential professionality, not only in the sense that they transform nontraders into retail traders and then some of the latter into professional traders: they also differentiate among retail traders, producing "elites" within that group. This differentiation can well become part of the "story to tell" when a student looks for a job in the financial industry. Seen this way, financial careers begin before a person has even started in the bank; they begin actually in the trading club. Transforming people into retail traders—in other words, creating noise—is indispensable, then, for creating information. An institution apparently situated outside finance, with a quasi-informal and voluntary character—the club—is no less an institution of finance than the investment bank that it seeks to rekey, with its departments and directors, the bonus system, and the selection process for its positions. This "fun" and "learning" mode (as Paul put it) of playing the formal structures and arrangements of an investment bank within small groups appears to be essential with respect to how behavioral expectations are created. One learns to be competitive not only on the job within the bank; one comes with this prelearned expectation from having participated in the trading club.

Based on the comments made by Paul and Mark, banks were more interested in supporting student clubs from the top end of the university rankings. (Tim didn't mention any support from banks.) This made me ask, What made banks donate to student trading clubs? Admittedly, the sums were quite modest when put in relationship to the balance sheets and the names of the donors. Yet, banks support more than just one club; from what my conversation partners were telling me, all the investment and trading clubs associated with top universities received support from banks, not only in monetary form, but also by facilitating speaker invitations, inviting participation in trading competitions, disseminating information about internships, and, of course, direct recruitment. These activities not only support pools of potential candidates for trading-related positions within the banks, but also enable early selection of those who may one day become professional traders or work on their teams. Financial institutions have to engage not only in morphing ordinary people into amateur traders, but also in separating those who can hope to become professional traders from those who will stay (for various lengths of time, of course) within the realm of retail trading. The work of separation entails a series of more formal activities, which are partly relocated within the structures of the banks themselves and partly hybridize the informal, minor-key modes of the trading club with the major modes of the bank.

Separating Professional from Retail Traders

There were at least two ways of organizing this work of separation: one was implementing summer internships, and the other was setting up an almost uninterrupted string of trading competitions, which could be very consequential in the banks' hiring process. The clubs were the intermediaries between students eager to do a summer internship in a bank, and the banks themselves. Clubs distributed information and application forms and organized the entire competitive process of getting an internship. Being involved in club organization seemed to play a role of increasing one's chances for an internship. An internship, in its turn, was seen as increasing the chances for a future job. A few times, I heard students voicing their expectation to be offered a job by the bank where they were doing their summer internship. I also discovered that club members had very clear ideas about banking hierarchies. Above all, they strove to get jobs with Goldman Sachs. Yes, some of the students I talked to got offers from Goldman Sachs. Below Goldman, there was a not-too-long list of names judged as good, below which was another tier. In a way, although I could not match this directly, there was a parallel between the way some members of the trading club sought to create a club-internal stratification, on the one hand, and the way they perceived job desirability as stratified, on the other hand.

Internships and trading club activities formed a mutually reinforcing mechanism, in the sense that at least some traders had become club members because of previous internships in financial institutions. After becoming club members, they sought to engage in even more internships. Mark, quoted earlier, had started trading because his interest in finance was awakened by an internship he had done when he was 17:

> MARK: I've told you already that I pursued the internships in such investment banks and I only ever apply for roles in sales and trading securities, so obviously it's totally in line with my career path. [. . .] So joining [college] obviously joining the Finance Society as a member for the first year and the Investment Club and you're open to a lot of people, who may have a lot of experience doing it, who share the same interests and it really spurred on since then, so I was really interested into this career and I attended all of the, all these seminars that the banks were holding, it must have been at least 20 or 30 seminars in my first year, within the first three months, so I was talking to all of these traders who were coming in trying to recruit people, talking, asking them questions, wondering what this whole industry was, and yeah, so that was sort of finding my ground and obviously, as I told you, in that April I then went to [bank] for a Spring internship, and them being an investment bank at the time, or, definitely meant I got a foot into the door and saw what was going on, so at [bank] it was the first time I spent an extended amount of time on the trading floor. I sat next to a Foreign Exchange salesman and I watched him do his job for around three to four hours and I really liked it. I liked what he was doing, I liked the pace of it and I like the whole nature of the role and of course by that time I already had my, had developed my interest and sort of curiosity in the financial markets. So, it's, just to sum up as a summary, it's really little things that has gone on in my life for the past three years that I've added

into my sort of pool of interest, of the markets and it's the act of being able to put one's sort of assists and allow it to fluctuate and controlling or having some control of what happens to that. So well of course if you were smart enough and if you were able to beat the market, to gain, and that is, I think that is what attracts me to the markets.

While the topics of competition and agency figure prominently in this account—and I will come back to both later—this cycle seems to play a very important role for transitioning people into trading. Being able to temporarily gain access to and observe financial institutions leads to becoming a member in quasi-formal groups dedicated to trading activities, which enables even more access to financial institutions. Of course, neither internships nor student societies are specific to finance, and one shouldn't minimize the relevance of perceived agency here. Yet, this account and other similar accounts systematically point to this transitioning as a social enterprise, not an individual, isolated one. It is also an enterprise that is not restricted to offering opportunities—understood as occasions to do something—but affordances, understood as occasions tailored (or related) to the perceived abilities (and status) of the participants. It would be mistaken to believe, though, that all members of trading clubs are exposed to this virtual cycle of internships and club membership. This is, after all, the "elite" Mark was talking about. Within one year of my observations, members of Tim's trading club hadn't yet managed to find a bank to support their activities. (Having followed their careers over the years, I know that Paul works now for a global investment bank, while Tim has remained a retail trader.)

The trading competitions (with which I will deal in detail in the next chapter) were a more exciting affair. Once a year, usually in the spring, banks organized trading competitions, inviting student trading clubs to participate. A trading competition, pitching against each other students from different universities, usually took a half day, sometimes a full day, in the banks' trading rooms. In this case, teams competed against each other in the physical environment of the bank. Online competitions could take up to a month and more. Winning such a contest or at least ranking higher up opened the door to the long string of examinations, interviews, and psychological tests that, for the lucky ones, ended with a job offer on a trading team. Clubs tried to send their best to these competitions, and the best way to identify the best was to organize even more competitions. The organization of clubs into groups, sectors, and committees facilitated this procedure, since it offered a way of monitoring performance continuously. In addition, however, clubs organized internal competitions, mostly half-day affairs, offering alluring prizes such as bottles of French champagne. (Since the legal age for alcohol consumption is 18 in Europe, this was an enticing prize.)

Trading contests, competitions, and, more generally, club participation are established ways of transforming young people into retail traders. With a bit of luck and application, all the club members can become traders provided they score well in competitions, pull their weight in organizing club activities, or get an internship. Then the lucky ones will morph into professional traders, something that takes a longer time. Once they enter this process, they will have to give up on being retail traders, or at least accept some serious restrictions. Tim, who is quoted above, had already indicated that he was ready to accept this. As one competition winner explained to me, being offered a contract by the bank meant closing all his trading accounts and opening a closely supervised one with his employer. Therefore, the winner in question planned to stop retail trading and fully concentrate on doing it professionally. The work of separation is thus brought to closure by clear, formal requirements with respect to status, but also with respect to what is permissible or not as a trading activity. The boundaries between retail and professional trading have to be kept in place once the processes of transformation and separation are brought to a close. During the process itself, which can take years, the distinctions are much less clear-cut.

Retail trading, then, was neither irrelevant "noise" nor something trading club members did just out of boredom. Neither was it the sort of activity one does in isolation and without any communication with peers (more about this later). Both participants and institutions were fully aware that retail trading as practiced in the organized form of the club was a significant credential when applying for a career in finance. On their side, club members groomed their trading biographies and fully engaged in committee memberships, meetings, giving talks, and picking stocks. They projected trading careers and goals both backward and forward. One young trader told me that he had started trading when he was 13. He would excuse himself from class at school to go to the restroom, and from there he would call his father on his cell phone, placing buy and sell orders. Being underage, he could not have a trading account in his own name; he had to use a family member as a front man. Another young trader told me that he wanted to go professional, make money, and then retire at 35, with the goal of buying a farm and horses. I tried to picture both scenes, frantic trading calls from a stall in a middle school restroom, on the one hand, and, on the other, bucolic pastures and horses, maybe with rolling hills. At least as relevant, though, if not even more, was the career goal formulated by Paul, who didn't want to work forever in an investment bank. He wanted to manage his own hedge fund:

> AP: So do you envisage then, a career in investment banking or in financial markets?
>
> PAUL: I do, but I don't believe in careers, I'm not very fond of them and I don't want to have one in the sort of, the sort of strict social sense of it. So I would much rather prefer and I do see myself, I don't know, being bankrupt for two or three times in my life and just getting bust on things that I do, and I would much rather prefer to have the adventure of actually doing something on my own and actually creating value for myself than, yeah, than putting my work and my labor towards someone else's added value. And I think that if you go from a very logical perspective, the fact that you are employed means that you add more value than you pay to you, to a company that you don't, you know, you actually add more value than you get paid, so otherwise you wouldn't be employed there right, so the company would fire you otherwise, so I think that very fundamentally it makes no sense for someone to be in a career. So I definitely want to start in investment banking. I have to, to learn somewhere, but my real aim is to become independent, maybe have my own hedge fund, maybe, definitely create something of my own, yeah, I wanna do that, I wanna create . . . [. . .] No, no, if in 20 years you call me and you ask me again, I am telling you that I am an investment banker, you can, whatever I am going to tell you, actually you probably are going to know that I am not happy, so if I'm really set on not having the typical career and then being whatever, a Director of some bank or Partner, whatever . . . no, that's not my . . .

The ultimate objective of being a director in a minor key isn't becoming one in a major key—that is, in real life. The ultimate objective transcends that—it is the apparent independence, but also the power, of having one's own hedge fund. These notions of independence and power, of "creating value for oneself" conflate social with monetary value, while reversing the relationship between individuals and organizations. Paul doesn't want to work toward adding value to organization—he dreams, though, of controlling organizations. He reconceptualizes "career" away from climbing the organizational ladder. Career means going bust a few times and having an "adventure"—as well as a hedge fund. Trading is a life project, not a career project. It is a form of conservative radicalism with established historical roots (Burns 2009, 189), one that does not reject forms of social organizations but rather claims to subordinate them to individual goals.

While these are some of the more extreme examples, they are by no means the only ones. Many trading club members didn't treat going professional as an aim in itself, but as a means of achieving something else (I will talk more extensively about this in chapter 7); at the same time, they actively worked, in a reflexive fashion, upon their trading biographies, well knowing that these counted when trying to get a foot on the ladder.

On their side, investment banks actively supported—financially and otherwise—the activities of trading clubs. They set up a complex, partly formal and partly informal recruitment process, which could last more than one year and included playful forms of competition such as trading contests, but also teamwork. Overall, it appeared that investment banks were interested in nurturing at least retail traders within a particular demographic bracket (young, still in higher education, studying at a prestigious university) with the aim of (willingly) engaging them in a process of finding potential professionality and of separating between amateurs and professionals. Yet, as I have said, not all student trading clubs appeared to be supported (financially and organizationally) by investment banks. There is competition for the banks' attention, but there are also entrenched, stratified recruitment channels that are difficult to widen or redirect. It is not enough to be a student at a top-tier university (see also Armstrong and Hamilton 2013; Rivera 2015). One needs to actively seek an elite position within that cohort, to create a documentable "story to tell." Lauren Rivera (2015, 154–155) emphasizes the role of emotions and passion in constructing a personal narrative during the interview process. For at least particular types of jobs related to financial trading, though, the narrative appears to be preconstructed by participants as documenting trading-relevant achievements and status positions prior to the formal recruitment process.

Trading clubs did more than just providing their members with immediate career opportunities. Not every member dreamed of becoming a professional trader, retiring at 35, and living on a horse farm afterward. In some specific cases, technologically savvy young traders got together and used electronic finance as a sort of real life laboratory for their ideas. They developed trading machines and tested them in the market, pooling together not so much financial resources as knowledge, imagination, and the discipline of research. While the perspective of a career in the financial services was not excluded here, it was more remote and less the ultimate goal than in other cases. Traders of this kind, at least those I saw and talked to, were exclusively technologically educated. They were studying science and engineering subjects; they engaged in trading not with the mere goal of immediately making money, but with the goal of testing a particular view or model of the world by means of making money. I will talk about them in detail when I deal with groups and group communication in markets. I would like to reiterate here, though, that the transformation process from nontrader to trader and the separation of traders, as supported by student trading clubs, are not merely selection mechanisms, in the sense that some young people will become traders and others will fail. They are diversification and stratification processes in which various affordances will lead to various outcomes. These processes produce not only skills but also relationships and stories (understood as the ability to invoke and mobilize one's own experiences but also to rework one's own biography recursively).

Latecomers

Trading clubs worked well as student recruitment grounds and as an institutional arrangement for morphing young men (mostly) into retail traders and then morphing some of them into professional traders. My next (admittedly rhetorical) question is, Did trading clubs work for people who were past their 20s, too? Yes, they did: both physical trading clubs and Internet trading groups were actively recruiting the interested (or the curious), making them into traders, and deploying considerable effort toward keeping them within markets. They were joined in this effort, more often than not collaboratively, by electronic brokerage houses.

During my ethnographic activities in electronic finance, I encountered numerous trading clubs and Internet groups that met regularly:

I know of three groups in London alone and have repeatedly attended the meetings of two of them, together with an audience of more than 50 people in each case. One of these clubs had a mailing list of more than 900 names, but the attendance at meetings was much lower. Club membership is not free: attendees of the London club I observed more extensively had to pay a fee of £30 (about $50) per monthly session, or purchase a six-month subscription at a discount (there were student discounts as well). While most members were London-based, a handful came from Continental Europe. In terms of age, the spread went from the early 20s to the early 70s. A majority (but not all) had college degrees and were men. I have been in Internet sessions with trading groups from the US Midwest. Some of these groups met at least once a month, for about one hour to 90 minutes (Internet groups) or up to three or four hours (in the case of face-to-face clubs, the members of which also socialized at the pub after hearing a talk).

At this point, I should add that trading clubs differ from investment clubs not only in style, but also in substance: the former are concerned with involving and keeping members in a regular and frequent activity by tying them to a particular institutional format (the brokerage house, the analyst), without having them delegate agency. Traders are supposed to trade on their own, and do so frequently. When traders decide to let a fellow trader manage their accounts, they delegate agency to an individual who is part of their circle, with whom they are in constant contact. Investment clubs, at least those I attended, delegate to institutions such as investment funds. Their members do not engage directly in a regular and frequent activity such as trading, but rather in delegation searches: finding agents with a good track record for money management. I attended meetings of investment clubs in the United States as well as in the United Kingdom, and in both countries they differ from trading clubs in their topics, interests, age, and wealth composition. The investment clubs I attended had an older and more well-to-do audience, and they discussed issues related to retirement provisions, wills, pension and trust funds, inheritance, and inheritance taxes. Trading clubs dealt simply with issues of buying and selling financial instruments on a regular and frequent basis.

Trading clubs and Internet groups exist to an extent also because of a process reverting the separation I previously discussed. To be more specific, the opposite of being recruited by an investment bank (or an exchange) as a trader can occasion the existence of trading clubs. Being

dis-recruited, that is, being fired by a bank, can lead to founding a trading club. We often wonder how people are made into professional traders, without thinking that the reverse can happen as well: professional
traders are made into nontraders, by, for example, losing their jobs, and
then they revert from nontraders to retail traders. We shouldn't think
that the professional lives of traders are eternal: among others things,
technological shifts (which occur rather frequently in finance) may put
traders out of business. Traders who have lost their jobs have several
choices: they can continue as retail traders; they can start an electronic
brokerage or work for one; they can offer educational services by starting a trading group or a club. In chapter 1, I discussed the case of Chris,
who was a trader in the pits of Chicago but had to quit when the job became physically too demanding and when technological changes managed to rip apart the social fabric of the pits (see also Zaloom 2006).

In some other cases discussed in chapter 1, changes in the tax code
provided the trigger for starting a trading club. Vince, the founder of a
London club, recalled that he worked as a consultant in the IT industry
when, in the early 1990s, a change in tax regulations introduced income
tax for IT specialists. As Vince's last job was the technical maintenance
of a very large corporation's trading room, he got his inspiration from
there and went into trading, later starting a fee-paying trading club. Yet,
although his career change was triggered by the tax code, and while acknowledging that he wasn't making consistent profits in his trading, he
described his motivation in terms of freedom from corporate life:

AP: So you prefer this activity to corporate employment?
VINCE: Oh yeah, yeah. Nobody used to like me in corporate life, I don't know
why, but no, I'm much happier doing what I'm doing. I like being in control of my own destiny, if you like.

Yet, the process of starting a trading club reveals that reminiscences
of corporate life creep through the back door. What is more, starting
such a club is a more organized affair than one would have expected in
light of the rhetoric of individualism. Vince had modeled the trading club
after a professional society and had institutional help in setting it up, not
least because his contacts from the professional society enabled him to
invite speakers and thus make membership in his club more attractive. I
encountered here the same process of rekeying that applied to the students' trading clubs: a formal institutional structure with major key goals

(advancing a professional career) is rearranged in a minor key, as an occasion for socialization and for meeting like-minded people, while keeping in place formal aspects (fee structure, invited speakers) that make it recognizable from the vantage point of formal institutions. If Vince invited speakers from the professional world, the latter accepted the invitation not only as returning a social obligation or because they wanted to promote a particular analytical technique, but also because the formal structure of the trading club was recognizable to them.

In most instances I encountered, clubs or even small groups had a member (if not a founding one) who was somehow tied to the financial services industry or was actively working in that industry. Communication among members, as I witnessed it, was indeed always genuine. Nevertheless, in the instances I encountered, the motivation to organize a group or a club did not appear to be something disconnected from the electronic brokerage industry or to connect with the said industry only at a later stage. Vince had started by advertising in forums, but later he also bought a mailing list, which served as a foundation for the club.

Trading shows are one venue where group members are recruited. There, group organizers rent stands, distribute flyers and business cards, and present their activities. Over my years of repeatedly attending these shows, I noticed that more and more sessions were assigned to the presentation of trading clubs and groups. What is the incentive for investing so much time in organizing a trading club? Socialization with like-minded traders is one incentive, for sure. However, in contrast to other groups I observed (and especially in contrast to those dedicated to building trading algorithms and to Internet groups), discussions within physical trading groups and clubs with nonstudent members never went into very specific details about who traded what precisely, how much exactly, and exactly when. They all stayed at the more general level of discussing particular market events or a particular analytical technique or strategy, or listing transactions completed, without specifics. On occasion, especially at the pub, some members acknowledged in my presence having lost money, without specifying how much. On one occasion, again at the pub, a club member noticed ironically that the organizer, who talked each time about his own trades, did so in the most general terms and without any specifics. When I asked the organizer about this, he said that he didn't disclose specific trades because doing so could have been construed as trading advice. The practice stood in stark contrast with that of

Internet groups, which admittedly were much smaller (about 5 or 6 members, as opposed to 50). Internet groups regularly talked in real time about their trades and disclosed specifics within the group.

Trading club activities mixed personal and impersonal interactions: formal presentations in a lecture format were followed by Q&A sessions and then by prolonged sessions at the pub, where trading was the main conversation topic. The audience didn't always absorb passively the wisdom of the lecturer. In several instances, when they seemed to disagree with particular statements, audiences sneered, laughed, or made ironic comments. During lectures I overheard snippets of whispered conversations indicating that some audience members were quite knowledgeable. This made me think club members were not attending meetings because they were completely ignorant and wanted to learn, but for some other reason. I decided to ask Vince (whom I have already introduced) about the members of the trading club and why they were attending regularly:

AP: And by way of demographics, how would you characterize your membership and your mailing list?

VINCE: Predominantly male. I'd say probably 95% male in all honesty, however, strange because female traders are supposed to be better than men [*laughs*]. I'd say that probably a quarter of the people who come along are professional . . . well I wouldn't say professional but full-time traders like myself. In the main several are retired indeed [from a regular job]. Several have just given up corporate life as I have too, to trade. And there are some people who still have a job but are very serious traders, you know, . . . trade large amounts of money, you know, on the side. There's one chap who owns several opticians and he day trades between patients and does very well. We also get, it's, there's quite a high churn, however, because people's perception of the trading industry is that it's easy money, and it's a myth perpetrated by education companies who will give you the impression that all you have to do is give them £5,000 or £6,000, spend a weekend with them, and on Monday morning you can start making £5,000 a week in your pajamas. Which is a total fallacy, and so consequently I get a lot of people who do come to the [club] and what they want to know is what is the button they need to push to make all this money without putting in any effort whatsoever, and when they find out there isn't such a button, they wander off and look for somebody who'll tell them which one it is. So there is a lot of that and probably the remainder tends to be made up of

graduates who come along twice to try to learn, get an idea of how to trade
in order to help them get a job in the City. So that's kind of, they're about
the three main groups I think.

In this account, there are at least three kinds of club populations.
There are the transient ones, "searching for the button" and leaving
when they are told that there is none. Then there is a transitional population, interested in changing their status from retail to institutional
traders. Finally, there is a stable population of traders who either substantially supplement their income from trading or aim at making a full
living from it (with varying degrees of success). When I asked Vince
about the sums used by club members, he said that very few had accounts of £100,000 (about $150,000) and more; the vast majority traded
with much smaller sums.

Yet, switching perspective from the founder to members of the trading club, how did they come to join the enterprise? I asked members of
Vince's club: in their accounts (and others as well), transitioning from
nontrader to trader is a slow process, in many instances occasioned by
everyday problems such as finding a way to save money, or simply learning how to manage one's own income. Jack told me how he started putting money into a pension fund but then tried to cut out the middle man:

JACK: The pension made quite a lot of money. I thought ah okay, yeah that's a
    great return, fantastic! But I wonder if I can cut out the fund manager and
    just, you know, go in and learn how to do it myself basically, and but I was
    sort of thinking about this over . . . Christmas, and in January I opened
    up a sort of stocks and shares ISA,[3] and it's quite interesting because that
    went up a little bit but then it also, then it started to drop and it sort of
    dropped off throughout the year. And also around about that time, Jan-
    uary, that's when I really started to think, okay, I wonder how this whole
    trading thing works, and so I started reading up about sort of various sort
    of web forums about how to trade in stocks, and I looked at sort of get-
    ting a . . . I got some books about how to, you know, trade, sort of more
    from a fundamental perspective, and that's probably sort of early Janu-
    ary and then throughout sort of January, February, I was sort of reading
    web forums, reading books about trading, not really focusing on techni-
    cal fundamental . . . just reading, and at the same time I purchased some
    shares. I purchased them with the intention of running them as a sort of
    like an "income fund" where basically the fund would grow through the

dividend reinvestment. Now of course, as you can imagine, in the last couple of months it's . . . the capital has been affected, but also the companies,
the underlying companies' sort of assets of, sort of earnings etc. and pre-
dicted growth have been affected so the dividends, some cases the dividends have been awful. But that was sort of, that was quite an interesting
experience, you know, sort of going through the mechanics of choosing
and buying, but I never really felt that I had a sort of like a proper system,
and so then, yeah, I went to the Traders' Expo back in February and that's
when I sort of first came across [Vince's club] amongst many other people,
and yeah it's basically, it's sort of . . . I've been on the hunt to try and work
out a way to make money from the markets and that's why I've come to . . .
I've come to more of a sort of technical approach to the markets. So that's
where I am at the moment, is . . . developing a sort of technical system that
I'm happy with, you know, so based purely on . . . purely on the charts, developing a method of . . . extracting money from the markets.

The redefinition of savings—extracting money from the market instead of setting money aside; doing it yourself rather than letting a professional do it for you—as a personalized activity (and as action) is seen
as the driver for this transformation, which cannot occur in isolation,
though. Its completion requires joining others. Jack's account points at
a distinction between accidental experiences and more systematic ones
("acquiring a proper system"). The latter requires being part of a group.
The transition from accidentality to sustained engagement with "working out how to make money out of markets," an engagement seen as essential for morphing into a trader, is made by becoming part of a group.
This account is echoed by other traders as well. Everyday issues of managing his own income had prompted Abe, who had an engineering degree and was based in the Midwest, to assemble his own trading group
after going through a process similar to Jack's:

ABE: I didn't really get much training there [in college], so outside of that, so
    outside of that I sort of took it on myself to . . . get involved and get hands-
    on learning, and that's where the process started, back in 2003, to educate
    myself. . . . So there was a lot of angst in the beginning, you know, par-
    tially just reflecting on the choices I made and not having some mentor-
    ship, you know, or guidance outside of just books and materials and, you
    know, things like that. So I started like my own trading group. . . . The ed-
    ucation program that I signed up for, the trainer for that education pro-

gram had other groups in the city, this was in [US state]. . . . And he was in touch with those group leaders and I was so energetic and I wanted to, you know, get involved and . . . you know, so I said, well the best way to learn is to start teaching, right? So I thought that also would give me exposure to some people who had been doing this longer than I had, so I contacted him and I said I would like to start my own group and I would like to be the leader of the group, and he put me in touch with people and then I contacted everyone, sent an e-mail out. We set up our first meeting in a library and we had a projector and a laptop and, you know, we started to . . . and then slowly started to evolve into a more tight group with, you know, having agendas that we wanted to discuss and talk about the market, talk about stocks, discuss the stocks people were looking at, why they would want to get into those trades, more swing trading, you know, type of stuff, so two to four week, six week long trades. Just talking through the mind-set of why enter, why exit and when do you want to exit and those kinds of things, so that's how I started. [. . .] We started to meet up at a Panera after that, so our first meeting was at a library and then after that we started to meet more often. . . . Once a month we would meet at a Panera . . . Panera Bread . . . y' know, which had free Wi-Fi and so we could set up a laptop.

Abe and Jack (and plenty of others as well) make it clear that simply reading books or attending a seminar will not make you into a trader. Joining a group is a significant process because it is in a group that the "mind-set of why" can be analyzed. That this mind-set cannot be idiosyncratic, that it cannot be a single person's mind-set, is made abundantly clear by traders. Trading is a social activity, not an individual one. What Abe and Jack also make clear is that initial (and rather trivial) motivations such as finding ways to save money (or managing one's income after graduation, as in Abe's case) are not enough as a driver of trading, because one needs, time and time again, to answer the question, "Why would I want to go into that trade?" This is a nonroutine question, different from, say, the decision to set aside every month a percentage of one's salary. Nonroutine questions are questions that need to be formulated anew again and again, and each time the answer might be different from the immediately previous one. The search for answers requires the "mind-set of why," which is social, not individual. Hence the group activity as the primary mechanism of becoming a trader.

This is not to say that the pattern of becoming a trader as member of a group is the only one. I have also encountered traders (a few) who were not fully integrated in a group (though even some of those kept in touch with a group) and who had taken up trading serendipitously (e.g., because of an ad placed in a medical journal or because going back to graduate school had confronted them with additional expenses). Social organization does not exclude serendipity or individualistic situations. This organization, though, shows that professional and retail trading are not two entirely separate domains and that transformations do take place in both directions. Professionals can become retail traders, and the other way around. These transformations take place regularly, in a reproducible fashion, and in social formats that include both formal and informal groups.

Coming back to my initial argument about noise: if we take this attribute as being affixed to categories of traders, then regularly, within the institutions of the market, noise becomes information and information becomes noise. I mean that the two social categories of professional and retail traders are much less separate from each other than one may think. True, boundaries have to be marked when the work of separation is achieved in individual cases: when this happens, individual trading accounts have to be given up. If we look beyond such rituals, though, no strict separation can be found over the life cycles of traders: retail traders can become professionals; professional traders can lose their jobs and turn to retail. The fact that the transformation is socially organized, and that groups play a significant role, should make us ask whether it is appropriate to think of market institutions only in terms of formal organizations, or in terms of the narrow confines of explicit, direct, and exclusive involvement in conducting transactions.

While brokerages, exchanges, funds, and regulators are market institutions, groups such as (student) trading clubs should be included on the list too, since they play a significant role in reproducing professional categories within finance. So should informal groups of traders, since (at the very least) they create a pool of shared experiences and knowledge that is intrinsic to being a retail trader. And because there is a flux between the two categories, one cannot devise a way of keeping such experiences completely apart and isolated from those of professional traders. Gary Alan Fine (2012) has argued that small groups are a fundamental mode of social organization, if not the fundamental mode, since it is in such groups that pools of experience within particular activities are produced. At least in finance, such groups maintain a fringe status with respect to the "big" institutions of finance; yet, at least some of them are essential with respect to how these "big" institutions are reproduced. Without the student trading clubs, for instance, it would be more difficult for banks to organize their recruitment processes and to separate future professionals from nonprofessionals. Similarly, without trading clubs and groups, it would be more difficult for former professional traders to redeploy their knowledge and skills. Seen this way, informal or quasi-formal small groups are much more than a fringe institution in the world of electronic finance.

In closing this chapter, I want to highlight again rekeying as an essential procedure with respect to how small groups operate. They do not simply imitate the formal structures of big banks, or their compensation arrangements such as bonuses, or their expectations such as competitive behavior. There is no "bonus" handed by student trading clubs to their presidents and vice presidents. Formality cannot be simply imitated within informal or quasi-formal settings. The expectations, rules, and structures of big banks can be rearranged in minor modes, though, and such rearrangements are crucial with respect to how formal, big institutions can live in symbiosis with small informal groups. The playfulness of minor keys needs to be taken seriously.

I will discuss extensively groups and group communication in chapter 5. For now, though, I will turn to another crucial aspect of trading—or at least one that is regularly touted as crucial and as making markets what they are—competitions. Until now, competitions haven't figured prominently in this analysis. Yet, we all know the saying "markets red in tooth and claw"—markets are seen as the epitome of unfettered competition, whether this is judged as good or as bad. For retail traders, where are this famed competition and the competitive spirit to be found? I have already discussed very briefly trading competitions as one of the activities of student trading clubs. But there is more to it than just that.

CHAPTER THREE

Taking On the Market

Competitions and Spectacle in Trading

Every year, in several large North American cities, in Western Europe (and now in Pacific Asia as well), trading shows are staged over two or three days in convention centers or hotels, attracting audiences of retail traders up into the lower thousands. They bear different names: the Money Show, the Traders' Expo, or the Forex and Options Expo. The organization behind these shows is a Florida-based financial media company called Money Show, which, according to its own website, produces about 17 shows a year around the world, in addition to seminar cruises and Internet shows. The shows are different from those addressing professional traders, who have their own, more complex circuits. I have attended several of these events on the East Coast and the West Coast and in London. The program is mostly the same, and it involves the same presenters and the same formats: seminars, live trading sessions, trading contests, and an exhibition where electronic brokerages, analyst firms, trading clubs, trading coaches, and publishers of how-to manuals distribute information. Some seminars charge hefty fees. Once I registered for the first show I attended, e-mails started flowing: brokers, education providers, coaches, analysts, strategy producers were (and still are) all vying to enlist me in their activities. Over the years, I have seen the same presenters do the same routine on the West Coast and on the East Coast, or in London and on the East Coast. The biggest events of all, however, are in Las Vegas and in New York City. In talking to attendees, I could see that some had come long distances: Midwesterners attending shows on the West Coast, Continental Europeans attending the London shows. In talking to some electronic brokers,

I could see that they take these shows very seriously and attend them: I have met and talked to the same representatives of significant brokerage houses on the East Coast and in London. With their mix of fun fare (there are prize drawings and trading contests), talks, demonstrations, and brokerage stands, trading shows are one of the main portals through which the curious make first contact with electronic finance. And then, of course, for those unable or unwilling to attend a trading show, there is still the world of the Internet, with its discussion forums, advice, sites, and webinars offering a glimpse of the claimed promises and rewards of trading. There is one element in these shows that deserves close attention: trading competitions.[1] They are staged in a face-to-face format, in front of a live audience of several hundred; they can take several days at a time; they can pitch teams or individuals against each other; and they can have sought-after prizes. They can involve amateurs, but also professionals. Overall, financial markets spend a good deal of time and effort on organizing trading competitions in a variety of formats and venues that, even in the age of the trading screen, are not at all limited to virtuality. What is more, these competitions, without exception, are carefully arranged. I have never witnessed a spontaneous contest or a mixup of competition formats. This indicates that competitions must be important; that one single format is not seen as enough; that it is not enough to have them once. They must be repeated periodically. While competitions are organized outside trading shows as well, it is at such shows that they unfold in front of live audiences, almost every day and sometimes more than once a day. True, professional trading conventions have their own competitions. But why is this competitive element so important that it is regularly staged at every single convention? Is it just to keep the audience entertained and ward off the dull times? As the most important shows are organized in Las Vegas and in New York City, trading competitions could hardly overshadow the entertainment opportunities available all around in these locations. What are they about, then? Why do staged, organized competitions figure so prominently in finance, when we should expect this to be the place where real, unfettered competitions dominate?

One could say, for instance, that competitions are staged as a means of attracting new clients by showing how traders win, particularly at those competitions that are enacted in front of a live audience. We should not forget that every competition of this kind has not only a winner, but also a loser. Audiences could be not only enticed by witnessing winning, but also repelled by witnessing losing. One could also say that competitions are organized to demonstrate trading technologies; during competitions, though, technology can fail in front of a live audience, and I saw this happening a few times. Finally, one could say that competitions are a means of breaking the monotony of trading and of offering a little more entertainment. But what kind of entertainment would be more of the same monotony? While in the audience of live competitions, I have witnessed enough moments of dullness, where nothing spectacular was happening. Trading competitions can be the antithesis of entertainment, although (to be fair) some contestants knew how to make spectacular introductions.

I will argue in chapter 4 that the trading screen itself is geared toward giving traders the impression of competition: that they bid against each other in an environment where skills and discipline are all that matter, in other words, an environment where one wins on merit and where fairness prevails. This argument also fits nicely with the trope of endless betterment required from participants in market competitions (Bröckling 2007, 102). For a very long time, competition has been—and it continues to be—an intensely used trope in the rhetoric of promoting various market environments, a trope that has been intimately related to various regulatory efforts as well, not least within finance. Besides much-touted economic benefits that can be found nowadays in every textbook—increasing efficiency, lowering prices, and so on—competition has been tied to moral issues, especially when it comes to justifying regulatory efforts (e.g., Stucke 2013, 165–166; Shionoya 1995, 13; Fourcade and Healy 2007; Zelizer 2010). Fairness and access figure prominently here; often, regulatory efforts to increase disclosure in financial markets or to limit particular types of trading have been justified with respect to the necessity of ensuring fair access for retail traders and investors (e.g., White 2015, 2014). More recent cases are provided by high frequency trading and dark pools: although these are completely different in nature, regulators have sought to limit both on the ground that retail traders have little access to them.

Competition appears, thus, not only as an economic issue but as a moral one as well,[2] especially in relationship to promoting forms of popular capitalism, or "markets for all": access and fairness (or winning on merit) figure prominently. In retail trading, which doubtlessly belongs to the "markets for all" category, the trading screen is set to give the impression (not to say the illusion) of a popular competition, open to all adults (I deal with this extensively in chapter 4). For participants, this is certainly an attractive notion. Most traders I have talked to, if not all of them, were enticed by the opportunity of meritocratic competitions, which they viewed in moral terms as well. The puzzle is, Can the trading screen alone sustain this enticement? Can competition as a moral issue to which participants adhere be supported solely by means of an anonymous medium?

If we are to understand what makes electronic finance attractive to traders, we need to solve the puzzle of how participation in competitions is made into a moral issue and sustained as such. And we also need to tie it to the previous puzzle, namely: Why are staged competitions organized so regularly, when we would certainly expect financial markets not to lack competition? The fundamental puzzle, though, is perhaps, What, actually, is competition? These puzzles hint at least at two aspects: since competitions are staged, we are confronted with the issue of rekeying, but also with that of transformation again. Competitions seem to be rekeyed in minor modes (as shows, exercises, etc.),[3] and since this rekeying is done for the benefit of particular audiences, we can legitimately suspect that they have something to do, at least in part, with the transformation of ordinary people into traders. But how?

Perhaps a good way to start solving these puzzles is to look at how the issue of competition has been dealt with in sociology. My focus here is competition as it is enacted in interactions, not competitions at the institutional level. As Erving Goffman (1983) once said, the interaction order is a sui generis one, and no matter how institutional setups favor, regulate, or control competitive environments, competitions will have to be carried out in interactions. Therefore, in the present context, I am less interested in issues such as competitions among brokerages than in a perhaps more basic issue—namely, what happens when two or more individuals compete with each other? And where does this incentive, or drive to compete, come from? I do not mean here psychological motivations, which may be as variable as they are hard to access. What I mean is, What conditions and restrictions does the interaction order place upon competitions, and what affordances does the interaction order provide to competitors and to their audiences, so that competition itself can take place? One argument coming from both Erving Goffman (1982) and Harold Garfinkel (1967) is that interactions place moral obligations upon participants: entering an interaction means committing, albeit for a limited time, to such obligations. If this is so, it means that even competitive interactions are not devoid of moral obligations and commitments, although these might not necessarily always fit explicit moral codes. This statement seems to be both contradictory and counterintuitive—competition should be "red in tooth and claw" (Mirowski 1994), implying among other things a lack of morality. Within political economy, of course, there is more than one notion of competition: there is free competition, there is perfect competition (Salvadori and Signorino 2013), but these notions are primarily concerned with how prices are determined with respect to supply and demand.[4] In the present context, I am concerned with the behavior of participants and with how interacting with each other in a competitive way places moral constraints upon this behavior.

How do we explain this? One approach would be to combine two answers coming from the classics—Georg Simmel's and Erving Goffman's. In his *Sociology* treatise, Simmel devoted substantial space to discussing competitions as a form of indirect social struggle, which cannot end with one participant triumphing over her or his opponent. Victory in a competition is only a means subordinated to the true aim of the entire competitive process, namely attaining social value (Simmel 1992, 323). Competitors are acknowledged and ranked by their public according to a set of social attributes (the most courageous, daring, cunning, etc.) that are regarded as being at stake in the competitive encounter. Accordingly, competitions *must* be witnessable; this distinguishes them from a mere fight where winning the prize is the main motivation—such as fighting over a cache of gold buried in a remote place (325). Incidentally, we can notice here that extreme sports, such as skydiving or off-piste snowboarding, where having a public in attendance is not the easiest thing to accomplish, go to great lengths to ensure witnessability (the participants wear cameras on their helmets, the competition is streamed live, etc.).

Since the true aim of competitions is attaining value—that is, being ranked according to social attributes—by definition they will have a moral component. "Moral" does not necessarily mean here something like "being good" according to some abstract standard of goodness. Neither does "moral" mean sticking to impersonal, normative prescriptions of "do's" and "don'ts." After all, cunning can be castigated in public discourse, while being seen as a social attribute through and through. And even if there is a discourse about gambling as being a "don't," participants engage in poker competitions, for instance. "Moral" means that participants in competitions have to adhere to the attributes or values at stake, and to acknowledge each other as adhering to and as compatible with them. This is why competitions go to great lengths to match participants according to what value is at stake. In a boxing match, we will not see an adult heavyweight matched with a 10-year-old, but in a chess match we might very well see a middle-aged man competing against a whiz kid. Matching is a social procedure of acknowledging similar affordances along a particular social attribute or group of attributes.

Because competitions are intrinsically moral along these lines (according to a morality that does not at all exclude deviations, transgressions, and infringements), they have to be organized, even when they appear spontaneous. A football match among amateurs called at short notice will be organized too, in the sense that teams and referees will be selected, duration will be more or less agreed upon, field positions will be negotiated, and so forth. Organization can take place in different keys: for instance, a football match can be organized as a rehearsal, a friendly match, a charity event, or as the "real thing." Organization includes matching—making sure that the competitors are compatible according to the social attributes at stake in the match, but also that audiences are compatible with the competitors. It includes witnessability too—making sure that what is going on during a competitions will be accessible to a public, directly or indirectly.

This brings me to the next aspect, which is no less important: Why should the public have a stake in this? Why should they be interested at all in competitions? Surely not as a means of pure entertainment: many actions undertaken by competitors are repetitive and not particularly entertaining. What is the stake of the public, then? The public's stake is that by witnessing competitions, they vicariously participate in encounters with chance, and they get the illusion of exercising free will, which otherwise they do not get to express very often (Goffman 1967). Competitors in a match are the public's representatives in this apparent exercise of free will, which occurs mostly in carefully controlled, if not staged, environments. Therefore, the public is as invested in the moral issues of competitions as the participants are. Directly or vicariously, participants in a game "creatively redefine the world . . . into decisional potentialities" (201). This means that the public of a competition participates vicariously in the social attributes at stake too, while being at the same time their judge: the public participates in being cunning, daring, gallant, and so forth, and at the same time is the judge of cunning and gallantry.

One consequence is that competitions bind public and competitors together, at least for the duration of the event. Competitions are struggles for acclamation (Simmel 1992, 328), not only acclamations of the competitors—of their skills, boldness, and so forth—but acclamations of the social attributes at stake too. In a boxing match, we acclaim not only the force or dexterity of the opponents, but also force and dexterity as socially valuable attributes. This means not only that a competitor who, say, is more cunning is acclaimed, but also—and at least as important— that cunning itself as a social attribute is acclaimed. This is the meaning of Simmel's argument that social values are objectively realized in competitions. After all, how should we know what endurance, or boldness, or cunning are if we cannot see them at work? Competitors struggle to have the attributes they embody and display acclaimed by the public. It is the only means for them to be ranked and to gain social cachet for what they do. This, among other reasons, is why the public can legitimately sanction transgressions during a competition by booing, even when such transgressions are ignored by the referees, or even if they do not neatly fit into the formal definition of a transgression or of breach of rules for that particular competition. Booing at the opera is an example here, since opera performances can also be seen as competitions on the expressive attributes of the human voice. Listening to music has a moral quality to it, which compels the public to react to how social values are displayed (Benzecry 2011).

Competitions objectify social values,[5] and as such they allow both socialization and the constitution of social identities. The self cannot be conceived without attributes such as "What does it mean to be courageous, righteous, clever, quick, witty, etc." These attributes are collectively produced in social experiences, not defined in an abstract fashion. Why are competitions a specific mode of producing such attributes of the self? Because competitions subject the collective production of social attributes to trials of chance. They are reached by social agreement, but the agreement follows trials of chance. It's agreement by trial, not agreement by negotiation or by ritual.

I shall return now to the issue at stake, namely trading competitions. What is the significance of the above arguments? My starting point was the moral issues implied by trading competitions. I have woven Simmel's and Goffman's argument together, trying to show that competitions cannot take place spontaneously or in the wild, that they are socially organized and regulated, and that this organization has to solve basic moral issues such as witnessability, proper display of attributes, and compatibility of participants and audiences. In a dispersed environment such as electronic finance, with its computer screens scattered all over the world, these issues would be difficult to solve. They would be difficult to solve for retail traders too, because retail traders are not concentrated in a few large banks. Even professional traders are not all concentrated in one place. The social attributes that a trader is expected to possess—what Caitlin Zaloom (2006, 136) calls the "trader-being"—need to be put on display to audiences of traders, not merely talked about in an abstract and general fashion. Experience of something like discipline or endurance is gained by witnessing discipline or endurance. Rekeying trading as performed competitions staged regularly around the world provides a way of dealing with such issues. Seen this way, activities that apparently are on the fringes of "real" trading take a much more central position, as carefully staged occasions for putting key moral issues on display.

If we think about trading as highly uncertain with respect to financial rewards—a majority of retail traders do not make money—then economic values and attributes like profitableness cannot be the only ones at stake. If profitableness (understood as the ability to make profit) were the main social attribute at stake, then a majority of traders would have shown over and over that they fail this attribute, and the attribute itself would have been socially devalued. In a trading competition, there is at least one loser for every winner, and both competitors can lose money. Yet, both competitors can show endurance, or boldness, or discipline— and can be acclaimed and ranked by the public for those traits. Virtues are talked about by traders time and time again. Yet, they cannot be only talked about. They need to be put on display during action, for large audiences to see, and what better way to do this than to stage competitions?

Boundaries

I have argued previously that competitions are socially organized and not free-for-alls. This social organization includes not only various keys in which they take place, rules, a fixed duration, a material setup, and the like. The social organization must necessarily include an awareness on the part of the participants of the kind of competitive situations they are in, and what these situations require from them. After all, we don't expect two contestants in a boxing match to continue the fight in the street or to take it into the audience. Even if this may happen from time to time, it is not part of the awareness of the boxing match as being bounded—that is, distinct from its environment and from other kinds of encounters (Goffman 1966, 151). In trading, the moral problem of boundedness comes to the fore in institutional transitions—that is, in competitive situations where individuals shift status from retail to institutional traders, or from "ordinary" traders to "trade leaders." In a manner akin to that of liminal situations (Turner 1964), where one goes into the tropical forest as a boy and comes back as a man, traders go into such competitions as amateurs and come out of them (some, not all) as employees of banks and brokerages. Yet, as in all liminal situations, the status of such competitions is unclear: is this only a game? How far can I go with my competitive drive? Are my former friends and classmates my competitors now? Do I have any responsibilities in competitions? Do I have any responsibilities if I win? All these issues require both setting limits to competitive situations and distinguishing situations where one is allowed to be competitive from situations where one is not.

Institutional transitions can take place in teams or individually. Investment banks regularly organize trading competitions as part of their recruitment process every autumn, enrolling final-year undergraduate students either individually or as members of a team. Competitors receive a set amount to trade, using the bank's trading platform within a set period of time. (Competitions on the bank's premises usually take a half day or a day. Online competitions take between a week and a month.) At the end of that time, the winner (an individual or a team) is announced. The criterion for winning is who makes the most return on the capital within the set time. The prize consists not only in an investment account but, more importantly, in increased chances for an internship within the bank. It also provides a valuable addition to one's CV. Small wonder then that such competitions are quite popular with students.

Competitions organized by investment banks can start with thousands of teams, only a few of whom will finish. Many teams will not trade throughout the entire allotted time, or will abandon the game. Nevertheless, what happens in such contests is that participants who make it through the entire game learn how to make decisions as part of a team. Competitive games are thus designed to replicate and anticipate real life organizational situations, where decisions are made in a team while profit is sought:

SAM: It was organized, they basically gave you access to an online trading platform, which was I think a virtual copy of the actual markets, so it gave you . . . I think instant access to the markets . . . that was pretty much it. [. . .] We met in the beginning and then we assigned roles to the, to different people, and then we didn't meet that much. We were more like, sort of [Skyped] all the time and talked and decided whether we like one position or not and then why that was, so if someone liked a position, why they liked it and which were the entry and exit levels, you know, which . . . and then we decided whether we wanted to take it or not.

AP: What was your role in this team? What did you do on the team?

SAM: We all had pretty much the same role. We all covered pretty much different aspects of the market. I covered currencies and government debt.

AP: And when you decided to do a transaction, did you have to get into touch with members of the team or . . . could you decide alone?

SAM: It depends on the transaction. If it's small, not necessarily. If it's not, if it's a significant part of our portfolio, we could chat about it, but it wasn't restrictive, so if you liked a position because of a recent, I don't know, news or something that was happening right now, then you'd go ahead and do it, and if you thought that your conviction was strong enough, that's ok.

AP: How much money did you have as a team?

SAM: We started out with 100 million.

AP: 100 million?

SAM: Yes and we made 21%.

AP: Profit?

SAM: Yes.

AP: And what was your time frame?

SAM: One month.

This account, provided by a final-year student who had been hired by an investment bank, describes how competitive games stage a decisional environment not dissimilar to that of a financial organization. The competition had been organized the previous summer by the career arm of another investment bank. The large sums of (fake) money, the division between discretionary and team decision making, the division of labor in covering various financial sectors, all rekey processes characteristic to investment banking rather than to retail trading.

I could add here what may be taken as obvious, namely that such games teach first and foremost how to be competitive. However, things are more complicated than this. The same behavioral traits can be seen as markers of competitiveness or not, depending on the situation. When I asked the same student whether there was competition among his friends who traded, he ascribed this notion to the institutional realm. If one were to be a big player (as he just had learned to be, with an—admittedly simulated—account of 100 million), one would need to be competitive, to act strategically, and not to disclose information. Yet, when it comes to the same kind of behavior among retail traders (and more particularly among friends), this is superstition, not competition:

AP: Now when you said that some of your friends trade, themselves, do you, when talking to them, do you also tell them concretely what trades, what transactions you've done and do they tell you what transactions they've done?

SAM: Yes, they, we exchange different types of information, sometimes. I tell them what I've done at which level I've done it, why I've decided to do it. Sometimes . . . we just express general thoughts about the markets . . . yeah, ok, sometimes it's very specific. Sometimes they will tell you where they've entered and where they've planned to exit. Sometimes they can be vague, depends how they feel, some people are superstitious and they don't like to talk about a position if they have it on.

AP: Is this because of superstition or is this because of them being a bit secretive and feeling that this is a competition?

SAM: Not with us, it's not a competition because I could not do anything to affect his position and he could not do anything to affect mine. If we were bigger players, which means that if my trading could affect the markets, then he would not tell me what his position was and I would not tell him what mine is, but given that we both trade in markets that we cannot affect, there is really no difference.

AP: Mm-hmm, all right, but you mention now superstition. Why, do you have a specific reason that some of your friends are superstitious about their trades?

SAM: Well, they wouldn't say they are superstitious, but I have noticed that sometimes if they have a big trade, so, for a significant amount of money, they would prefer not to tell you what the trade is before it's actually done, so, it's . . . I guess they are superstitious, I guess you can call them superstitious.

Friends who trade tell each other what they are doing, except when they have a large position. This is when they become superstitious. Big-

ger players with large positions that can affect the market are not superstitious, though, when they are not disclosing information. They are
competitive. In the same breath of argument, competitiveness is seen as
the capacity to affect each other, the capacity of one's actions to have an
effect on other people's actions—something that in this account is restricted to the institutional domain. Yet, this is exactly what is learned
in trading games when you enter against teams you do not know personally. Competition becomes thus a moral issue, circumscribed to particular environments: one is allowed to be competitive there, while the same
behavioral traits will be something else in a different setting. This aspect—the fact that being competitive is morally acceptable, though only
when carefully bounded, is strongly echoed in another account, from a
student trader who avoids getting involved in a second trading group exactly because of issues of competition:

AP: Do you mean that there is no competition within your group?

RICK: Absolutely no. Absolutely no competition [*laughs*]. 'Cause our first
goal is to get students to understand and to learn so that when they get internships they'll know. If we just wanted to be making money, well there's
another thing. Like [name] and [name], they're in [trading group 2], which
they created for themselves, and they have personal meetings together
where they invest more thoroughly. I'm not part of it. I was asked to be
part of it last year but I decided not to do it 'cause you know with school,
with my portfolio, the portfolio within the [trading group 1], I didn't know
if I could even balance another one with even more money, so I told them I
wasn't too confident, . . . maybe next year. So if we wanted to make money
we just stay all together and not really care, and I know our CVs would be
just as good, like yeah, we're trading at [university name], this is the profits
we're making etcetera. But this is really good learning and teaching experience and it's really fun to see the success we have right now.

The trader talking here was (at the time of the conversation) the president of one of the United Kingdom's largest student trading clubs, with
members' own capital of £97,000 (or about $150,000). Two group mem-
bers (former club presidents) had decided to form an additional group,
where they traded with their own money and their own trading strategies, without leaving the first group. Some might think that this dual
membership would raise at least issues of competition, if not conflicts
of interest that, in their turn, might affect social relationship within the

group. Yet, the issue of competition was carefully bounded to the goal of making money ("if we just wanted to be making money"), while the group's goal was to prepare members for future internships ("our first goal is to get students to understand"). This careful separation of goals, on the group level as well as on the personal level ("I didn't know if I could even balance another one with even more money") indicates that competition was seen as a moral issue, permissible under certain conditions but to be avoided under the given circumstances ("we just stay all together and not really care"). This points to the fact that competitions are not only bounded in a formal manner, by establishing their duration, participants, means of competing, and so on. They are also bounded in the sense that participants have to make judgments about which situations allow competition and which do not, and how to handle the separation of such situations. At the same time, competitions, even when they take place, are subordinated to a more fundamental goal: keeping relationships going. The social fabric is not allowed to tear under their strain.

Compatibility and Witnessability

If competitions appear to be accepted under particular circumstances (but definitely not all the time and not everywhere), this means that efforts must be deployed not only in organizing competitions, but also in persuading audiences that competitions are fun and enjoyable. Thus, the organization of competitions implies not only a material setup, logistics, and rules, but also—and at least as importantly—the quasi-simultaneous deployment of different keys (Goffman 1974, 44): competitions as spectacle, as exercise, or as the real thing. If the quasi-simultaneous deployment of different keys is necessary because it is not self-evident to audiences that competitions are acceptable and enjoyable anytime, anywhere, and with anybody (a reticence that has been articulated above), then it means that keys that are apparently minor (competition as an exercise or as a spectacle) can actually play significant roles.

Competitions as exercises are strongly present in institutional transitions. Transitioning from the status of student (and amateur trader) to that of employee of an investment bank or of a hedge fund implies, more often than not, taking part at least in one competition, as I have previously shown. How do competitions as spectacles work then? In fact, they are strongly present both in the world of institutional traders and in that of retail traders, and the most adequate places for the competitions are professional conventions and trade fairs, not least because those venues provide relatively large audiences for such spectacles.

At the professional conventions I attended, both in the United States and in Europe, multiple competitions were regularly organized, though in formats that were not directly related to trading: in the exhibition hall, for instance, a major stock exchange would organize a table soccer competition, witnessable by all participants and with prizes such as a bottle of champagne or a ticket to a sought-after football game. Over two days or so, participants would sign up and enter against each other, being gradually eliminated until the finale took place during the last lunch break on the second day. Audiences would come by and watch for a few minutes and then leave, but at regular intervals the next phase (and especially the finale) would be announced over the public address system.

It is interesting to note, even if in passing, that the exhibition floor, where most competitions are organized at trade fairs and professional conventions, hosts another very significant activity: gift-giving. Every exhibitor will come prepared with goodie bags, which, of course, vary in quality and significance from pens and notepads and plastic toys to expensive bottles of single malt whiskey. Generally, professional conventions distribute more expensive gifts than conventions for retail traders, but the intensity with which these gifts are coveted both by professionals and by retail traders is remarkable. (At the close of a professional conference in London, I passed a dressed-up gentleman carrying three large, almost overflowing canvas bags and talking on the phone: "Darling, I've got great stuff for the kids.") Some gifts are given out more liberally, but the more expensive ones are kept for close business friends. (At another professional conference in London, a broker friend told me "Oh, we've got to go to the brokerage A, they've got good whiskey and I'm friends with them. Don't you want a bottle?") The close coexistence of gift-giving and competitions in the relatively restricted space of an exhibition hall is significant because they embody such contradictory principles: while competitions are meant (in theory) to highlight the powers and virtues of meritocracy, to show (not tell, show!) that the most skilled win, that the games are fair, and so forth, the lively exchange of goodie bags (and the intensity with which they are coveted) is meant (especially at professional events) to consolidate economies of favor (which are very much alive) and to perpetuate business grounded in forms of reciprocity that are far from the egalitarian and meritocratic spirit of competitions.

Outside exhibition halls, nontrading competitions can be directly woven into the presentations. At a presentation on high frequency trading that I attended at a US professional conference in 2013, I found on the seat a device similar to a TV remote. The presenter announced right at the start that there was going to be a multiple-choice quiz and that two mini iPads were the prizes. All we had to do was to press the number for each answer on the remote. The participant who was quickest in hitting the right button got the highest marks, the second-quickest got the second-highest marks, and so on. Since the remote answer devices were linked to the seats we were seating on, the winners could easily be identified. Then the (very technical) presentation on high frequency trading started, interspersed with quiz questions. After each question the percentage of correct answers from the audience was displayed on the screen behind the presenter, together with the two fastest hitters for each question.

Some questions were very technical in nature and directly related to the technological infrastructure of high frequency trading; some were about general culture, though related to communication (for instance, about the Trojan War). I must say that I took part in this competition (and was second-fastest for some questions) but was dismayed to miss the one about the Trojan War (8 members of the audience of about 100 got it right, though). Later, at the elevators, I saw the proud prize winners being congratulated by other competitors. It looked and sounded as if they already knew each other.

In the situation I was part of, it was hard to distinguish between the audience of a technical presentation and participants in a competitive quiz, or between the presentation itself and the competition, since the latter two were interwoven, not only in the way questions were interspersed with the presentation, but also in the way the technological setup of the presentation itself was used for giving feedback in real time about how the participating audience performed in the quiz. This particular competition achieved several things: first, it concretely and specifically established compatibility between the audience and the presentation. It showed the entire audience in real time not only how many of them knew about the Trojan War, but also (and perhaps more importantly) how many knew specific things about microwave technology, and how quick they were. Being competitive was entertaining, and the prizes were really coveted (judging at least from the postcompetition comments at the elevators).

Why are so many apparently meaningless competitions being staged in a key that has nothing to do with serious talks given to professional audiences? My answer is that they are not meaningless at all, and that they are not ultimately meant to entertain or alleviate the supposed dryness of technical presentations. They are meant to contribute, solving at least two interrelated key moral issues. The first is the compatibility between audience, presenter, and the topic of presentation. Is one quick enough with one's answers? As quick as microwave transmission of data (metaphorically speaking)? The second key moral issue is witnessability. In auctions, for instance, witnessability is solved by allowing only a "two at a time format" (bid and counterbid; see Heath 2012). The rest of the audience witnesses the competition and has the opportunity to participate in it at available slots. In electronic finance, competition has a different format: the fastest arrival in a queue. Orders arriving in a queue are not directly visible to an audience assembled in one place, like an auction room. Theirs is a dispersed audience of traders sitting in front of their screens. Yet, a competition such as the one described above makes the queue visible—and thus witnessable—to all: fastest answers are displayed to all participants, with the name of the respondents. The seemingly arcane structure of the market becomes suddenly visible and intuitive. Thus, an apparently minor, peripheral element—a competitive quiz—reveals its organization as homomorphic with placing orders on electronic exchanges. What was previously considered arcane and hidden is displayed for all to see and experience.

The loci where compatibility between competitors and the audience as a moral issue comes to the fore are provided by the trading competitions organized at trade fairs for retail traders. Competitions here are organized both on the exhibition floor and as presentations in seminar rooms, in a format not far removed from the one described above. On the exhibition floor, an area around a podium will be marked off and seating for the audience will be provided (the audience can reach around 300 people for a competition). A trading competition will be part of the formal program of the fair and will usually be scheduled so that there is minimal overlap with other activities. On the stage, two tables with two laptops will be set up: behind each table, the trading screen (which appears on the laptop) is projected on a large screen for the benefit of the audience, so that everyone can see what the trader is doing. The format of trading competitions is a relatively rigid one: there are always two traders entering against each other. They compete with currency trading against indices, or on a one-minute time frame versus a five-minute time frame. The duration is usually between 30 and 45 minutes, at the end of which the winner is declared (the trader who made the most money during that interval with the same starting capital). The competitors are allowed to set up their trading screens and accounts in advance, and the audience is in many cases informed that the trading accounts are set for the purpose of that competition (implying that they are demo accounts, not real-money accounts). The competitors can be broker dealers, technology providers (e.g., chart providers), or "educators"—the latter meaning that they offer personal coaching, seminars, weekend retreats, and other kinds of "educational" products (the number of the latter is remarkable). An emcee (there is always an emcee) introduces the two competitors to the audience, lets them present themselves (and the products they offer), starts the game, coordinates the Q&A sessions during the dead times of trading, asks the competitors about their strategies and the rationale for their decisions (as these decisions are made), compares the results, declares the winner, and lets both competitors comment at the end on what they did right and what they did wrong.

Such competitions have a thinly disguised aim of selling to audiences a particular product, perhaps a charting software or a particular trading method. Yet, the act of persuading the audiences is formatted as "I'll show you that my product or method is better than his" (competitors are overwhelmingly men), and therefore participants have to stick to and fully participate in the competition spectacle, or they will fail by definition. That the competition is a staged one is clear to everybody, but this doesn't change anything with respect to the participants' necessity to seriously and fully engage in this rekeyed format. That is, competitors will have to seriously try to win, even if everybody knows that the accounts do not have real money in them. (If you cannot win on a demo account, how can you win with real money?)

In order to be able to engage, though, competitors have to solve at least two moral issues: are they compatible with each other and with their audience? How can they be valued by their audience, and how can they value their audience? Compatibility cannot be reduced to a purely informational aspect, since it entails not only how all the parties involved maintain the ongoing situation, but also the chance of transforming at least some individuals in the audience into future customers. Competitors want to sell something to the audience. The audience, in its turn, has to make a judgment: is this the right thing? Compatibility was a moral issue in the quiz discussed previously, but it can become more complicated when competitors and audiences are allowed to interact directly and talk to each other instead of just pressing a button on the remote control.

A first aspect of compatibility in trading competitions is that the profits at the end of a competitive round appear to be plausible and in line with the kind of profits the members of the audience would expect themselves to make. According to my field notes, these profits were $8, $520, and $850—perfectly plausible from a retail trader's point of view.

A second aspect, at least as important, is to make sure that the competitors are compatible, while remaining different from each other. Nobody wants to see a 10-year-old junior league player being pitched against a professional footballer: that would be considered unfair, and in the world of sports, rigorous institutional mechanisms are set in place to minimize if not outright eliminate such a possibility. (That is not to say that a junior league player and a professional footballer cannot play against each other in a different key, such as practicing or relaxing.) In trading competitions, however, which lack such an institutional setup, it is the task of the emcee to establish and maintain compatibility *and* difference throughout the competition, for the benefit of the audience, through talk. Usually, establishing compatibility between competitors for the benefit of the audience allows the emcee to simultaneously tell the audience that the competitors are like them and that the competitors have an edge (or a difference).

In one competition I witnessed, the emcee started by asking competitors A and R how they traded and what they traded, as a means of showing that they were both alike and compatible with what the audience could be:

EMCEE [TO A.]: How many trades do you do per day?
A: Three up to 40 per day, would stop by noon.
EMCEE: Looking at the highs and lows?
A: Based on the A pattern . . . [AP: the A pattern was the proprietary trading strategy promoted by competitor A].
R: I typically do two–three trades per day, Last week I did about five. . . . Typically I let the market give me what it's gonna give me.

The range given by A is so broad that it leaves room for his competitor to assert that he is similar (does a number of trades per day that is within A's range), while keeping a difference at the same time (R's statement is that he "lets the market give him"). In the course of the competition, such compatibilities and differences have to be made visible all the time. Otherwise the audience could not follow the differences in action. This is why in every trading competition, without exception, the emcee feels compelled to act in the manner of sports journalists on TV broadcasts, the comments of whom make the action intelligible for a remote public.

Gameworthiness

Not only do the competitors have to be compatible among themselves and compatible with the audience; they have to be gameworthy too. After all, what good is it to witness a competition where the contestants cannot display the social attributes audiences expect from them? Later on, in the same competition, as competitors A and R buy and sell, the emcee intervenes with comments and questions:

> A: for every trade I make I have a $18 potential profit. I made $50 on a trade. . . . The cash market closed here [points cursor]. it's gonna come down here [points cursor]. I'm expecting to come down here [points cursor]. Right now there is high probability of . . . I don't care about the cap.
>
> R [INTERRUPTS]: Can I just say, I've been doing this for a long time—I've added a new position. . . . For every contract you have when it moves 10 ticks against you . . .
>
> EMCEE [TO R]: . . . never add to a losing trade . . . But you're adding. Why?

The situation from which this excerpt is taken is that until this moment R has not been doing so well against A. He has been losing money continuously. As A tries to tell the audience that he has made a $50 profit on a trade and that his positions are potentially profitable (which does not mean much), R interrupts him and asserts his gameworthiness ("I've been doing this for a long time"), and he announces a new position immediately afterward. At this point, the emcee intervenes and asks why R is adding to losing trades (going against received wisdom), giving R an

opportunity to explain his decisions. The job of the emcee is to thus provide slots for the competitors to explain their actions, to visualize their
expectations on the trading screen (with the help of the cursor), to justify their decisions, to offer repairs of unfavorable situations (explaining losses away as temporary), and to distinguish themselves from other
competitors at every point in the game. Not rarely, the slots provided
by the emcee are used by competitors to offer audiences metaphorical
statements such as "The market talks to me"; The market is "a big giant
crowd"; "I know I'm right, not wrong yet"; "It's a psychological game."
The capacity to philosophize about the game while playing it should signal audiences that one making such statements has reached a certain
level of knowledge and resilience. At the same time, since critical moments can arise in the game, when one competitor continuously loses or
when both of them lose money, showing or at least asserting that one is
gameworthy becomes a critical moral issue. Otherwise, what fun would
it be to watch two very unequal players competing against each other or
two bad players competing against each other? The structure of the competition itself needs to provide for the necessity of visualizing and/or asserting gameworthiness at critical moments, and it does this by layering
upon the emcee features akin to those of a sports commentator in addition to those of a referee.

In some competitions, displays of gameworthiness on the part of the
competitors can take spectacular forms involving considerable show-
manship. Some participants will prepare spectacular "trading routines,"
which they will perform (with some variations) at various trading conventions. At two different conventions I attended (one in London and
one in the United States), the same participant (the founder of an electronic brokerage that he later sold to a larger one) appeared before an
audience of about 300 in the following manner. Facing the audience and
with his back to the projection of his own trading screen, he started giving trading orders to his assistant (who was sitting behind him on the
podium with a laptop), without turning even once to see what was being put on the screen. He started his trading with the following exhortation to the public: "You wanna see something, you wanna see the explo-
sion? I'll start out with the futures and I'll start out with smaller futures.
[Without turning around, to the assistant] ready, Joanne? Sell one S&P
future [waits for confirmation], sell another S&P future [confirmation],
sell a bond future three times. [Orders further trades.] [To the audience]
are you ahead of me?"

All in all, 43 trades were placed within 35 minutes, actions that were announced as "building up portfolio" and "creating inventory." A margin of $100,000 was requested. The trades themselves (the S&P futures) were presented as "the Taco Bell of trade," implying a low level of sophistication, accessibility, and low price. As I was watching the trading screen behind the presenter (though "performer" would perhaps be a better term), I noticed how the numbers changed: an initial loss of $250 mutated into a profit of $700 (a differential of $950), to be reduced moments later to a profit of only $400. During the show, the performer asked the audience how many were risk averse, and three hands went up.

After the competition I talked to members of the audience (who had traveled from the Midwest and from the West Coast to observe it). They told me that people were dazzled by the rapidity of trades, not all of which could be followed. They were puzzled by the performer's placing them one by one (which drove up commission costs) and noticed that not all the trades were executed. Personally, my conversation partners "would have gone for the pennies," implying that they would not have held the positions for as long as the performer did. The aim of the performance, though, was not to realistically replicate what a retail trader would do. It was not a trading lesson. It was meant to dazzle the audience and to show the gameworthiness of the performer—that he could do trading in an extraordinary way, like no other.

Not only do the competitors have to be gameworthy. The audiences have to show gameworthiness too. Since the audience participates vicariously in performances like the one described above, audiences have to show that they are worthy of this encounter with chance, worthy of being there. When the performer asked how many were risk averse, only three hands went up. I didn't see this reaction as reflecting any stable, deeply ingrained, favorable attitude of the audience toward trades they barely comprehended. They had to signal, however, that they were worthy of witnessing a man confronting chance, and such worthiness does not sit well with admitting risk aversion in public. The competitive quiz I participated in at the professional convention was designed to test the gameworthiness of the audience by mixing technical questions with cultural ones and by giving them feedback in real time about how many had answered correctly. In both cases, the audiences had to show, in different ways, that they were gameworthy.

In other situations, during trading competitions, conflicts can arise between presenters on stage and the audience, when the audience is insulted as unworthy. At one presentation I attended at a trade fair, the speaker, who was trying to mobilize the audience of about 100 attendees for his training system, said to them, "They told me you guys are dumb, but they are clearly wrong." Only moments later, while the competitor was answering a question from the audience, the following exchange took place:

TRADER: You should talk to your coach.
MAN FROM THE AUDIENCE: That's me.
TRADER: Then you should tell your coach that he has an idiot for a client.
[a few moments later]
SAME MAN FROM THE AUDIENCE: Don't you think coaches fleece you?

Exchanges such as this one point to the possibility that the relationship between competitors, or presenters, and their audiences can become a problematic one and that it entails moral aspects. Both sides need to treat each other not only according to the conventions of polite public behavior, but also as worthy of what the competitors are doing and the audience is witnessing. In other words, as a condition of being engaged in this game of trading, they must treat each other as worthy of it.

Finally, there is another element competitions as spectacle are meant to show audiences, not just tell them about: the traders' attributes, which are intrinsic to their gameworthiness. At trade fairs that target retail traders, a lot is said about trading discipline and about the virtues that make one a trader. Discipline, courage, resilience, sang froid, all these are moral virtues trumpeted as intrinsic to being a trader. As we already know from several studies, these topoi are not specific to the retail sector: many a professional trader will talk about the need for discipline, for instance. Some "education" providers specialize as coaches for traders—intending to teach not trading as such, but the virtues of trading. Yet, this creates a problem: if virtues are so much touted, where can a trader witness them directly, as embodied by other traders? In the days of the good old trading floor, one could easily observe what other traders were doing and could judge directly who had discipline and who didn't. In electronic trading, this is not so easy, since there is little possibility, if any, of directly observing what other traders do. Moreover, direct observations of virtue would require showing some examples that, for instance, typify what resilience is, examples that could serve as a benchmark. This is where trading competitions come into play. At the same time, displays of gameworthiness are not all the same: they leave room for comparisons, rankings, and degrees and hence can become status attributes (Geertz 1977, 444).

I argued above that trading competitions are not exact replicas of real retail trading. They are not keyed as real trading, and the key is exhibited there for all to see. In fact, retail traders participate only in some of them; in others professionals (brokers, mostly) compete against each other. While some elements are realistic (the wins, for instance), others are definitely not (e.g., placing trades in a rapid sequence, lot by lot, and with one's back to the trading screen). Therefore, the aim is not to teach traders the "how to" within the space of 45 minutes, but to make something else visible. Competitions are displays of gameworthiness, but as such they must also display the social attributes at stake in particular situations. Patience is paramount. In one competition I witnessed, one of the traders had placed his bets on the Euro's going down against the US dollar, but the Euro kept going up. He was determined to stick with his method; as the end was approaching, he addressed the audience directly this way: "We might sit here doing nothing for hours, but if we are following a method, we are doing our job and we are waiting for an opportunity."

Because it was clear that he was going to lose the game (his competitor had a small profit of $215, and he had losses), he addressed the audience again: "I'm not here to make excuses, but to teach you. [. . .] I was one of the unlucky ones I guess. [. . .] This is what this show is about, getting education."

To this the winner immediately replied: "This is what this show is about, getting education." Education about what? Not necessarily about the fact that one of the contenders had made losses and the other only some modest wins. At the same time, during this end-of-game exchange, which took less than a minute, several qualities were displayed: one of the traders acknowledged losses and displayed resilience; the winner graciously acknowledged that the show was not about him winning, but about "education." The closing sequence ran counter to the opening statements, which promoted the winner's method (obtained, he said, through an epiphany, or divine revelation) against the loser's (called the "blue line" method). Suddenly it wasn't method against method anymore; it was about displaying patience, resilience, the capacity to take losses and the capacity to behave graciously (see also McCormick 2014, 2264). All in all, then, spectacular competitions can be seen as live displays of gameworthiness in more than one sense: they contribute to showing audiences their own compatibility with trading, but also display the moral virtues touted so much in relationship to trading.

One question remains, though: how are the attributes put on display in trading competitions rekeyed in the "serious," the major key of trading? After all, the gameworthiness of traders is shown in a spectacular key, which does not replicate real trading. I think the answer to this question is this: even if the spectacle of trading competition is in a minor key, it needs to be taken seriously by participants. In other words, traders engaging in spectacular displays of gameworthiness need to fully commit to them. Therefore, what is displayed is not minor versions of trading attributes, but full-blown ones. The audiences engage vicariously in them. Spectators watching traders compete gain an experience of what it means to be patient, or daring, or cunning, an experience that can be replicated, exercised, enlarged, and consolidated in the major key of "serious" trading. An amateur football player might try to replicate a cunning pass seen in a memorable match. An amateur pianist might try to replicate the delicacy of a legato heard in the concert hall. Having seen firsthand what it means to be daring, I might try it myself while trading. Experiences of trading attributes are produced thus along a continuum of keys rather than in a single one. In order for this to happen, however, trading attributes have to be put on display for all to see.

Vicarious engagement with gameworthiness is present not only in a staged format, but in real trading as well. In social trading, participants have the chance to shift their status from "ordinary" to "star" trader. They are ranked according to a series of standardized statistical criteria such as return on capital, a risk metrics (usually the standard deviation of returns, indicating how volatile their returns are), strategy, and length of activity, but they will not have to disclose how much capital they have at their disposal. Rankings are periodically reviewed, and traders might lose their "star" status. Some newcomers may become stars too. At stake here is not only the prestige of being a "star" trader, but, more importantly, the fact that social trading platforms encourage "ordinary" traders to entrust their money to "star" traders, who will act then as quasi-fund managers. Entrusting money means here that "ordinary" traders will sign up for automatically copying the trades of the "stars" instead of making their own decisions. The "stars" will take 20% of the profit they generate for the "ordinary" traders, and the trading platform will take a

2% management fee. At stake in such competitions is much more than the feeling of being a "star."

The logic of the competition is selecting the most reliable, skilled, and resilient traders, and then the rest of the community signs up to copy them. "Copying" should mean (and is understood by participants as) the simultaneous and automatic replication by followers of each and every trade done by "stars" (however, imitators can opt to select only specific trades to copy). We should expect followers to sit back and enjoy their profits, together with the thrill of well-executed trades, but without the stress or the effort. Such a logic is the apex of vicarious engagement: an audience who plays along and witnesses the game at the same time. While the logic of classical vicarious participation implies that spectators at a football game, for instance, participate with fateful encounters via their representatives on the field (the players), vicarious engagement goes one step further: members of the audience choose their own personal representatives to engage them in the game. In the case of the audience of a football game, engagement of this sort might be limited to placing bets on the outcome of a game; the moves of the players on the field, taken one by one, will not be immediately consequential for the audience. The spectators at the football game do not directly feel a tackle by an opponent. In vicarious engagements, they do. And it can be very painful sometimes. This is revealed in moments when the leadership status or the logic of the game—namely, copying—are called into question, as I discuss in the following chapters.

A particular form of vicarious engagement in electronic finance—and I do not mean here mere participation, but engagement—copying means playing with the champion traders, becoming part of them on the trading screen. "Becoming part of them" is more than a metaphor: since followers entrust their money to champion traders, theirs becomes part of the (hopefully winning) trading capital. It also becomes possible to divide one's capital among several traders and engage vicariously not with one but with several champions at once. In horse races, betting does not mean that bettors will take the same steps as the horse. In copy trading, champions and their followers are supposed to become one (in principle), since every trade is automatically and instantaneously replicated. (The technical minutiae of replication present a different picture, though.)

Does this mean that competitions such as the ones presented and discussed in this chapter make trading virtuous, or moral? Erving Goffman noticed that the attractiveness of engaging with fate, as provided by competitive sports, but also by trading or gambling, resides in the affordances it opens to self-determination, in the sense that it is in and from such situations that the participants can get a sense of making their own decisions. In fateful situations (which include competitions), "chance lies in the attitude of the individual himself—his creative capacity to redefine the world around him into his decisional potentialities" (1970, 201).

Of course, a true realization of the self is not guaranteed in fateful situations, but the latter appear to offer the one genuine chance in this respect. Yet, such a realization is dependent on moral issues, on showing "major forms of character that bear on the management of fateful events" (Goffman 1967, 218), such as courage, gameness, gallantry, and composure: "a fundamental trait of character from the viewpoint of social organization is integrity, meaning here the propensity to resist temptation in situations where there would be much profit and some impunity in departing momentarily from moral standards. . . . Integrity seems especially important during fateful activity that is not witnessed by others" (219).

Fateful activities in electronic finance are hardly witnessed by larger, compact audiences, in the same way they would be in the trading pit. This, perhaps, is why it becomes so important to rekey trading and put it on stage in such a way that it becomes available to and witnessable within the confines of physical copresence. Spectacles such as trading competitions make electronic finance a public affair, which is an attempt to solve its moral conundrums. Of course, under the given conditions, the integrity Goffman talks about does not mean the absence of deceit, of cunning, and the like. Integrity means sticking to aspects such as compatibility, gameworthiness, resilience and, yes, cunning and risk-taking too.

Integrity, courage, gameness, gallantry, and composure all are carefully and periodically enacted in front of large audiences, so as to show everybody what trading is about: as the performers say, educating the audience. Such enactments of virtue, sometimes dazzling, may make audiences forget to some extent that they take place in exhibition halls, at organized events, only a few feet away from an economy of gifts and of reciprocal favors, which is not brought to display as being virtuous. Fateful competitions are organized dates, in the sense that they are supported by organized, institutional setups that, during the game itself and for all purposes of the game, remain mostly hidden from view or are designed in such a way as to make sure that they interfere minimally with what is witnessable in the fateful occasion.

Trading competitions thus remain mostly conjured up illusions (yet both essential and attractive ones), which can (and will) be easily frayed away in moments of real trading, when orders are not executed or when the platform freezes. They are essential because they display (albeit in a staged fashion) and do not just talk about moral issues intrinsic to the idealized (even, perhaps, romanticized) notion of trading that participants find so attractive. Yet the scaffolding on which this morality is erected is that of organized trade fairs, where I never heard any broker acknowledge to an audience that he was actually taking the counterpart in the trades put by his clients. I cannot find a better ending to this chapter than this one: "To satisfy the fundamental requirements of morale and continuity, we are encouraged in a fundamental illusion. It is our character. A something entirely our own that does not change, but is none the less precarious and mutable. . . . We are allowed to think there is something to be won in the moments that we face so that society can face moments and defeat them" (1967, 239).

CHAPTER FOUR

Rituals and Illusions of the Trading Screen

W hen I started this project, I was offered the opportunity to see a retail trader at work in front of his screen. I met him at the door of his office, and since we didn't know each other, I was asked to turn around as he punched his name and password on the keyboard of his laptop. I had of course promised that all private information would be kept confidential and that I would anonymize everything. My interest and attention were drawn primarily to the screen: hundreds of flickering cells, some blue, some red, some green, and some yellow, with numbers and letters in them, changing all at once, several times per second. I counted them later and found that there were 346 cells on the screen, which, as I learned later, was a Nasdaq level II screen.

It was puzzling, because it seemed to be far, far away from the relationship-based trading that characterized the pits of old: there, each trader had to face others, shout, gesture at them, and constantly compete for their attention. This doesn't mean that the pits and trading floors of today are lacking in screens: quite the contrary. There are plenty of information screens around. And yet, in the pits of the past, at least, the main mode of conducting transactions was the face-to-face interaction.[1] If in this old world of face-to-face interactions, trading meant establishing and maintaining relationships, however fleeting, what does it mean now, in the apparently flat world of the screen? Do clicks on screen cells provide enough substance, enough of the stuff relationships are made of? Or has trading been hollowed out of any relational content?

Ethnographers have answered these questions in the negative (e.g., Knorr Cetina and Bruegger 2002; Zaloom 2006; MacKenzie 2017). We know that electronic markets aren't atomistic. And we know that so-cial relationships provide the scaffolding upon which trading activities are mounted and assembled together. We also know that interactions in electronic markets have features different from those of face-to-face interactions. We assume too that the relationships supporting retail trad-ing aren't necessarily similar to those supporting professional trading. If retail trading is different from professional trading, then the scaffold-ing upon which it is mounted must be different too. Above all, we as-sume that these interactions and relationships, at least in the domain of professional trading, are (exclusively) conducted in one basic, major key: they are "serious," they are "for real," they "mean business." The scaf-folding of transactions cannot be anything but a solid, serious one. And yet, the screen can be engaged with both individually and group-wise; it can be displayed, played with, and commented upon in front of audi-ences. It can be used in face-to-face settings but can also be duplicated on other screens—for instance, in situations where a trader can broad-cast his actions to a remote audience while displaying his trading screen on the audience's own screens. The screen can be frozen in a snapshot, which is distributed to other traders, posted online, or used in com-plaints against the brokerage when the latter is too slow or prone to tech-nical breakdowns.

What if this scaffolding includes not just one, but several keys? What if it contains variations from a single, exclusive, major key—variations from "seriousness," if one wants to put it this way, and what if such varia-tions are critical for what is going on?

Managing Trades and Traders

I focus here on what makes retail traders different both in their work with the screen and in their relationships. In doing this, I am examining not only differences within one and the same basic key (that of "serious-ness"), but also how variations on this key make retail trading what it is.[2] I am taking a less beaten path and asking first, What happens with an or-der once the trader clicks "buy" or "sell" on the screen? Where does that order go? Who takes care of it (or not)? In taking this path, I see social relationships as being incorporated primarily (though not exclusively) in the material tangle of order signals that are sent from a trader's screen and arrive somewhere else.

In the world of professional traders, a trader's orders are matched with similar counterorders put in by other traders. This can happen anonymously on electronic trading venues, or it can happen in direct, trader-to-trader transactions, of the kind investigated by Karin Knorr Cetina and Urs Bruegger (2002). Usually, professional traders maintain relationships among themselves and with brokers, among whom orders are distributed for execution (Kellard et al. 2016). However, not all traders are human: some are robots or algorithms designed to place certain orders when specific parameters are met. Often they will interact with other algorithms in their search for order execution (MacKenzie 2017). Since the effects of such interactions are not always foreseeable, and because algorithms can go awry, they require constant monitoring by their makers. They cannot be left unsupervised. Nevertheless, whether humans trade with humans, or algorithms with algorithms, an order placed can be seen as a search (anonymous or not) for a match with a similar counterorder. The outcome of the search is that a relationship, however fleeting, however quick, is established: a match has been found. Orders queue up in this search for the most possible rapid match (Pardo-Guerra, n.d.). We can see this as a finance version of a strategic speed dating game, in which suitors on both sides try to outfox others and be the first to find a match on a bare set of minimal "attractiveness" attributes. Matchmakers (such as brokers) might intervene in this game, but the game itself is ultimately about rapidly finding a match with another trader.

I initially assumed that broker dealers catering to retail traders would ultimately act only as intermediaries, taking a cut from the bid-ask spread, and that orders would be forwarded to an exchange or would be matched over the counter. In other words, I assumed that retail traders would trade with each other, in the way professional traders do. I later learned—and it was confirmed by various sources, brokers as well as regulators—that many trading platforms operated by broker dealers do not send any orders to the exchanges, but take the counterpositions to their traders' positions. I once attended a workshop at which one panelist, from the Federal Reserve System, acknowledged that many orders placed by retail traders never "reach the market." She meant that the orders are not being traded against each other on an exchange such as, say, the Chicago Board of Trade, individually or in aggregated form; the counterpart is taken by a broker dealer.[3] This might evoke the world of casinos, of roulette and blackjack tables, where the house takes positions against the clients.

Some broker dealers aggregate the orders and send them to another broker who collects aggregated orders from various broker dealers and executes them in the market. Aggregating orders is called in broker parlance "masquerading," meaning that similar orders are stripped of their identifiers, lumped together, and then sent for execution. As one broker explained it to me, traders all too often overlook the word *dealer* in the term *broker dealer*. Broker dealers will offer retail traders bid-ask spreads that approximate the quotes on the exchanges and which are not necessarily (and not always) the ones at which an order will be executed. Dealers taking counterpositions to their clients will either conduct transactions of their own against other dealers, or will aggregate ("masquerade") orders and send them to another broker, to be executed in the institutional market. Each of these modi operandi poses special problems for the dealers.

Does this mean that at least some retail traders are not in a market, actually? If we look at who actually takes the counterpositions to their transactions, then the answer is no: traders are not in a situation where they directly compete against each other. Traders perceive themselves as competing against each other, and against other types of traders, when this—at least when some broker dealers are involved—isn't actually the case.

Brokers who receive orders from their retail clients have to decide whether to take the counterposition or to wait until more similar orders come, bundle them together, and send them for execution to another broker, who will trade them in institutional markets. In currency markets, for instance, bundled orders can be traded among brokers. If brokers decide to bundle retail orders and send them further up the line for execution, the profit will come exclusively from the difference in spreads. At the same time, additional costs will be incurred, since the second broker (the one used by the broker dealer) will have to be paid a commission. If the broker dealer decides to take the counterposition to the clients' orders, profits are potentially higher, but risks are higher too, since some retail clients might make money on their trades. As retail traders leverage their trades (up to 400 times their actual capital, in unregulated markets), a winning trade conducted by a retail trader with relatively large actual capital might bring the broker dealer into a very bad situation.

This, among other reasons, is why broker dealers do not really like retail clients who deposit very large sums into their accounts. True, such clients are rare, but they do exist. One broker dealer complained to me that he had one client who deposited more than $1 million into his trading account; he, the broker, didn't know what to do with him. The sum was too large: with the usual leverage of 1:200, that client would have been able to move, in principle, $200 million worth of trades at one time. One winning transaction could have simply wiped the broker out, since it was the broker who would have been forced to pay out the client. The ideal retail trader for broker dealers is one who has between $500 and a few thousands in her or his account.

The problem of taking counterpositions to the clients' orders is compounded by the fact that at the end of each trading day, broker dealers need to know how much profit they have made and how much capital is available for the next day. If there isn't enough money there, a broker will have to borrow from other brokers, and this will put a dent in their profits too. Statistically seen, only a very small fraction of retail traders make consistent profits. The traders themselves (most of them, anyway) know this, and broker dealers know this too. The fact that most traders do not make consistent profits does not mean that they do not make any winning trades. When this happens, if a trader's broker has taken the counterposition, the broker has to pay out the trader. These payouts reduce the broker's daily operating capital. A day when several traders win is a day when the broker has to make several payouts, and this affects how much capital is available for the next trading day. In the world of electronic trading, when positions are not held for a long time, such an event becomes a very significant issue.

Conversely, since retail brokers deal among themselves or (in forex) with the banks in order to counterbalance the positions they take against their clients, they have obligations toward each other or toward the banks. When the retail traders cannot pay, brokers still have to honor their obligations. A sudden spike in the exchange rate means that retail traders may be wiped out but cannot pay the large, leveraged sums they owe. However, banks will still call on brokers to pay their debts. This can cause losses in the hundreds of millions and send brokers straight out of business (Golovchenko 2015).

The pressure to break even or make a profit on a daily basis confronts broker dealers with a significant, real time problem: as the orders from their clients come in, brokers need to decide then and there when to take the counterposition and when to bundle the orders and send them further up the line for execution. In a way similar to that of the retail traders managing their trades, and unbeknownst to them, broker dealers need to manage these very same trades too.

What appears to be a simple transaction, then, becomes the object of management efforts on two sides: the retail traders and the broker dealers who have to decide what to do with a particular transaction in the moment when it happens. Broker dealers have an array of decision tools at their disposal, some of them more sophisticated and some less so. Among the less sophisticated ones are changing the spread at which a transaction is executed, or delaying its execution, or both, or, in some extreme cases, freezing the trading screen so that for a while at least, no more orders can be placed. A change in the spread at which a transaction is executed is called by brokers a slippage, a term that evokes a minor accident beyond one's control. From the perspective of traders, slippages, delays, and screen freezes appear mostly as (annoying) events attesting perhaps to the poor quality of the trading software, but not as management tools used to deal with trades in critical situations. Yet, change the perspective and they can become essential to managing transactions. Among the more sophisticated tools that have only recently begun to be developed by broker dealers for managing the transactions of their clients are stochastic models of the order flow, which integrate the risk features of the clients, based on their financial metrics. While in the past broker dealers catering to retail traders did not have the analytical capability to develop stochastic models of their order flow, a change had begun to occur as I wrote this book. Larger brokerage houses are able to hire quants to develop stochastic models, and some smaller brokerage houses are operated by brokers with engineering and mathematical training that enables them to develop such models.

The Illusions of the Bazaar

When I was trading, the screen gave me the impression that the trades I had placed on it—buying five e-mini Nasdaq contracts, for instance, or Euro contracts—would have at the other end an unseen trader who truly had five e-mini contracts to sell. In other words, the awareness that my transactions belonged to a community of traders interested in and dealing in similar instruments created the feeling that this community acted as a sort of bazaar (Geertz 1978). Some traders would put up some Euro contracts for sale, while people like me, shopping around, would become interested and buy some, and the other way around, all the time. Since I could look around for price and volume, and since I could "shout out" that I was looking to buy five e-minis on the Nasdaq index, the screen at first gave the feeling that it was indeed like a bazaar. I am saying "bazaar" for at least two reasons: first, because the order size was relatively small:[4] nobody bid or asked for hundreds of contracts, let alone thousands. It felt as if each participant had only a few items displayed on the table. Second, the awareness that all participants were retail traders carried a sense of equality of status: I assumed that they had different degrees of financial power and skills, but I also assumed that they were all nonprofessionals like me. We were all participating in these egalitarian exchanges, far from the world of professional traders.

The carefully maintained appearance, namely, that traders encounter each other in a bazaar of contracts and that they deal with each other in a competitive yet egalitarian environment obscures the considerable efforts put forth by all parties in managing trades. It also obscures the fragility and tension inherent in the broker's position, in the sense that brokers, while working for their clients, necessarily have to play against them too. The traders are a boon for the broker—who doesn't want to have clients?—but can become disruptive to the brokers' finances too. They shouldn't have too much in their accounts, but not too little either. They should win, but not too much and not too often, and if possible several should not win at the same time. Their trades have to be managed, and not simply managed in the sense of being executed, but in the sense of being decided upon: what is to be done with them? Are they to be kept, or are they to be bundled and sent away? Trades and trading situations have to be managed with an array of tools ranging from stochastic modeling of the order flow, at the one end, to staging "slippages" and other technological "glitches," at the other end.

This unspoken and asymmetric double set of activities, in which traders manage their trades while being managed (together with their trades) by their broker dealers, lies at the core of what trading means. "Management" here means not simply routine maintenance or execution of transactions. There is little routine in this. Nor does it mean simply caring for, in the sense of traders caring for their positions while brokers care for their traders. There is care, but not only that; there is much more.

What is presented as management has more the features of a strategic interaction, in the sense of being problematic, consequential, and dependent on other traders' moves in one and the same horizon of experience (Goffman 1967). Traders play (aka experiment) with trades. They manage portfolios. They try to infer or guess what other traders are doing as a condition of their decisions. Brokers need to decide what to do with the trades of their clients, and with their clients' accounts, as these trades happen. Both are symbiotic strategic activities—in that they depend on each other, but also in that they grow on each other.

The relationship between traders and brokers is both strategic and asymmetric, in the following senses: (1) while brokers see what traders do, traders cannot see what brokers do with their trades. The brokers' screen configurations are, as I have observed, entirely different from those traders work with. (2) Brokers manage the trades of their clients, as well as the clients themselves, yet this management remains unexplicated. As such, it has to resort to "accidents" (quote slippages, screen freezes) as management tools. (3) The (unexplicated) management of trades and traders is essential for the reproduction of the trading relationship. Without it, the broker would run the risk of bankruptcy and the clients' capital would be jeopardized.[5] (4) Because this management remains unexplicated, traders must maintain the impression (if not the illusion) of freedom to enter into transactions with counterparts who are retail traders like them. The trading screen is configured in a way that enables activities such as reciprocal observation of orders, giving the impression that actions are undertaken with (or against) other traders. In other words, if the orders placed by traders are managed on the back stage, the trading screen is the front stage, where activities are configured in specific ways, maintaining the appearance of full autonomy. It is an appearance that is crucial for the activities at stake. Just pause for a moment and try to think what trading would look like if the screen was configured around individual transactions with the broker. (5) Since the screen is the front stage on which traders appear to be entering transactions with (and against) each other, it has to enable basic operations (such as observation) both as individual *and* as group activities. Traders sit on the same front stage—metaphorically speaking—and they are provided with perception and action elements enabling them to relate to what each other is doing.

Observation and Relationality

When I started my second round of trading, in October 2009, I spent two days deciding what to put up on my trading screen and how. I started with a "trading matrix" on which I could put the contracts I wanted to trade. I started experimenting first by putting the British pound and the Euro, but then I discovered that I could trade contracts on any of the following (and combinations thereof), as I wrote down at the time: "Corn, soybean, currencies, indices, oats, rice, wheat, gold, silver, copper, platinum, palladium, cocoa, coffee, cotton, orange juice, sugar, crude oil, heating oil, natural gas, gasoline, feeder cattle, lean hogs, pork bellies, live cattle, DJ Euro Stoxx, Eurex Dax, Eurex Bobl, Eurex Bund, S&P500, Nasdaq 100, Russell 2000, Nikkei 225, Dollar index, Australian Dollar, British Pound, Canadian Dollar, Euro, Japanese Yen, Swiss Franc, Euro Dollar, Mini Dow Jones, Dow Jones, Treasury notes 5 years, Treasury notes 10 years, Treasury notes 2 years, Treasury bonds, Federal funds." And I was just an amateur. I could in principle observe all these contracts, but I had to make a selection. Next came building my order book, where I had various choices of action, such as transacting at the market price, transacting at limit, stop transacting, or stop at limit. I could place orders that would automatically cancel other orders or which would automatically trigger the execution of one or two more orders. To do this, however, I needed to first select and then assemble together the contracts I wanted to watch: I had to choose and build my world in the market, observe it, and only then trade.

I found myself opening the trading interface every morning and asking in my trading diary: "OK, what do I want to watch? I need to assemble the boards."[6] But this could not be done without learning all the securities codes, and I had better learn how to recognize them at a glance. And I needed to know what every one meant. Assembling the boards—even I could see this—meant thinking about what kind of securities I need to put together in the same window and how the different windows I assembled would relate to each other. I ended up with currency, indexes, treasuries, and commodities boards, but later I split the latter into metals and agricultural produce. I was somehow uncomfortable seeing hogs next to platinum. I had to put them on different boards, simply because seeing them made me think of how they could be or could not be related. In other words, by forcing me to operate with boards, the trading screen was also making me search for and produce accounts of the possible dynamics of such worlds made of platinum, gold, frozen orange juice, hogs, the Australian dollar, the Euro, the mini S&P500, and so on.[7] What counted as information was the product of my activities (Lynch 2014, 326), which had to be accountable. Before thinking of any possible strategy, I needed to do all this: it took me the better part of three consecutive days and continued over the next trading period. Only then could I start observing the screen.

While the totality of all available contracts is the same for everybody using the same platform, and while in principle individual combinations of contracts (or commitments) are infinite, traders are aware that they need to be where the action is—that is, they need to find and observe the contracts or commitments other traders are interested in. They do so in part by a trial and error process—that is, by playing around with trading boards and seeing where there is more activity. In part, such choices are motivated by past experiences, reading, attending trade shows, and the like. Thus, communities or groups of electronic traders are self-constituting through a process of observation combined with searches, a process through which mutual orientation is achieved: I am sticking with those traders who seem to have experiences (and interests) similar to mine, although I do not have any idea who they actually are. The entire work of observation is geared toward finding "opportunities." As a female trader told me once, observation is not passive; it consists of "digging." I observe orange futures on my screen, but at the same time I observe what other traders interested in orange futures are doing, and I have to decide whether I want to respond to and be a part of what they are doing.

Continuous observation was crucial to understand what was going on, as well as to be able to engage in action. When I started my experiment, I was spending all day hunched over my laptop without taking many breaks. I started putting trades on the screen, and I discovered that I had better not go away from the screen or do anything that required my attention for, say, 20 minutes at a time. I learned this the hard way: I once spent 20 minutes answering e-mails during trading hours, without checking what was happening on the trading screen, only to discover that I had accumulated substantial losses.

Talks with traders have again and again confirmed that observation takes most of their time: in fact, the more experienced traders are, the more time they will spend on observation, conducting fewer transactions per day (see also Sicherman et al. 2016). When Jim started trading, he spent 40 hours a week on observation and conducted about 20–50 trades per week, but he trades less now. Tim spent 5 hours every day on observation and made 1 trade every week. Chris and Terry spent 20 hours every week too, although Terry had reduced to 5 hours. Matt and Ben spent about 20 hours per week on observation as well, while Sam and Ron spent substantially fewer hours at the time of our talk, after initial periods of intense observation. It appeared that although the number of weekly trades was in inverse proportion to the experience of the trader, the number of hours put into observation stayed more or less the same or diminished at a slower pace as experience increased.

In this process, it is essential to be able to recognize at a glance what is going on, and this requires learning by heart the codes or acronyms of the contracts on screen. One of the challenges I had at the start was to make sense of, for instance, ES9Z and YM9Z, which I had put on my board the day before. I had to go back and look up what they meant: one was the E-mini S&P 500 (12/09) and the other was the mini Dow Jones (12/09). And then the @ED7H (that was a Eurodollar 3/17 contract traded on the Globex). I wrote in my trading diary that learning all the contract acronyms was like learning a language, without which I would not be able to communicate with other traders. All this learning couldn't be done in any other way than by observation. Of course, there were "dictionaries"—lists explaining what "ES9Z" was, and I learned to translate the entities' names into natural language, but they needed to be recognized and made sense of at a glance and without thinking, in the same way that we understand "dog" or "chair" without pausing for reflection. Indeed, looking at the instant messaging of traders, I could see that they casually, without any reference or explanations, used not only acronyms but also nicknames in talking about their observations, while they were conducting them: the Cable, the Loonie, the Kiwi, the Yuppy are common references in screen-relevant communications.

Learning acronyms and nicknames also means learning how they are (or might be) connected to each other, and how to gloss such possible connections. The logic of the trading screen itself makes this an inherent feature of observations, so that a trader is forced to develop accounts of the worlds configured on the screen. Let me explain this: I had started by putting acronyms on my screen: PL9U (that's a palladium contract), ZG9ZC500 (a gold 12/09 eCBOT call), YM9Z (mini Dow Jones 12/09 2200 call), and I could go on and on. Each one of these was a temporary

relationship (a contract), consisting of a reciprocal commitment scheduled to end on a specific date, with a specific outcome for me. What was I
to do now? Should I take these commitments as unrelated to each other,
as singular and isolated? Should I sort them and start building piles of
similar commitments? Should I combine them? Should I start thinking
about how they influence each other? Which one(s) did I want to enter?
Traders need to figure out how these commitments are related and what
the consequences are for their positions. In doing this, traders also observe each other's commitments.

Thus, the front stage of the trading screen primarily provides observational relationality. Traders relate to each other through observations
(augmented by various communication formats, which I discuss in chapter 5). This requires that they try to identify not only various types of
participants (for instance, who is a human being and who is a robot), but
also which of the flickering numbers is the trading "me."

Traders need to establish through observation where they are in the
world of the market at a given time. Where have their transactions gone,
how many are waiting to be executed, what is the situation of each transaction, and what is the overall situation of their positions? This is the es-
sence of what is called managing a portfolio. Traders need to observe
what is happening to other traders' transactions and provide a relatively
consistent account (albeit consistent only with the needs of the moment)
of what is happening to themselves in relation to other traders. I will il-
lustrate this with two excerpts from two different trading days:

> EDDIE: Okay, what I generally try to do is I try to sell it up. I use my own mov-
> ing averages on the options. I like to sell at . . . here's my average, what
> I've sold them for: 134.6. Now, it's higher. But I don't really want to sell,
> I mean, the lowest I'll sell is about 150. What I try to do is, anytime I can
> incrementally increase my average, I'll go ahead and take it, a little at a
> time. Just to get it up. And then when the stock pulls back, and it goes be-
> low that, I'll buy some of them back. So . . . I mean, I don't know if that
> sounds crazy, but . . . see, like right here, I've got 52 and a half cents. And I
> sold—that was mine, I think. I sold a bunch of them. And what I'll do is, I
> got ready to put in this order for—buy them back at 45.

When I was sitting next to Eddie in front of his trading screen, he
pointed with his finger—for my benefit—but also with the cursor all the
time to his positions, because he needed to see where he was with his

transactions at a given moment. He also needed to identify whether the transactions flickering on the screen were his ("that was mine, I think"). This was necessary because he was buying and selling continuously his own options, among others, I thought, in order to create the impression of demand for them. He was acting for the benefit of other traders, but this incessant buying and selling required him to observe continuously the traces his own actions left on the screen. In the excerpt below, which is from a different trading day, Eddie enters an imaginary dialogue with other traders, as if they might buy his contracts:

> EDDIE: Yeah. I hate it, really. And I . . . did a little nibbling on Apple Com-
> puter, just . . . well, I did, well, I sold 200 puts. Or two contracts for my IRA
> account because Apple Computer's been doing very well, very strong, its
> sales are strong, and the price is . . . the analysts have been boosting the
> price to like $78 a share. It went up above 70, came down to about 67 and
> change, so I said, well, I don't mind actually owning the stock. This is
> more . . . like, if someone wants to sell it to me for 65, I'll go ahead. You
> know? Pay me $1.20 a share so I get it for like $63.80.

Is there a trader, a real one, other than Eddie's broker, willing to sell him options on Apple at the specified price? A trader with whom Eddie enters a real transaction, no matter how fleeting? What matters more, perhaps, is that the process of observation itself forces Eddie to react as if there were one. The necessity to find himself on the screen, together with the need to rationalize his own trading decisions, makes him ask an imaginary other trader to give him what he wants. The screen fosters relationality—that is, the ability to relate to others as if one could enter a transaction with them.

Observation is inherently differential, in the sense that it does not result in a homogenization of commitments, but a differentiation. Some retail traders will surely want to sell Euro contracts when I want to buy, as I can see clearly on the screen. Seen from this perspective, trading communities are certainly observational communities, in the sense that their members do not trade directly with each other, but they observe each other all the time. While traders observe each other, they are also observed as a community by broker dealers, who in their turn observe more accurately what other institutional players are doing; retail traders have no chance to observe directly what broker dealers are doing, though they can make observational inferences about what institutional traders are doing. In this sense, the capabilities and possibilities for observation are asymmetric—dealers and institutional traders see more and have more accurate lenses than retail traders do.

Fabricated Observation

In some situations, observation apparently morphs into something like a ritual, during which audiences are bestowed the gift of observing the market directly through the eyes of a "master." This conjures a specific, fleeting relationship between the said "master" (or a "queen") and that person's followers. The audience is summoned to share the master's screen and observe what he is doing. Followers may be scattered across several time zones but respond to the master's call—sometimes in the wee hours of the morning—almost unfailingly. I once took part in such a ritual in which East Coast audiences had to gather at 3:00 a.m. because the master was trading at the opening of the London markets. They didn't fail to show up.

At first sight, this appears to be a rekeying of naturally occurring joint observations. Building on Alfred Schutz's metaphor of observing a bird in flight, Karin Knorr Cetina and Urs Bruegger (2002) implicitly underscore the egalitarian nature of coordinated observation in professional trading. Participants focusing their gazes on a price movement are, in the given situation, more or less the same. Of course, differences in skill and acuity can and will be revealed. Nevertheless, subordination to the charismatic force of a "master" is not asked for when professional traders jointly observe price movements. While implicitly egalitarian, joint observations exist in retail trading as well; the format of seeing with and through the eyes of a master trader, of accounting for what it is seen through his voice, is most probably specific to this domain. The ground level of trading activities would be rekeyed then as a ritual (Goffman 1974, 48) in which audiences are summoned to submit themselves to the vision of a master. And yet, it is more than that: this is a fabricated ritual (156), not in the sense of being "invented" or "fictional," but in the sense of being an intentional effort at managing observations in such a way that the audiences come to see the difference between themselves and said master. In a ritual, efforts (collective or individual) at observing prescribed steps will lead to a specific, witnessable outcome. We see because we have followed the rules of seeing, as exemplified in front of us.

In a fabricated ritual, a person or a group will manage a process at the end of which they will be able to claim that they can see differently (and better) than their witnesses.

Fabricated observations usually take about one hour—but they can be longer than that. The master (that is, the operator of a trading room or of a brokerage service) will trade live. What the audience sees on their screens is the master trader's screen. The audience can see the cursor moving around, the master's actions, as well as his performance during that period. (In these rituals, many master traders operate with special trading accounts.) The replicated trading screen can be accompanied by commentary or dialogue (sometimes there is an emcee as well), or by an instant messaging box where the audience can ask questions and the emcee or the assistant of the master trader posts comments and (occasionally) answers questions too. The size of the audience varies from a dozen to a few hundred, depending on the prestige of the "master" or the "queen."

Deploying fabricated observations is not without challenges. The mere existence of different time zones can pose serious problems sometimes. I once signed up for a live trading session scheduled to take place at 2:00 p.m. GMT, or 9:00 a.m. EST. I logged in, and the emcee welcomed us and gave a short introduction of the master trader. And then I waited, and waited, and waited, together with all the other traders, and it turned out that there was no master trader at all. The emcee was audibly trying to find that trader, but after an hour or so she gave up and the webinar was canceled. A few months later, I flew to the East Coast to interview the broker dealer firm that had organized the webinar and asked, among other things, about that event. I was told that the master trader was based not on the East Coast, but in California, and he had simply slept through the event, missing his live trading session.

In the absence of such mishaps, however, the audience will witness the market through the eyes of the master and will account for what is going on through the master's voice. Speaking rights are clearly allocated. Members of the audience do not talk to each other; they do not ask each other whether what they are seeing is right. They talk to the emcee or to the master. They can address questions, but they do not comment on the master's actions. The master, in turn, can summon the audience through questions, as well as through comments. I participated once in a fabricated observation where a member of the audience typed in a question before the master had given the start signal, only to be rebuked, half jokingly, by the emcee, with "Quiet. Master G is asleep." The participant in question replied, "Sorry, I thought it was 3:00am eastern." (The session was supposed to start at 3:00 a.m., and it was 14 minutes past.) Once the master has announced that he is "here," he will be greeted by the audience. He will announce himself a second time before the session can start:

> MASTER: And what you can expect from me is breakoutdown of trades, I'm a scalper, so you will get entry, target and stop loss from different pairs. Make sure to write down [these] levels and jump with us in the trades. IF market is quiet you will receive a lesson about money management, risk reward or market commentaries. I'm always looking for trades and you will receive those entries before it happens.
>
> For all new members, we recommend the following. Sit back, relax, enjoy and experience the opportunity to look over the shoulder of Master Traders as we trade and make Pips for our team. After a few days, you will get accustomed to a very unique style that has [been] proven and used successfully by hundreds of traders around the world.

The exhortation to jump into the trades with the master can be seen as self-serving, of course. If it was followed, it would create the appearance of a movement in a particular direction. Nevertheless, the master cannot know how many in the audience will follow his call. While there is a promise of revelation (entries will be received before they happen), the audience is summoned to absorb the experience of looking *as if* they were physically copresent. In a manner reminiscent of trading competitions, the master claims gameworthiness for him and his team, and he will be acclaimed for it by the audience:

> NEIL J.: £$ 1 hour MST taken out 5260.
> MASTER G: Yeah is sitting there Neil. I don't jump on whatever trades and sometimes I don't trade if my levels don't occur. So trading is about patience and analysis. Is a very difficult business but you are with real professional Forex Traders.
> NEIL J.: Very true GIO.

This session starts at 3:00 a.m. EST and stretches over four hours. Some of the participants wander out because they have to go to work, while some latecomers join in. The duration makes repeated assertions of gameworthiness a practical necessity: the audience needs to be reminded regularly that they are in good hands. While rituals of this sort can be (and are) used as a means of attracting new potential clients, they also spread particular perceptual explanatory patterns as well as action prescriptions, of the sort "When you see X, do Y." The master is seeing all the time things others might not see and is looking to do this or that action, should a particular situation occur: he sees buyers coming, he is looking for pullbacks, he is looking to sell at target, but is also aware of reactions. In short, he is in a state of permanent alert and is aware of the momentariness of situations. At the same time, he keeps reminding the audience that the environment they are in has unseen dangers lurking. Nevertheless, he still hopes to be "blessed" to see what he hopes to see. When members of the audience ask about "jumping in," they will be reminded that it is dangerous and that they can be hurt in seconds. This is apparently paradoxical, since the audience is supposed to trade, and hence encounter chance. They are supposed to make judgments and take risks. At the same time, they are summoned to defer to the judgment of the master, to his (in)sight, to his acumen.

The audience is warned of lurking dangers, which only the skill of the master can avoid. Fabricated observations provide for slots where encounters with the unexpected, fortuitous or not, occur. Every now and then, a member of the master's team will burst in announcing that something has happened, that they had such and such an encounter. These are treated by the master as completely objective and external events, as out there, never escaping the master's eye:

> [MASTER G'S TEAMMATE] GBPUSD: Closing 1/3 at 1.5265 for +115 pips. Closing 1/3 for +20 on TM; Holding 1/3 for 1.5085.
> MASTER G: I see that thanks Bill.

Bill, a member of the master's team, announces that he has made pips —that is, profit—only to be summarily dismissed with a thanks.[8] Such announcements happen several times during the session and are greeted with "nice and sweet trade" or "awesome job," or ignored. Of course, fabricated observations can only benefit from a good incantation that turns trades into pips. And it always helps to send signals to the audience that one's traders are really making profits. During all this time, it is not obvious that the master actually makes any trades, although he is "looking" to buy or to sell at particular prices, or is giving "targets."

What is observed here, then? Not so much actual trades (only their announcement can be observed), but the practical claim of a "master" of observational mastery. The master sees everything in front of him, is aware of the danger, has the required virtues and wisdom, is ready to share it with a public, is ready to guide the public in "jumping in," but is also ready to hold that public back when necessary. Fabricated observations are participative observations of how claims to charisma, to more power or more skill, are formulated as practical acts. This has very concrete consequences: on what grounds can the audience follow a summons to do as they are told? In situations such as these, on the grounds of the master's claims to a superior power; the claim itself (not so much empirical evidence supporting it) is displayed in front of them.

From Observation to Action

The logic of action is presented at trade shows and in seminars as a very simple one: "Cut the losses and let the profits run." In practice, this is not so easy to achieve, because, for example, notions such as a profit or a loss are abstract. Traders need to identify at a given moment what is a profit and what is a loss in the situation they are in, and for how long the said transactions are going to remain a "profit" or a "loss." Moreover, "letting the profits run" is inherently temporal—for how long should or could traders "let profits run," and when should they realize that something is a loss and needs to be cut?

At any given moment, traders act within a "found" pattern that precedes their decision—a pattern provided by the previous actions of other traders, but also by the trader's own situation. That is, it matters whether traders are in plus or minus on specific transactions, how many of their orders have been executed, and with what results. It also matters whether traders are within margin—that is, whether they will be allowed to put an order, according to whether they have used more than a set percentage of their deposit.

Within these constraints, several types of actions can be roughly distinguished. In practice, with a few exceptions, they will not be encountered as "pure" types, but rather as mixed up in the flow of trading activities. The one exception here is perhaps construction, in its more complex forms: building up trading robots and quantitative models requires particular skills, as well as a degree of concentration and an amount of work, so construction tends to be a distinct set of activities.

In observations, traders engage with what is happening in front of them, without necessarily providing direct responses to these happenings. Observation does not have the direct and immediate reactive component, although it can be undertaken in preparation of a response. In action "with the screen," traders directly and immediately respond to what is going on by engaging with the numbers flashing in front of them. They insert their own actions on the screen, modify the numbers, and directly intervene in the play. This kind of action is what is generally and somewhat amorphously called "trading." It takes place much less frequently than observation but perhaps is much more intense. Its subtypes are "playing" a trade and "managing" a portfolio.[9]

"Playing a trade" can usually mean executing transactions with a very short time horizon without integrating them into one's portfolio: it is a burst of activity, which will cease after a while. It can mean being constrained to have short time horizons because there is not enough money to "roll" over, or to manage trades. It can also mean that a financial instrument has suddenly become attractive, without necessarily fitting with one's portfolio, so that a trader might be tempted to "play" that instrument. Or it can mean that the instrument is riskier than others, so that a trader might want to "play" with it first and see what happens. "Playing" a trade, then, generally means lack of durability and limited knowledge of how an instrument will behave when traded, but also willingness to take a risk and to learn thus about particular instruments. Eddie, whom I previously introduced, played all the time:

> EDDIE: Google was interesting, it went up to 431. [. . .] And then it pulled back. It went down to 395 yesterday. Sunk like a rock. And then it, by the end of the day it was up to 405. So I'm actually thinking about playing some Google options. It's a strong stock. I mean, I'm just purely speculative . . . but, you know, quick in-and-out kind of thing. Let's see, what else am I looking to do? I bought some Sohu.com.

Among the kinds of activities that make up action "with the screen," the most important one is provided by managing existing trades. True, playing or experimenting with a trade may be dominant in the incipient phases of trading, when novice traders set up their screen and try their hand for the first time. This doesn't mean that more experienced traders do not play around or experiment; they do. Beyond the incipient stages, however, the dominant kind of activity is managing existing trades or managing a portfolio of trades.

When the trading screen is set up for the first time and the first trades are put through, an "inventory" is built, as a broker explained once to his audience. This inventory may change in time, but it will completely disappear only if all positions are liquidated.[10] Otherwise, it needs to be managed—taken care of on a permanent basis, either in its individual components or with respect to the linkages among such components. Once a transaction is placed on the screen, it cannot be left there on its own. It will need to be taken care of—observed, watched to see when it is executed, its implications analyzed. Most times the work of managing a trade will lead to even more trades, since the conditions under which trades are executed rarely match a trader's initial expectations. Managing a portfolio is nothing else but trying to manage one's implicit relationship with one's own broker, while seemingly engaging with other traders. The broker's response to trades—that is, the broker's execution, delay, or "slippage"—will lead to responses (aka more trades), which in turn will generate further responses by the broker (in the form of price spreads). This system of response actions creates "positions," understood as tensioned and strategic relationships that can be neither abandoned nor brought forward without qualities like patience and resilience:

> TIM: If you have trust in your system, this is to be able to, like, stay in a position whilst it's retracing against you, and not to be constantly going in and out of the market I think requires a lot of discipline and it's quite addictive. Watching charts is the only way I can describe, so that you, but you need to be able to, you can not, to hold back and try and wait for what is a signal and not just trying to force a trade into it, like you just, like you . . . many people seem to get to a point where you just want to see a trade for yourself, and it's really important I've found to just try and step back and try and not be so deeply involved into it. Which is difficult, I'm not gonna lie.

Staying in a position—that is, keeping up a tensioned relationship—requires qualities intrinsic to the gameworthiness of a trader. One has to hold back and wait—a leitmotif of screen observation. One needs the right amount of involvement—not too much and not too little. The response needs to be the right one. All these elements that appear crucial for action—what is the right amount of waiting, when is the response right—cannot be determined according to a set of general rules; as Tim says, one needs to follow one's "own rules." Relationships are unique. If we switched perspective here and looked at such relationships from the viewpoint of the broker, this uniqueness would mostly go away. Brokers focus on managing what counts for them as "difficult" relationships, with traders who have too large accounts or who too often go out of margin.

The vocabulary of care, of being close to one's positions (one needs to become comfortable with them) and judging "how much on something" is the right amount, suggests that the work of managing a portfolio is directly related to the perceptual effect of the unfinished, never-ending market flow on the trading screen. Managing a portfolio does not mean sitting there and observing one's own positions on the screen; it means continuously adjusting here and there, selling a bit of that (if one has too much of it) or buying a bit of the other (in case one has too little): taking money off the table and leaving money on it all the time. This continuous, never-ending work of adjustment, undertaken simultaneously by traders, is what gives the trading screen its flow.

Taking a position is not easy: it requires, as some traders explained it to me, being comfortable with the security (even if that security can be a "fight"), but also being patient and disciplined (on which, more later); if one is impatient or inexperienced, one might prefer to "scalp" (that is, quickly buy and sell the same security within a short interval), although scalping can be problematic in itself. Taking a position also means having enough money to be able to "hold on," weather transient bad moments, and "roll" positions into the future. Another trader I talked to saw managing positions as an ideal limited both by insufficient capital and by lack of patience. Taking and holding a position means holding on, being confident, having the financial and mental resources to wait:

SAMANTHA: Oh, yes I am still trying to decide . . . to stick with a pair rather than when it doesn't behave as I think it should, to lose confidence and move off to another pair, and the problem with this Aussie Dollar is that the carry is so high that was a problem, I was wanting to short or I had shorted and it didn't drop for . . . literally weeks or days and days and days and days and I just saw my carry interest getting bigger and bigger and

bigger and bigger and bigger and then you're kind of locked into it because
you don't want to drop it because you are convinced it is going to go soon,
but at the same time you can see the carry going against you and so really . . . that's what I would like to do. I would like to have just a few trades
and one or two pairs, but my confidence level isn't enough, you see when
it, when it dropped the other day I thought, wow, now is a good chance to
go long and I can earn carry, but I had so little confidence, I did, I went
long and I came out after about an hour, I thought no, it is going to keep
going, and of course it didn't, it went up and it didn't go all the way up, but
it's been up long enough to have earned quite a lot of interest, so . . . so I'm
still too amateurish, Alex, unfortunately I don't know how long it takes.

While in Samantha's account, managing positions as the gateway into
a "stable" trading relationship is marred by her lack of confidence and
money, there is another aspect that intervenes here and makes managing positions a fragile undertaking: margin calls. In my second round
of demo trading with a US brokerage, I discovered—rather suddenly—
that I needed to have a minimum percentage of my initial deposit there,
and that I could not deplete everything. As soon as I went below that
percentage, my trades were blocked.[11] For real money traders, this can
be a serious problem: I have repeatedly seen instances in which, after
two warnings, the brokerage automatically liquidated some trades so
as to bring the trader back into margin. More important, perhaps, being forced to return within margin, especially if it happens suddenly, can
jeopardize future trades: plans need to be thrown overboard or adjusted
so as to respond to calls for returning to margin. Thus, one of the paradoxical features of trading is that traders have to project actions into
the future while the future can be undermined by their present situation. This means that traders need to answer the question "What to do
next?," and any answers to that question will depend on their answer to
the question "What is the situation now?" But the "situation now" can
change so suddenly—and so detrimentally to the trader—that tentative
answers to "What to do next?" have to be thrown overboard. Traders
have to attend to and reconfigure the "now," and then start reconfiguring the future based on the new "now."

Managing positions, then, becomes inherently unstable work. The
broker's margin calls (expected or not) can be seen as akin to soured
moments in a difficult relationship, to tensioned interactions, arguments,

or disputes capable of jeopardizing the future of the relationship. One doesn't want that; patience, carefulness, and feeling are required to avoid such tensions as much as possible.

Being in a difficult relationship can still be seen as a privilege. A bad relationship might be better than no relationship at all. Nevertheless, maintaining (or managing) a relationship, even if it is only with one's own trades and with one's own broker, requires not only patience and other skills, but also a strong sense of identity. And, as is true so often in life, it requires money too. Bar all these, traders contemplate—sometimes with resignation—the option of scalping, or going quickly in and out of a trade:

> SAMANTHA: My point there being that I would like to, first of all I know what kind of trader I would like to be, which has taken me a long time. I would like to be a position trader. Now I don't think you can be a position trader with $250. Unfortunately you can take, you know, one position and you can . . . you can sit there and at the end of the month you will have, you will have got $280 or something, but I know if I scalp I can make a whole bunch of money really quickly, but then I invariably get into terrible problems afterwards, so . . . I know that I would like to be a slow trader. I would like to be a position trader. I would like to stick to either one currency or . . . one type of pair like a carry trade or something like that. I would like to listen to the economic words and understand what is happening, but I get so bored, because it all takes so long. Now I don't know what guys do in big companies when they position trade, I mean what do they do? In between, they go to work and they just look and see that it's moved three pips and then they go home?

The trope of "understanding," which comes up repeatedly in the accounts provided by traders, puzzled me at first. How can one do—again and again—something that one doesn't understand? However, after a while I came to realize that "understanding" does not mean "having an idea" or "making sense" of something. It means being able to relate the temporal horizon of one's actions to the temporal horizon of a justifying narrative.[12] The temporal horizon of the action itself and that of the narrative are intimately related: the account "I did X because Y happened" needs to develop its inner time, and this time needs to match that of action. For instance, we can give accounts of what we said in a meeting at work today, and why, but, in order to be effective, such an account needs to have a temporal horizon that matches that of the work rhythms and work relationships. This is why we might start by presenting the discussion at that meeting, the issues at stake; putting them in the context of work relationships; sketching participating characters and their interests or positions, and so forth.

When the horizon of action is extremely short, a matter of minutes, it becomes very difficult to develop a corresponding account. There is simply not enough time—time as the stuff to build an account from. Actions with an extremely short horizon lack understanding, not in the sense that participants are not aware of what they are doing, but in the sense that it becomes very difficult to develop an account intrinsic to action. This is why traders use the interstices in trading, the moments when not much seems to be going on, to build accounts, justifications of their own trading decisions. Seen this way, idle interstices in trading—of which there are a lot—are not idle at all; they are actively used to construct rationales of decisions. At the same time, producing accounts is not a merely discursive rendering of why a trader made a particular decision, but a more complex activity of searching for, identifying, and examining visual patterns on the screen, putting together various bits and pieces of information, and trying to infer the reasons for other traders' decisions.

The lack of patience that Samantha is complaining about (together with her lack of money) keep her in the inferior position of a scalper. In her account, however, there is a hierarchy of "understanding" directly related to her ability to take positions. Being able to match actions with justifying narratives is something Samantha imagines "the guys in big companies" are much better at. They have the money to buy time to think.

Maintenance Work

When I asked traders what they did with their portfolios (a collection of existing outcomes of past transactions, as shown on their screens), they unanimously responded in terms of maintenance, or keeping things up and running. This was their primary task, and a more important one than making money or executing a trade at any given point. Executing trades is subordinated to management work. One has to "go out" to do a trade. More important than doing a trade, any trade, are taking and keeping positions and developing "a sense of comfort" with a security.

One usually "rolls" positions, keeping them into the future, albeit in modified forms. Ideally, one has to "run the profits," although this isn't easy. Managing a portfolio has its pitfalls too: one can have "too much on something"; in general, one needs to decide when to take money off the table and when to leave money on the table.

Managing a portfolio of trades requires projecting oneself across various temporal relevant horizons, not only in terms of "positions," but also in terms of personal commitments and constraints. Tax time, or college tuition due dates, are important. From the viewpoint of retail traders, managing a portfolio of trades fuses together personally relevant time horizons (my taxes, my payments, my financial commitments) with institutional time horizons (such as dividend payment time), integrating one's personal world with the larger world.

It is not only constraints such as tax returns that determine how a portfolio is managed and how its performance (or lack thereof) is explained: family commitments can also intervene in the everyday work of managing a portfolio or in rationalizing its performance. Eddie systematically engaged his spouse in observing and commenting upon market actions. When it came to explaining the outcomes of his trading over the recent past, he commented that the decisions to sell from his portfolio were dictated by his family needs, but also that these needs put pressure on him to perform:

> What I did, for this year, I took out a chunk of money to pay bills, and set it aside and, just, this is it for the year. Now, I'm going to have to do that again probably in the end of December or January for next year. But, it basically, I mean, the house is paid for, so we don't . . . you know, and then we just cover our monthly bills, so . . . well, you know, I mean, this whole education thing has been so outrageously expensive. [*laugh*] And it put a lot of pressure on me, financially, you know? And I made a lot of mistakes because of it, and right now, like I say, that's one of the reasons I'm . . . right now, I'm just hell-bent on getting, building up my finances this year.

A trader from the East Coast explained to me once that when he decided to focus more upon managing his portfolio (he had been laid off and had more time on his hands), the first key steps were identifying "underutilized money" ("money sitting in cash, doing nothing" is apparently bad) and defining portfolio goals in relationship to taxation. He had to manage his portfolio in relationship to transaction costs, including not only fees, but also taxes. This meant that in some cases decisions about what to sell and when to sell were shaped not necessarily by the value of an equity at that moment in time, but by how the amount of money resulting from that sale would be taxed: "Here you've got . . . fortunately, I've owned this fund, so [*laugh*] for about 10 years, I guess I've gotten 12.55 there, even though this one has a high expense ratio, but it's in my taxable account, so I'm going to keep it because of the embedded capital gains." The relevance of taxation has been recognized by banks and brokerages, which around 2005 started offering "tax efficient" products such as exchange traded funds or, in the United Kingdom, contracts for difference and binary options (an upscale name for what is essentially a bet, but a tax-free one).

Overall, then, what does online trading mean? While existing ethnographies have looked at (online) trading in the basic key, or mode—that is, as a "serious" activity that is "for real," trading is much more than that. The basic key can be seen as "signal," as something serious and informative, different from the "noise" of rituals, of fabricated observations, of the front-stage illusions of the screen. And yet, all this noise is woven into the basic key of retail trading and shapes it. We cannot fully understand how its assumptions work if we do not understand what happens to orders. We cannot grasp how the differences between "masters" and "followers" are produced within the act of trading (and not simply within its institutional setups) if we do not pay attention to the rekeyings and fabrications occurring not far away from, but layered upon, this basic key. This noise contributes to making the basic frame of trading what it is, and this noise helps make the other noise, the retail traders, what they are: groups summoned to subordinate to and follow "masters" and "queens," groups summoned, within the very act of trading, to think that they are in need of endless betterment.

A crucial feature of electronic retail trading, then, is the interactional richness and complexity of tightly laminated keys and fabrications, of which the basic key is rather "as if for real" than "for real." Yet, from the viewpoint of traders, it has to be taken as "for real." While traders strategically engage screen representations, broker dealers strategically engage customers and their trades. The fabrication of competition allows brokers to take the counterpositions to their clients, while leaving the latter with the impression that they are entering a contest with each other. This is probably nowhere more visible than on the trading screens of brokers and traders. The setup of the retail trading screen is completely disjointed from that of the broker dealer screen: the former presents an environment not only where the actual counterpart is absent, but also where this absence leaves plenty of room for building up a fiction of multiple equals as counterparts. The setup of the broker dealer screen brings together actual counterparts. This setup disjunction acts like a one-way mirror, allowing dealers to see what their clients are doing (yet without the possibility of intervening), but never the other way around.

Is trading a staged encounter with fate, then? When sitting in front of the screen, traders need to engage the fiction of multiple, equal counterparts in a major key. They need to address seriously and to respond to what other participants in the world of the market are doing. Awareness that actual counterpositions are taken by brokers would not change anything in this requirement. The key is locked in.

Ethnographies of the basic key of trading have stressed particular features of synthetic interactions, such as response presence and temporal co-orientation (Knorr Cetina 2009). Perhaps another major feature can be added next to synthetic interactions: the lock-in of the key that establishes the mode of action. While brokerages create the illusion of competition among clients (one could say, they fabricate competition), they can create this illusion only in a serious way. They are committed to the action too, so they cannot extract themselves from their obligations. In face-to-face interactions, a situation can easily change from seriousness to joking and back to seriousness. Interactions in situations such as those provided by the trading screen cannot be easily rekeyed by participants. Going back to Erving Goffman's argument that encounters with fate are carefully orchestrated, one could add: trading is carefully orchestrated as variously keyed activities, but the orchestration itself cannot be done except in a major key.

CHAPTER FIVE

Talk in Trading, Talk for Trading, Talk of Trading

Group Communication in Electronic Markets

I have argued that the key is locked in: that is, even if participants are engaging in an illusion of trading against peers, they have to take relationality seriously and commit to it. The next question is: How do concrete and specific relationships emerge out of relationality? And what kind of relationships are these? I start again with a puzzle.

Communication and Relationships

Financial markets are regularly celebrated as the pinnacle of individualism. We would expect traders, especially in electronic markets, to conform to this stereotype and carefully avoid revealing to each other what they are doing. After all, in theory at least, every one of them is there to make money, and they compete against each other over information (Vives 2008; Peres 2010; Fuzhou and Liu 2012). The standard rationale is that each trader is on the hunt for information, and every bit of information she obtains will shape her decisions, so why share it with others? One could argue that traders will talk to each other in order to obtain information that is not available otherwise, but in electronic finance a wealth of information is readily available on the trading screen. One could argue that traders will try to elicit private information, but what would be the rationale for disclosing private information, when having it is so advantageous? Furthermore, one does not expect this kind of infor-

mation to "move markets." Why would I want to know what other traders like me are doing at this or that moment? And aren't their actions
reflected in the price movements I see on the screen anyway? If traders share information, how can they trust that they aren't being manipulated? To avoid harm, they will keep their cards close to their chests, and
even if they talk to each other, it will be in order to bluff, raise (or lower)
the stakes, give false impressions when convenient, and the like. All in
all, they will use a communicative arsenal intended to induce particular impressions, which in their turn will give them (potentially) a specific
advantage. Since they all know or expect this (bar perhaps a few naives,
who will quickly learn their lesson), why talk to each other?

The argument that communication serves exclusively strategic purposes sits at odds with my previous arguments, namely, that competitive settings need to address moral issues before participants engage in
them and that the trading screen is geared toward generating relationality. According to the first, competition is not unfettered but is carefully
bounded, and it does not exclude, but rather demands, cooperation. According to the second, if trading requires relationality, it is hard to imagine relationality without any form of communication. Relationality cannot be maintained exclusively by expression games and deceit. It cannot
occur without genuine communication.

In the old days of trading pits and floors, traders communicated on a
regular basis, since trading meant shouting at each other, waving hands,
making eye contact, and such. Making a transaction meant talking (or,
better said, shouting). In other words, trading meant a string of perfor-
mative utterances. In addition, in those old days, and especially among
professional traders, talking to each other was not restricted to the trading floor. Most, if not all, knew other traders and were part of more or
less tightly knit networks that socialized together after the trading hours.
At restaurants and watering holes, a lot of information was circulated
about the state of the world, the situation of various stocks, or the ru-
mored intentions of this or that player. This practice continued in the
early era of computerized transactions, when professional traders transacted via proprietary messaging systems (Knorr Cetina and Bruegger
2002), and when trading desks in the same trading room collaborated on
transactions (Beunza and Stark 2012, 2004).

We can say, then, that various forms of communication in financial
markets, in a restricted sense (leaving out the shows, the fairs, the seminars, and all satellite activities), had these purposes:

1. Communication was the vehicle of transactions. There would have been no buying and selling without oral communication or, somewhat later, proprietary messaging systems.
2. Communication was a vehicle for strategically circulating information within networks of traders who knew each other. Included here are communication as a means of deceiving and manipulating other traders (Harrington 2009) and communication with key holders of information (such as market makers), from whom hints and suggestions (if not exactly detailed information) could be obtained. But also included are judgments and evaluations of transactions, glosses, representations of past transactions as exemplary (in a positive or negative sense), and communications of previous trading experiences.
3. Communication was the vehicle for organizing local collaborations, with a view to conducting transactions. Communication, then, was shaped and constrained either by locality, or by networks, or by a combination thereof. Traders talked to each other because under the given circumstances talking was the most efficient way of conducting their key activity or of creating favorable conditions for this key activity.

We can call the first form talk in trading, because conducting a transaction meant talking. The second form includes what can be called talk of trading, meaning swapping experiences of past transactions. The second and third forms include what can be called talk for trading, because here talking prepared the grounds or the conditions for conducting a transaction, while not necessarily being coextensive with the transaction.

In electronic finance, all these particular constraints seem to have disappeared. A transaction is just a click away, not a shout away. Not to mention that information, any kind of information, is available online at any time and in real time. Not just price and volume information, of the type it might have been difficult to obtain previously outside a network, but also expert opinions, judgments, recommendations, and much, much more. On top of all this, while location certainly plays a significant role for professional traders, it is much less relevant for retail traders. Professionals are mostly located in the City of London, in Canary Wharf, in Lower and Mid-Manhattan, or within a few square blocks in downtown Chicago. Retail traders are located everywhere. With a few exceptions, such as trading clubs, there are few opportunities for retail traders to talk to each other. And why should they?

Electronic retail markets must be a very silent environment, then. Click, click. Yet, the existence of trading clubs, the regular meetings, and the "elite" groups within these clubs indicate that communication has a much larger presence than we would suspect. The question is, To what extent is this communication consequential? To what extent does it affect actions and decisions, and how? From the start, I was struck by the amount of talk present in markets. Traders talked all the time. They had their own messaging systems. Then, around 2009, social trading emerged. That means trading platforms with built in messaging systems. They became quite popular. Traders seemed to talk at least as much as in the old days in the trading pits, if not more (although comparisons might be difficult). They talked to family members when trading from home; they talked to other traders whom they didn't know much about. And they talked to traders they knew somewhat better. Why so much talk? What did it accomplish, when there was apparently nothing to accomplish by talking?

The list of apparently puzzling behaviors doesn't stop here. Not only did traders talk to each other, but they revealed transactions to each other. Why would they do that? These transactions did not move markets, and, besides, there was actually no market to move (since broker dealers were counterparts). Why would they spend time on talking instead of focusing on transactions? Was talking not distracting them? Then I thought, talking is perhaps a way to kill time, so maybe they talk to each other when the market is slow, and they stop talking when the market gets busy. If this is true, then we should see more talking when there is less trading, and the other way around. I decided to take a closer look at one of the social trading platforms, one that has more than 6,700 active traders. One of my assumptions was that traders who chatted more would be trading less, because they would be just too busy posting messages. Then I assumed that such traders would not get much attention—that is, their messages would be viewed seldom, because other traders would get distracted by reading the musings of a handful of traders who just didn't trade. The third assumption I made was that, overall, trading times and talk times would not overlap at all. When things were slow, traders would find time to talk, and when things were getting busy, traders would trade. In other words, trading and communication were inversely correlated. Admittedly, this was only one trading platform, but it had 6,700 active traders, and hence it could offer some good insights into communication.

My first surprise was that, generally speaking, trading time and chat times were not separated at all. Traders chatted when not trading and they chatted when they traded. Sometimes chats were not accompanied by any trading activity, and sometimes they were; in some cases, chats occurred during intense trading activity. This raised the issue, What were they chatting about? Perhaps topics and interventions from other traders play a role in who talks to whom and when.

Over twelve months, the community participated in 2,356 discussion threads, grouped into the following categories: questions (1,048); positions (692); market commentary (228); technical analysis (177); poll (121); technical indicators (58); news reports (20); and economic events (12). Only a minority of these threads concerned news or economic events. A good number of them (about 5%) consisted of opinion polls among community members, while the vast majority fell under just two categories: "questions" and "positions." A "question" can actually be no question at all, but a summons to look at a price movement and comment on it. For instance: "take a good look at the usd/gbp, It's been on an 800 pip move so look for a fallback to 1.4775 area." A position can be a personal disclosure such as the one called "Bozo move": "I closed the wrong trade, which was hedged and it stopped me out of 4 trades. I'm so upset. Mental note pay attention to which trade you're working with."

These statistics indicate that traders—at least in this community— were less interested in commenting upon events or news (generally, information coming from outside the community) and more interested in discussing particular price movements, as well as in revealing or judging their own transactions. If this is so, it is not lack of information or the difficulty of interpreting external information that prompts communication, but something else. Why should somebody disclose an infelicitous trade instead of keeping silent about it, especially since there is no constraint to do so? Or why should somebody publicly anticipate a price move instead of keeping it to himself?

The second surprise came from looking at the posts with the highest number of hits. The more hits a trader's post gets, the more popular she or he is. Other traders spend time looking at them, and these traders spend time writing posts. Hence (I expected), they do less trading and perhaps they also have fewer winning trades. However, it appeared that the more popular traders (in terms of hits) were also those who traded more: the correlation between post views (how many other traders read somebody's post) and that author's number of transactions was 0.10. Therefore, communication doesn't mean lack of trading activity; communication is neither ignored nor completely amorphous; there are both followers and followed among traders (at least in communication); communication and trading are somehow related. But how?

In face-to-face trading, talking was a vehicle of transactions, of circulating information, and of organizing collaborations. It had to be used by traders, for lack of any better alternative. It was seen as being outside trading, because we conceived trading as an essentially individual activity. However, if we look at trading as a collaborative activity, then communication does not appear anymore to be an external prop. When I refer to trading as a collaborative activity, I do not mean incidental collaborations (of the kind we see in some trading rooms). I mean that trading has by definition to be collaborative.

Why is that so? Trading as collaborative, instead of competitive? I have previously discussed trading competitions. Now collaborations? Yet, the two do not have to be mutually exclusive. While competitions can be staged in a spectacular form, collaborations can take place offline and online, in a less spectacular, though not inconsequential, fashion. If we seek an answer to these questions—Why is trading collaborative and Why do traders talk—perhaps a good way to start is to look at the groups and communities who talk, how they are organized, when they talk, and what they talk about (Fine 2007, 243). In looking at groups in electronic markets, we should pay less attention to whether they meet face-to-face, online, or a mix of the two, and more to what they actually do, and how talk contributes to what they do. But we should also look at sustaining collective identities in electronic markets (if these exist). It has been argued that collective identities depend on shared rituals, which in their turn cannot dispense with face-to-face presence, or at least with visual representations of human bodies (R. Collins 2004, 53, 59). Electronic markets, however, are devoid of such visual representations: they are all about flickering numbers. Does this mean there is no other way of creating and sustaining collective identities—collective not in the sense of large market crowds, but in the sense of organized groups with distinct identities?

There are further aspects to consider here. Groups can do more than one thing: the student trading clubs I discussed previously, for instance, were organized as recruitment grounds for professional finance jobs. Yet, to attain this ultimate goal, a club's members had to engage in trading activities that required regular talk. The questions are thus, How does this talk contribute to trading? To what extent it is consequential with respect to trading, and To what extent does talk as a "unit of activity in

its own right" (Goffman 1981, 131) shape interactions within groups, allowing us to distinguish among various types in electronic finance?

If talk contributes to trading, then to what aspects or parts of trading? The view that communication arises from the need to get trading-
relevant information (e.g., price and volume) assumes that talk is a vehicle to obtain key decision-making ingredients, mostly as part of an
economy of favors. The view that communication arises from the need
to collaborate assumes that different skills, embodied by different people, must be brought together in decision making. The first sees communication (talk) as essentially transactional. The second sees communication as essentially a consensus-building tool. Traders talk to each other
because they need to transact information (mostly as a form of reciprocal gift giving); or traders talk to each other because they need to reach
consensus, to harmonize different, though not necessarily conflicting,
points of view. That is the consequentiality of talk in and for trading—
neither transacting information nor consensus building can be achieved
without communication, and trading decisions require information or
consensus (depending on which view we favor). Sometimes trading can
even require a combination of the two, although one of the two elements
will remain the primary one.

Are there other forms of consequentiality as well? I will look at this
issue based on what groups do in their talking. At least the following
kinds of groups can be distinguished based on what I have observed:
(1) operations groups; (2) experiential groups; and (3) managerial groups.
I will discuss them one by one, starting with operations groups.

Operations Groups

One of the instances of group communication that comes closest to the
more traditional situation of shop floor talk is seen in the process of
building and running automation projects. This might not be the largest chunk of activities in retail trading, but it is nevertheless a very significant one. I call it operations talk (conducted by operations groups).
Operations groups are small groups that coalesce around building, testing, and operating a trading machine, in the form of either a quantitative
model or a trading algorithm. Subdivision and collaborative dissent are
the prominent features of operations groups. Some operations groups do
not want to reach consensus. They want to produce and maintain dis-

sent—at least for a while—as essential for the goal of building trading machines. While forms of dissonance can arise in trading rooms and can be used in constructing arbitrage strategies, they are not a design principle of trading rooms. Rather, various trading desks organized around various evaluative principles (which are not necessarily conflicting) will collaborate when need arises (Beunza and Stark 2012, 209). Dissent, though, is not mere dissonance. Dissent is the conscious organization of collaborations around conflicting principles.

In operations talk, small groups of traders will get together to build, test, and use quantitative models or trading robots. It is implied in many situations that one and the same group will build and test both a model and a countermodel (i.e., a second model based on theoretical assumptions completely opposed to those of the first or using a completely opposed technique). Since commercially available robots are highly mistrusted, savvy traders (at least some of whom hold advanced degrees in engineering and the natural sciences) will build their own robots. These groups are different in their composition, organization, and operations from the collaborations encountered in institutional trading rooms, where traders from different desks will come together in order to plan and execute a trade.

First, operations groups are not necessarily located all in the same place. One group of about six people that I encountered had some members in London and some members on the East Coast of the United States. Second, operations groups are not necessarily homogeneous by way of education and institutional positions. Some groups come from the same background in signal engineering or operations research, but some others have a lead figure holding an advanced degree in the natural sciences, a subordinate figure holding a less advanced degree (e.g., a lead figure with a PhD and an apprentice who is a doctoral student in an unrelated field), and other members who may not have a college degree. This is so because operations groups are involved not only in building but also in using quantitative models or trading robots (aka algorithms, or algos).[1] Operations groups can be hierarchically organized, with a lead developer and users following the developer's instructions; such groups are involved not only in building and testing models or algos, but also in using them. Building, testing, and using appear to be seamless, rather than discrete activities. Based only on test results, one cannot predict how a model or an algo will behave in a real market environment— for example, whether it will be stable, under which conditions it will work well, under which conditions it will be profitable or not.[2] Therefore, operations groups will continue to function for a while at least after trading algos have been uploaded.

This bundle of rather complex activities makes constant communication necessary, both off-line and online. When building a model or an algo, some groups will meet and establish the core hypothesis or principle, which will be then encoded and tested. In some cases, this core principle will come from the lead developer and the encoding will be done by an apprentice. Such groups can develop and test a model and its opposite. The group will split into subteams that take conceptual positions against each other. One of the team leaders from a group developing quantitative models explained it this way:

TED: Yeah, yeah. And my approach will be looking at historical volatility. You see someone else in my group wants to look at something called the implied volatility, which looks at for example the Black-Scholes formula to try and calculate the volatility of the stock price, so we're taking different routes. No one's actually come up with codes yet because it will take, from conception to actual running of the code it takes some time. There's a time to take for the investment, but once we get the models running we can make a lot of investments very quickly, as we just run our code for different stock prices, but we're still in the process of writing our code. [. . .] I'm using an auto-regressive, so basically it makes the assumption that previous values, previous days' stock price, depends on, has a relation with the future price, so there's a correlation between the past and the present. And so I use past data to calculate parameters in my model, and once I have the parameters in my model I can then calculate things like mean and variance, which I can then design a normal distribution, a statistical distribution to try and predict with a certain degree of probability what the price will be in the future—whether it will go up or down, what level will be in the future. So that's my approach. The other person's approach, which looks at implied volatility, looks at a specific, it looks at the Black-Scholes formula. The Black-Scholes has an underlying assumption of the data being normal or the process being normal, and from, so it's a normal distribution basically, so from that, knowing what the historical data is, you plug the data in and I can't remember how they're doing it, sorry, so they're doing it using just the inverted Black-Scholes formula, so they look at the data, calculate probability and once they know what the distribution is they invert it to calculate the mean and variance, so that's what they're doing to calculate, that's their modeling approach, whereas for their model, underlying assumption for their model is that the past, the present day value is independent to the past day value. So any value in the future is just independent, so there's no correlation between the past and the present. That's what their assumption is when they're carrying out their modeling.

In this account, the collaborative work is consciously organized around conflicting principles, meant to replicate conflicting views from finance. The aim of the collaborative enterprise is to build a machine that in the end will transcend oppositions:

> TED: Either there's independence or there's correlation. There's only two, you
> know . . . possibilities. And so you can't just go down one or the other. You
> have to generally look at both just so that you can, 'cause if you have two
> models, right, which are completely different in their underlying assump-
> tions but they give you a similar result, that's a strong case for investing in
> a particular security if two different models give you the same, so . . . that's
> also one of the rationale why we're choosing two different models, or two
> different approaches, because if they agree, it means it's a good invest-
> ment basically as well.

Some may say here that these are not just two different, but two completely opposite models, and if results fit both, some additional explanation is needed. Nevertheless, from the viewpoint of group work,
it is worth noting the division of labor that has teams within a group
not only collaborating but also taking conceptual positions against
each other. They produce dissent within the group on purpose. This is
not the same with having conflicting views supported by two separate
groups. Being in a team doesn't necessarily mean sharing the same
views: those who believe in historical volatility and those opposing it
may well work together. While controversies and dissent in science have
been often tied to groups working separately and competing with each
other for resources and for winning over audiences (e.g., Latour 1988;
H. Collins 2004), groups such as this internalize dissent. In this case,
the group of eight was split into two teams of four, each modeling opposite assumptions, and each team was split into subteams of two each.
This complicated division of labor required, as one would expect, a lot
of talking:

TED: Ah me, okay. I've split again. I've split my team up into two members so one which goes down the implied volatility and one which is going down my route. Now . . . our general group meeting will be every week or every two weeks approximately, but I'll meet with my, the person who I'm working with, my partner, the person I'm paired up with I meet pretty much every week to discuss models and to come up with proposals, for example, so whenever there's a proposal we'll meet quite often because we need to prepare our proposal and come up with the numbers to give to the people, so we'll meet very, quite, we'll meet often if that's the case, but you know we meet regularly to discuss the models and how we should approach everything. . . . Well there are I guess they're debates with regards to which direction we should go, but there's also, you know, because we don't, all of us don't have a complete knowledge of finance. We're all learning and so there may be misunderstanding with certain ideas and it takes time to iron out those misunderstandings so that we can get a consensus and agreement, so generally we're still debating. There's no serious conflict as it were. I mean there's no shouting or abuse. It's early for that. [*laughs*]

The very nature of the work—building and testing models based on opposite theoretical assumptions—makes dissenting collaboration necessary within the group. In contrast, perhaps, to forms of collaboration seen in other domains, where group members coordinate various skills and expertise in accomplishing a task (e.g., Hutchins 1995), this form of group work is built on dissent. Dissent, of course, doesn't necessarily mean "abuse and shouting," as Ted put it, but in some cases it can lead to rather fragile group dynamics. I talked to a trader who was active as an apprentice in a different group (of 6) involved in building, implementing, and using a trading algo. His group had split from a larger group (of 20 traders) because the former group leader kept changing the strategy (that is, the theoretical principle on which the trading pattern should be built). After the split, this second group coalesced around using one trading algo provided by the lead developer.

While in Ted's group all members were working toward advanced degrees in engineering and the natural sciences (that is, they all were MS and PhD students), this second group (let's call it Phil's group) was much more heterogeneous. It was scattered: the group leader had a PhD from a US school, was in his 50s, and lived on the East Coast; the apprentice was 21, pursuing a science degree at a UK university, and lived in London; the other members of the group were in their 30s, did not have advanced degrees, and were all living in eastern US states. The core was formed by the leader and the apprentice, and their mutual trust was grounded in having revealed to each other the code of their trading programs:

> AP: So if I get it right there is a relationship between you being able to receive a code and you developing trust in the codes of, and you following the signal?
>
> PHIL: Hmm, yes.
>
> AP: You'd follow a signal, you said, based on you having time to trust the signal because you trust the code?
>
> PHIL: I trust the code, I trust the signal, I've seen it, in action, so I'm yeah, I can place a trade based on that.

Why, then, were the other members accepted, since, in Phil's account, they could not code or develop a trading model? As in Ted's case, Phil's group blended model development and testing with use: but while in Ted's group developers were also users, and they were all together as postgraduate students, Phil's group was dispersed, and the distinction between developers and users, as well as the group hierarchy, was more marked. Ted's had a complex division of labor and clear leadership positions too, but trust did not seem to depend so much on revelatory acts, since all participants saw each other face-to-face on a regular basis. In Phil's case, reciprocal revelations and a capacity to understand (code) were seen as the foundation of trust, but also of the core relationship between master and apprentice. The other members were followers: they were taken care of and talked to, but they clearly occupied an inferior position. When I asked Phil why he trusted them, the answer revealed a reason different from that for trusting his master:

> AP: How often do you communicate with this group?
>
> PHIL: My current group at the moment? I suppose almost every day, I have the group open on Skype all the time, so I have my, like multiple monitors set up in my room, so then, but because most of them are based out in the United States, so their main time of activity is whilst I am asleep, so normally I would sort of wake up in the morning and read what's, read what they've been chatting about, and then if some other came on later on in the day I would sort of, well again I would go and chat or offer up, offer up any indicators that I had made, or again or if [name], the mentor-leader

had any more developments, he would tell us, so we are, we yeah, we've all become quite close actually now. [. . .] We talk about a lot of personal stuff as well, as I say they call it our little family group.

AP: How did you come to trust them?

PHIL: Over time really I guess, as I've been speaking to [name of the group leader] for eight months or so now I think . . . and yeah, I, at first didn't really volunteer much personal information, and I sort of guess I don't do a great deal, but . . . I had, sort of grown to trust them and they sort of talked about their own personal lives. They've been helpful when I've asked for help, so yeah so.

This points to a series of aspects that help explain why in electronic finance, in one and the same kind of market (all participants above traded foreign currencies), we encounter neither a single dominant "style," strategy, model, or algorithm of trading, nor an infinity of styles, but a finite variety. Trading is not an individual activity: it involves groups, or little "families," each with its own "signal" or machine, which is collaboratively achieved. These "families" are not necessarily egalitarian: they are organized, differentiated, with well ascribed positions, and different members perform different tasks. In the case above (and it was not the only one I encountered), the core relationship in the group was a charismatic one, from a mentor-leader to his apprentice and to his followers.

The fact that attachment to a particular machine or signal is not a matter of merely knowledge, but also of belief, supported by complex relationships, helps explain why such models are resilient. They cannot be easily displaced and replaced with "better" or more profitable ones, since such a displacement would entail reconfiguring the entire set of group relationships. This is what had actually happened with Phil's group, which split from a larger one when strategy was changed. Discontent with the fact that strategies were changing all the time, Phil's group split away and decided to follow a new mentor-leader.

In a manner similar to that in which a dogma cannot be true or false, but is embraced by followers, a strategy or a model's unprofitableness (at least for a while) does not mean that it will be immediately abandoned. This fact helps to explain why we see an overwhelming majority of (retail) traders losing money but not abandoning trading: one cannot abandon social relationships or commitments so easily. And the standard notions that noise is unstructured and disorganized and that retail traders act on a whim, or without thinking, or without much knowledge, are quite unfounded. Noise is very much structured—if it were not, it would dissipate. The structure of noise is provided by communication and, largely, by social relationships.

How consequential is talk with respect to trading in operational groups? Ironically, the ultimate aim of these groups was to eliminate communication from trading by developing and implementing a machine—an algorithm or a quantitative model that would allow for the execution of transactions without direct human intervention. This would be a step further from human traders who click buttons on their screens. Yet, the more effort was put into eliminating communication from transactions, the more necessary communication became, because this very work of elimination could not be done without talk. In Ted's case, the group's cultivation of dissent as part of the model-building process required talk. In Phil's case, the more hierarchical structure still required communication, between mentor and apprentice as well as between these two and the users of their strategy. The production and use of trading tools, even if the latter are designed to be communication-free, requires talk. With trading automation, talk-in-trading (that is, talk as the form of conducting transactions) seems only to recede in favor of talk-for-trading—that is, communication geared toward the production and maintenance of trading tools.

I say this because implementing an algo is not the end of talk. First, algos have a finite life in the market: the average life of a trading robot is three months, and in some cases algos will be active for only one week. This means new algos will have to be developed, tested, and implemented periodically, making group collaboration—and talk—a continuous necessity, not a singular occasion. Algos cannot be developed individually, owing to the sheer complexity and amount of work involved. Working algos have to be monitored permanently because they can go astray. As Phil indicated, the fact that the group had a working algo didn't mean that they ceased communicating. Far from prompting silence, automated markets merely change the preponderance of forms of talk.

Experiential Groups

While operations groups coalesce around a particular style, strategy, or model, experiential groups are somewhat more diffuse, in the sense that their members do not necessarily share the same style. They may adhere to different views of what is a good or a bad trade, and yet they will communicate with each other during trading very regularly, sometimes on a daily basis. One such group I observed over more than one year was based in the Midwest and central Canada: its members were all middle-aged males, ranging from the mid-30s to the mid-50s, with different professional and ethnic backgrounds. One of them had worked as a professional trader decades before, and one was still working for a brokerage house. I met some of them in person as well and interviewed them. Over the period when I was a member in their group—they knew who I was and what I was researching—they instant-messaged almost every day, during trading hours but also outside them.

In addition to this group, I observed, over more than 18 months, the members of a social trading platform talking to each other. I was a member on this platform and joined groups of traders who, using the platform's proprietary messaging system, were talking to each other every day on various issues related to trading. Over 12 months, there were more than 2,000 conversation threads of varying lengths. Some of them continued for a few minutes, while others stretched over months.

Why did these traders in the Midwest group talk to each other? They were different from the operations groups discussed above. They did not use or develop the same model or trading strategy. Were they trying to get trading tips from the former trader or from the broker? Over one year, I only once or twice witnessed communication in which the broker was asked technical questions about accounts, and that broker never tried to peddle products or to advertise the services of his own house. Why, then, were they apparently wasting time instead of focusing on trading? I will argue here that the answer lies in the group members' need to check their trading experiences against the experiences of other traders, to find similarities and differences, and to build a pool of shared experiences with others. These shared experiences contribute substantially to producing local cultures (Fine 2007, 238) as ways of perceiving, judging, and acting that are layered upon each other and pressed together, or, using Goffman's term, laminated (1974, 82).

Without being able to know whether what one sees on the screen at a particular point in time is consistent with what others see—both in terms of the visual experience and in terms of judging the character of this experience—a trader can hardly make decisions. It is not a mere matter of coordination, although coordination is involved. It is a matter of establishing whether the visual display of data is experienced similarly by other traders. A particular number on the screen changes suddenly (they do this all the time), but is this particular change worth paying attention to? How does it translate in terms of action taken by others and in terms of responses to such actions? These questions cannot be answered without finding out whether other traders have seen this too—that is, whether the change has entered their structure of relevance (Schutz and Luckmann 2003, 252; Heath et al. 2002). In other words, when seeing a change, traders need to find out whether others have seen the same thing—whether there is mutual orientation to it. Even if traders do not trade against each other, this mutual orientation still needs to be achieved, and it requires communication.

Establishing this sort of experiential consistency requires that a trader check it against other experiences as it happens, and not merely that the experience be recounted to others after it has happened. We need to take into account that most traders (particularly in foreign exchange) trade from charts. They see an array of zigzagged lines on their screens, with numbers moving up and down, placed at particular points on the lines. That is the basis for their decision making. The visual experience of a line moving up or down needs to be ordered alongside experiential types in order to be used in a trading decision—what kind of situation is that? Where and when has it been seen before? Do others see it in the same way? In other words, (visual) experiences of the trading screen, even when they are idiosyncratic, are so in opposition to a shared pool of experiences. Traders will first need to build such a pool before resorting to judgments about which experience is solely theirs (i.e., "I've seen something others did not see"). There cannot be only idiosyncratic experiences. Even if we assumed, by way of a thought experiment, that traders had gone to the same trading school and had learned together how to recognize experiences, this could not possibly cover all the range of experiences and situations they would encounter in trading and could not act as a memory store to be recalled in every situation (Hindmarsh 2010, 221–222).

Hence the necessity that traders find experiential types together during action, an activity that cannot unfold without communication. Since communication cannot take place at the overall level of a community of all traders (one cannot have tens of thousands of conversation partners at once), it is the group level that is the most adequate for this. In turn, this has at least two consequences: first, different groups will generate different experiential types, which do not necessarily overlap and might even be contradictory across groups. Second, to generate shared experiential types, group members will have to reveal to each other what they are doing (or what they have very recently done). This runs counter to the received notion that trading is a strategic (aka competitive) activity devoid of any cooperation. Trading may well include competitive elements, but such elements will never work without cooperation. Cooperation in this case does not imply bringing together different skills and layers of expertise. Cooperation implies coordinating different experiences and building common experiential types.

This assertion actually is valid not only for experiential groups, but for operations groups as well. It is only that the type of experience is different. Whereas the groups I call experiential build shared pools of experiences of human observation and action, operations groups generate shared pools of experiences with constructing and operating trading machines.

I encountered at least four types of sharing experiences: jointly establishing observational relevance; sharing (in the sense of disclosing) trades; sharing experiences with trading procedures or strategies; and jointly constructing regulatory and economic interpretations. I will start with coordinating screen observations:

> [t1] CHRIS: So you were thinking higher USDCAD?
> [t1+35"] CHRIS: i.e., no significant correction?
> [t1+13'08"] JAMES: no bias yet on usd/cad
> [t1+13'26"] JAMES: uso chart looks interesting in comparison
> [t1+1hr55'31" | Edited t1+1hr55'39"] JAMES: i see usd/cad going to 1.0380
> [t1+1hr57'59"] CHRIS: Yes, I was expecting more of a pullback before continuing higher, no?

Chris and James, each on his own trading screen, and physically separated, look at the trading chart of the US dollar (USD) against the Canadian dollar (CAD). There are other participants in the chat who do not intervene at this moment but can observe the exchange. The issue is how to see the USD against the CAD—that is, figure out where the line on the trading chart will go. Chris asks James whether he sees the currency pair going higher (which means a price increase of the USD in CAD), and James states first that he has no bias, but then, almost two hours later, he announces that he sees the price now (namely a higher one). Of interest here is not only that James needs time to see (first he has no opinion and then he needs two hours to form one), but also that "seeing" is meant here anticipating where the line will go next (and it goes against Chris's expectations). Anticipation is not the same as forming the abstract expectation of a number such as 1.0380 but, very concretely, where to look next on the chart line, what point on that line to focus attention on. This sort of anticipation (which occurs on small time frames) cannot be undertaken in an idiosyncratic and isolated way: traders need to check their anticipations against those of other traders, to be able to make adjustments to their own ways of seeing things. Such adjustments would benefit little from expert advice offered in isolation from direct screen observations. Looking at the screen, forming anticipations, and adjusting anticipations go hand in hand. This kind of synchronicity can be achieved by talking to fellow traders while looking at the screen, not by checking every now and then some expert advice. This may help explain why, during all my years of observation, I seldom saw professional expert advice taken seriously during trading. Traders much prefer to talk to and pay attention to what fellow traders, in a situation similar to theirs, say.

This is a type of "seeing" that is different from the ritualized ones practiced by "master" traders, discussed in chapter 4. It requires not submission to any special powers of observation claimed by a master, but rather a collective search for relevance. It is not grounded in revelation, and therefore it is uncertain. It is not geared toward formulating action prescriptions, but rather toward producing momentary discoveries, from which action can start.

Not only do traders coordinate with each other's observations and anticipation, but they also disclose their trades to each other, as they happen or shortly afterward. Sharing trades is one of the most puzzling activities. Why would traders tell others what they are doing, as they are doing it? Two group members had the following exchange, while two more (including the ethnographer) were present without participating:

[t1] JAMES: usd/chf shorts
[t1+26"] THAD: I literally just shorted that on the 15minute
[t1+49"] JAMES: good stuff lol
[t1+1'7"] THAD: I dont know how good it is . . .
[t1+6'24" | Edited t1+6'34"] JAMES: yeh its in the right position if the yens are strong

[t1+6'42"] JAMES: sell position that is
[t1+7'01"] JAMES: moved just 11 pips since the open though
[t1+7'48"] THAD: looks like its taking a breather
[t1+8'10"] JAMES: but is still going to short
[t1+8'45"] THAD: it's looking that way, It could reverse again though

While the overall conversation is longer and had started before t1 (when the exchange begins), quite a few things happen during less than nine minutes. James starts with a general statement about usd/chf (US dollar against the Swiss franc) shorts. Thad announces that he has shorted the US dollar against the Swiss franc, and he receives confirmation from James, but he has doubts. They are looking at 15-minute trading charts, something Thad mentioned after the opening (hence James's remark about the right position if the Japanese yen remains strong—they are betting that the US dollar will weaken against several currencies). They both agree that shorting is a good move, although Thad expresses doubts again.

One of the remarkable things here is that Thad and James are not afraid to disclose to each other (and to others who are present but don't intervene) what they have done in real time. They do not keep their trades secret. They try to evaluate whether shorting is the right thing to do, and the answer is not clear-cut. It all depends on whether the dollar is in the right position, but this position is not easy to judge from what they see, apparently. It hasn't moved much, though it could. They are trading on a 15-minute chart, which means that they are looking at this interval for price movements, and this is the time frame in which they must make their decisions. In this context, it is difficult if not impossible to draw upon any information such as macroeconomic data, central bank announcements, and the like, simply because none of these might happen within the next 15 minutes (or in 15-minute intervals, for that matter). Still, both James and Thad need to try to estimate whether what they see on their screens (the "position") is going to change within the given time frame; how it is going to change; and whether the consequence of what they see (i.e., sell the US dollar) is the right one. Such estimates cannot be idiosyncratic and need to be achieved jointly with other traders. It is interesting to note that Thad continues to express doubts but nevertheless does not reverse his decision. He sticks with short selling.

So, why do traders disclose trades to each other? I would say that this happens because traders need not only to anticipate where the line will move—in a very concrete fashion, anticipate where to look next on the screen. They also need to anticipate how to respond best to such a movement. What would be an appropriate response is not a decision to be made in isolation: it is a matter of judgment, and judgment cannot be other than social (Vargha 2013, 42). Therefore, as the natural continuation of establishing observational relevance, traders will have to show each other what they are doing (or what they recently did) and seek opinions on whether it is the appropriate action. Would another trader do the same thing in this situation? Well, the best way to find out is to ask another trader, and this means disclosing one's own trades.

To better evaluate the consequentiality of this talk, we can ask what would happen if there was no conversation in this situation. Thad could have only, say, his own stream of consciousness without James intervening and without Thad's reactions to James's. What we would be left with is Thad's statement that he had just literally shorted. Then what? Where to look? What to do? Action would stop for a while, because there would be little means, if any, to progress from what Thad had done to the next step. Such a progression implies both making judgments about what has happened in the immediately preceding step and building anticipations for the next step. I would argue that talk proves its consequentiality in this transition from one step to the next. Talk helps build trading sequences that otherwise would be difficult to achieve. Now, some may say here, can't we find situations and moments in which traders are entirely alone? My answer is yes, we can, and these are the situations in which we can observe traders talking to their reflection in the trading screen (as I have witnessed many times). Being alone does not mean that talk disappears.

At other times, group members will announce to each other what they have recently done and what they plan to do, or what they do in particular situations:

[t1] VICTOR: FYI—I have sold EUR USD at 1.3597 with a stop at 1.3648 profit at 1.3546. it's going my way, down, so I am scaling in another sell trade. fyi.
[t1+14hrs17'20"] CHRIS: I am curious, do you guys typically scale into or scale out of trades? For example, i took the most volume at the bottom of the EURUSD trade. i lightened up as we blew through resistance. At the "top" I take very little on, but still keep a "toe in the water" to participate.
[t1+14hrs26'44"] CHRIS: What do you do?

[t1+14hrs26'58"] JAMES: i usually scale in
[t1+14hrs27'39"] JAMES: and use fibs for levels
[t1+14hrs28'15"] JAMES: s/r same thing s what you mentioned

There are three traders chatting here, including James, from the previous excerpt. Early in the morning, Victor has announced what he is trading and that he is going to scale in on a trade because things are going his way. After the announcement, there is a break of 10 hours, a short chat about quantitative easing in the United States, and then the exchange above. Fourteen hours later, Chris asks around whether others scale in or scale out of trades and discloses what he is doing. (Scaling in a trade means entering initially just an amount of what you actually intend to put in, and scaling out of a position means liquidating it bit by bit and not all at once.) James intervenes then, announces that he is scaling in, and confirms Chris's procedure. Not only has Victor disclosed a trade and a procedure (scaling in) in the morning, but hours later, in the evening, the topic has not gone away. Scaling as a procedure becomes the issue on which traders swap experiences. The question is not how to do textbook scaling (or what the experts recommend), but what others "typically" do. Chris wants to hear what the experience of the others is with this procedure. An expert recommendation, addressed to an abstract "public," would be too remote from the situation Chris is in. James does not volunteer a general recommendation, but a confirmation that he does the same thing—and with that, a confirmation that Chris's experience is not idiosyncratic but shared by other traders he knows (from chatting).

Members of trading groups also seek to arrive at joint interpretations of new rules and regulations, or economic policies. Quantitative easing (for example, the Fed policy of pumping money into the economy by buying Treasury bills) or the regulations of the CFTC (which would cover retail traders) have been among the issues that need debate and joint parsing. These can also become occasions in which traders share information or reveal to each other aspects such as the (overseas) accounts they have. With that, not only experiences *in* trading, but also experiences *of* trading are shared with each other:

[t1] AARON: Hi Guys,
[t1+5'58"] AARON: Regarding the new rules on Forex. Does anyone know

what the ruling is on if US citizens can open up an account with a foreign broker? i have looked all over and talked to some current forex brokers and no one seems to know what the ruling is for sure.

[t1+6'46"] PHIL: it seems like the rules restrict US citizens to US regulated institutions

[t1+7'12"] PHIL: i read an article on it . . . let me see if i can find it [inserts source]

[t1+12'18"] PHIL: i am part of a trading group in geneva switzerland and one americn there just filed for renunciation last money . . . he trades for a living and has done quite well for himself. all of the EU nationals that he trades with use off-shore corporations because they aren't tax on foreign-source income, as well as foreign-source cap gains

[t1+25'15"] AARON: Thank you for the info Phil

[t1+27'16"] AARON: A lot of my clients have corporations overseas to trade from and do business from. It sounds like that is going to be a thing of the past. I have been getting a lot of questions lately on where people should start an overseas company.

[01:39:38] VICTOR: [. . .] This will affect my trading greatly, I barely have adjusted to 100:1, and now that it's going to 50:1, my income will be cut in half. So I am probably out of the game at this point. But I will keep playing around with it. Essentially I will need to risk twice as much to make the same amount, or double my capital in the account to make the same amount. I was working with 400:1, so this is a huge drop down to 50:1.

Aaron, who is a broker, opens the conversation by asking the others for information about the new CFTC rules (debated in the fall of 2010). Not only is information volunteered from available sources, but traders also volunteer information about other experiences they know of, as well as evaluations about how the new regulations will affect their leverage. Leaving aside their expressed distaste of the limitations on leverage, or on opening offshore companies for trading, they reveal to each other how they are trading (what kind of leverage they have been using), but also possible ways of avoiding restrictions. This sharing of experiences of trading—what I know from a group in Geneva, or what my leverage was—points to a communicational mechanism that compensates for the lack of trust-building, face-to-face interactions. After all, what keeps these traders talking to each other almost every day, over such long periods of time, when they haven't seen each other at all, or hardly at all? It cannot be just access to sources of information or the detection of supplementary ones that might be missed otherwise. The reciprocal disclosure of experiences and situations one has been through appears to be a necessary element in constituting trading as what it is: a joint, social activity where participants face common (external and internal) constraints and where they search jointly for action opportunities. How could we imagine trading without shared experiences and without building common pools of such experiences? If the latter were not necessary, numbers flickering on the screen would bring most action to a screeching halt, because traders would lack the essential means of generating anticipations—where to look next and what to look for next. Anticipations and expectations cannot be idiosyncratic except as marginal cases, as contrasts to the ones produced by groups.

Managerial Groups

The third type of groups I have encountered among traders is what I call managerial groups. I do not mean that members are managers; what I mean is that such groups are concerned with how their money is being managed, not by them, but by others. Retail traders have usually been thought of as trading (and therefore managing) their own money. That is why some, at least, have wanted to avoid institutional fund managers. With the advent of social trading—that is, of Facebook-like trading platforms, rankings of traders in terms of their success can be (and are) posted on the site for every member to see. Social trading sites have developed proprietary metrics for ranking successful traders, which can include, among other things, the ratio of winning to losing trades, the amount of time elapsed since starting trading, leverage, strategy, and return on capital.

Since all traders on a site can see who are the most successful ones among them (according to the site's metrics), some, at least, will think it is better to entrust these better traders (also called "trade leaders") with their money. (Earlier, I have called this vicarious engagement in markets.) Trade leaders will then trade with their own money and with the money entrusted to them by other traders. In return for their skills, luck, willingness to take risks, and so forth, they will take 20% of the profits, and the site will take a 2% administration fee. This is nothing but the hedge fund model applied to retail traders: a trade leader becomes the money manager for other, less successful traders. (As of this writing, this model is completely unregulated.) In theory, the more traders a leader manages to attract, owing to his success (these traders are overwhelmingly men), the more capital he will have under his control, and the larger the transactions he will be able to operate. The other traders (the "investors") will receive 78% of the profits made with their capital, and everybody will be happy.

What is more, it becomes possible to select not just one trade leader to follow, but several. An investor could put, say, 25% of his or her capital on Jimmy, 15% on Tom, 30% on Harry, and 30% on Dick. Then, according to who performs how, these percentages could be shifted around. Jimmy, Tom, Harry, and Dick would then become investments that have to be managed. If, say, Jimmy doesn't perform according to expectations, the money would be withdrawn and entrusted only to Tom, Harry, and Dick. This would mean that an investor would acknowledge that the above four (or three) are better than her or him at trading and entrust them with money but at the same time monitor their performance and shift money around, if necessary. Investors and investees would become a tight market unit, a group whose members would manage each other. Such a construction is not hypothetical. It exists in the real world. When a social trading site started the automated copying program, it created a portfolio of seven traders with allocations ranging from more than 30% to less than 10% and invested real money to see how it would perform. The interesting aspect of this type of group is that it is anchored in a series of tensioned assumptions: there has to be reciprocal trust but little knowledge between investors, on the one hand, and the investees, on the other hand. There has to be a hierarchy, so that investors acknowledge their money managers (or investees) as more skilled but control them as their investments. The money manager is also an investment, not only somebody who manages investments. This is a social group, but social issues such as conflicts, cooperation, and the like are not factored in.

One of the first questions arising here is: How can this investment program be reconciled with the hard statistics that indicate only a tiny minority of traders earn money in a consistent way? If traders were to sign up to copy those who are better and earn consistent money, then surely the proportion of earners would grow larger. In other words, if, say, 97.5% sign up and copy the 2.5% who are earning consistently from trading, then the 97.5% would also earn consistently (albeit less, owing to the fees), and everybody would be happy. If, on the other hand, 50% of all traders earned consistently, there would be little incentive for the other 50% to entrust their money to the first half. From the perspective of the second half, chances are 50-50 that they too could earn money consistently. The model of hedge fund managers, by definition, works on the assumption that very few can be successful consistently in markets. It actually replicates the distinction between "noise" and "information" within the world of noise traders. In this way, a hierarchy is replicated in the trading system, with the best traders at the top. Overall, what we would see here is more or less passive groups who let their money be managed by the best among them. There is a clear hierarchy, and there is little controversy, or communication for that matter (since copying is automated).

The picture I have painted above might be plausible if we assumed that traders compete against each other. In that case trade leaders too would compete against each other. The best would attract more investors and the rest would lose their ranking. This explicit logic of competition hides the fact that traders take positions not against each other, but against broker dealers. Since traders have accounts with various dealers, it is difficult to see this as competition and as grounds for the selection of the best traders.

The reality of such groups is different, though. As I was trying to find out how many investors decide to copy a trade leader, and obtain data about it, I talked to a broker dealer who was acquainted with the matter. He told me that copying was not clear-cut at all and that the brokers themselves had difficulties with it. Traders had the option of decoupling and recoupling themselves to their "trade leaders," a platform feature they made use of. This means that they didn't actually copy indiscriminately everything the trade leaders did. Sometimes trade leaders decided to copy trades of their followers, perhaps thinking that the followers' decisions were better than their own. Sometimes the followers copied each other's trades and ignored what the trade leader did (as members of a group, they could see each other's transactions). Overall, it appeared that copying was not a simple matter of following somebody, but rather a selective process.

Copying trades did not function smoothly. It was supposed to be instantaneous, but in fact it was not always so, and even a small delay in the execution of copied trades could lead to results different from those of the trader being copied. There were situations in which trade leaders were making a profit, while followers were incurring losses.

Still, why wouldn't somebody follow an acknowledged leader and an accomplished money manager? I turned to the discussions in the community of social traders, in the hope of getting some answers to this question. And sure enough, there were plenty of discussions. It appeared that some trade leaders could have very bad days when almost half of their portfolio was wiped out—and with it, a corresponding share of their followers' portfolios as well. Since copying trades was not the object of a formal contract, there was little that losing copiers could do except vent their anger and frustration. One could argue that similar things happen to professional hedge fund managers as well. The main difference, I think, is that investors with professional fund managers do not get to see every single trade the latter make, and how much they may lose in one day. They get only quarterly statements, not an overview of all transactions that fund managers make.

As it turned out, some investors at least resorted to due diligence: in one case I observed, they reconstructed the trades of one trade leader not from his metrics, but from his tweets, and they found that according to tweets he was losing money, while his trades on the social trading site were profitable. This forced the trader in question to justify himself and disclose the transactions he had made from one of his accounts. At the same time, a debate was triggered about the accuracy of tweets, reminiscent of many academic debates about how to measure profits. Another type of due diligence was that some investors contacted trade leaders directly and asked them what kind of trading they were practicing. Additionally, they were checking discrepancies between their (supposedly copied) trades and those of the trade leaders, asking publicly for explanations. This led to the following conversation:

TRADER A: I just checked the updated graph of the new [trade leader X] whom I've been following since [day d]. On his account he is up by half a percent between [day d – 1] and [day d]. On my account I had 2 trades by him executed and they lost me a total of 35 pips. On the second trade I got slipped 11 pips, so he would have lost only 24 pips on the two trades. Thankfully he trades with very modest leverage, so the loss only amounts to about 0.7% of the allocation. Something needs to be done about this. There was no significant volatility in eurodlr after that, so how could he have turned the loss into a profit without the followers catching those trades???

TRADE LEADER X: I'm absolutely gutted that people lost money following me on a day where I (eventually) made out. I would be very interested to know which trades followed, which slipped and which didn't get taken at all. To this end I would appreciate it if you would contact me direct at [e-mail address] so that we can compare notes. In the meantime, the only palliative might be for me to move my account from [broker One] (who routinely offer a 0.9 pip spread) to [broker Two] (where it is more like 2.5 pips). This would reduce the risk of my trades not following across the community. This is something I will trial in demo, alongside [broker One], for a pair of weeks. I'll report what I find on this forum.

This exchange is part of a much larger discussion on the execution of copy trades and the relationship between trade leaders and followers. Questioning or contesting the execution of copy trades implies either an element of dishonesty (why did the leader make a profit and I incurred a loss when I was supposed to automatically and instantaneously copy his trades?) or a technical glitch (why were the copy trades executed at a different spread—or slippage—from the leader's?), or both. In the larger discussion, it emerged that many followers of that particular leader were signed up with broker Two, while the leader himself was with broker One (who had better conditions), and this was offered as one explanation for the slippage. The trades with broker One had to be replicated by broker Two, and this implied a time delay and a slippage. Hence the reaction of Trade Leader X, who declared himself gutted and offered to compare notes, to trial a new account with broker Two (without abandoning his own account, though), and to report further in the discussion forum.

Vicarious engagement (of the kind discussed in chapter 3) implies reciprocal moral responsibilities, which can go beyond mere copying and which come to the fore in debates, in critical situations. Relevant in this context is that the transparency of social trading sites works against the idea of a stable group hierarchy, since few mistakes can be hidden (for long enough) and there is no time for repairs. Any top position is inherently fragile, and the higher up one is placed, the deeper one can fall. One of the most heated debates I witnessed on a social trading site concerned the same top-ranked trade leader (the one whose tweets were checked). Four months after the tweets debate, he lost 40% of his account in one day. A flurry of furious posts followed, such as this one:

TRADER B: well today [trade leader X] just blew up. he lost something in excess of 40% of his account in ONE DAY . . . . complete idiot. so, until today, i was very pleased with the [program]. but now, it makes me scratch my head and question if ANY of these trade leaders have any idea how to manage risk. I feel like i am such a noob at forex trading, but even I have a rule on how much i will lose in one day, and STOP at that point, and same goes for a month. If i lose more than that % of my account, i do not trade. it would be IMPOSSIBLE for me to lose 40% of my account in a day or even a month. i think it is INSANE. I have no idea how [name] has a risk rating of [x] when he obviously was using some trading bot with an AWFUL risk/reward ratio and obviously NO cutoff. many [program] investors lost gigantic chunks of money today as he was one of the most followed traders. a similar thing happened with [name] just a few weeks ago . . . all of these "leaders" are blowing up, and it is making me very concerned

TRADER C: Saying that [trade leader X] just blew up is putting it nicely. If you look at his twitter account [twitter handle] you'll see made 200 trades that lost over 13,000 pips in 9 hours! He should be black listed from the "trader leaders" program.

If this is reminiscent of furious investors rising against company management, it is also indicative of the fact that a "fund manager" is also treated as an investment and monitored continuously. Investors such as the one above offer not only speculative explanations for why things went wrong (he might have used a trading robot), but also trading prescriptions (such as using stop losses) and comparative judgments (this would not have happened to me). All of this reveals the tensions inherent in a group that is supposed to be hierarchical and have (more or less) passive followers but is anchored in egalitarian communication and where the leaders are treated as investments.

If we look at the two situations discussed above in contrast to each other, when both leader and followers lose big money, it is deemed idiocy. When only the followers appear to lose some small amount, it is categorized differently and triggers an obligation to engage further: opening a new account, discussing one-to-one, making more information available. These are obligations that work in the absence of any binding legal contract between leaders and followers and which are implied in the institutional position of the leader, who has transited from ordinary trader to a new status.

Yet, with the exception of situations in which trade leaders lose large sums of money, there was little disdain and few insults for them. It seemed that basic communication norms prevailed, and even during complaints, investors took care to state publicly that they were not criticizing the trade leaders. Why were they willing to engage in such groups? To be sure, nobody forced them to take part in this social engineering experiment. They could participate in social trading without copying other traders. The dissatisfaction was palpable, yet they engaged in these activities. During the period of my observations, I saw only a few traders leaving the program. Why were they sticking with it? Of course, one could say that in the program they put less effort into executing trades themselves. They put a lot of effort, however, into due diligence and into monitoring what their trade leaders were doing. One could also say that they wanted to make money by letting the trade leaders work for them. Judging from the number of complaints in the community, making money in this way was not certain at all: quite a few were continuing to have losses. Perhaps it all boiled down to what one of them said:

> TRADER: I am not really satisfied with [program]. I will handle my account If I am psychologically prepared to trade. All I need to do now is fixing my emotion. I am doing excellent trade when I am in demo. More so, we should not trust automated trading because market is so dynamic and is it [*sic*] so confined to one's not so perfect perspective.

If this excerpt expresses a more general opinion, then the reason why at least some traders join and then stick with managerial groups is that they want not just to see traders who are prepared to trade, but they want to participate with traders who are prepared to trade. It is a form of vicarious engagement that goes beyond mere spectatorship (Goffman 1967, 195). In groups like this, members are truly, literally invested in those who are prepared to trade. Yet they do not do it themselves, because they think they are less skilled, or unprepared, or not there yet. Then, what other solution is there than to participate with somebody who is ready to trade, to invest oneself in another person, and to establish a quasi-symbiotic relationship of close monitoring? There is a difference between vicarious participation of the kind spectatorship at a football game provides, and vicarious engagement, where one invests oneself, puts oneself at stake in the decisions made by a "champion" or a "leader." In vicarious engagements, one expects an experience of "performance." When this (all too often) does not materialize, very negative reactions follow, which stand in stark contrast with the readiness to lose money in one's own trading (I discuss this in chapter 7). The failure of "performance" is a failure of supposedly meritocratic, market based hierarchies as well.

I have discussed three types of groups that are active in electronic trading and the complex organization of their activities. Most trading in electronic markets takes place in groups, not individually, and is anchored in communication. On a higher level yet, I also wanted to uncover at least some of the structural aspects of "noise." The notion that at least some of the trading activities (and in electronic finance even more) are noisy in the sense of being disorganized, uninformed, volatile, hard to rationalize, and so on, needs to be revised. So does the notion that such activities are confined for a considerable part to retail traders. In fact, these activities are diverse, complex, and impossible to accomplish alone. They demand organization and various skills. We should see (electronic) finance in terms of groups rather than as noisy swarms of atomized participants.

What is the consequentiality of talk in electronic finance? Talk differentiates and structures participants: it binds them to specific tasks; it produces pools of shared experiences and judgments; it channels vicarious engagements, as well as collective controls over these engagements. Is all this consequential with respect to transactions? My answer is yes it is, and in more than one way. By building pools of shared experiences, talk also bounds the types of transactions that are feasible in relationship to these experiences. By making group work possible, talk makes algorithmic trading possible. By channeling group controls over vicarious engagements, talk forces corrections of play—that is, of engagements gone awry. Electronic, apparently mute, markets are necessarily in a state of talk (Goffman 1981, 130).

CHAPTER SIX

Trading Strategies

Traders build shared pools of experience in observing, acting upon observations, using trading tools, and "performing" in trading. They act as members of groups. And yet, they see themselves as autonomous decision-making actors. How is this possible? I will try to answer this question starting from examining strategy, a much touted notion and one that is routinely taught in business schools.

Strategies and Plans

Usually, when we think of a market strategy, the analogy that immediately comes to mind is that of military commanders who devise and apply battle plans. A battle plan created in the sandbox—the classic modeling tool of the military—will try to anticipate the moves of enemy troops; it will devise countermovements and responses to counter-countermovements. It will also create surprises and ambushes, while trying to outguess the opponent. Something similar must occur in markets, where traders will apply carefully guarded plans, will make use of disguises and concealments, and will try to infer other traders' strategies from the pieces of information they receive.[1] Market action has strategies, in the same way ballroom dancing has its strategies, understood as imagined and shared futures which support broad, long-range plans (Fine 2015, 31). Even management textbooks that say a strategy is not a plan end up defining a strategy in terms of a plan, as choices regarding where to play, how to play, and how to win.

Perhaps having a strategy is the epitome of market action—being able to devise a plan (ideally, in secrecy) and then successfully apply it. The number of military analogies used in the description of markets—with famous speculators akin to generals who overcome their opponents by applying a carefully laid out strategy—could easily make us think that this is the case. At the opposite end, we encounter those arguing that practical actions—and especially those of the technologically embedded kind, which would include online trading—cannot be the application of a plan (Orr 1996; Suchman 1987). Devising a plan ex ante and then merely applying it (under all contingencies and with limited resources, even while revising and adapting it) would mean that each step of the application is recognizable as corresponding to a rule of action specified in advance. In that case, a strategy, together with the corresponding counterstrategy, would be entirely programmable and foreseeable. If a strategy is entirely foreseeable by the competitor, it does not make sense to devise it, let alone apply it. This is why developers of trading robots go to great lengths to hide the source code of their robots and regularly change the code; once a trading robot becomes known (in the sense of revealing its rules or its code), it becomes useless. And this is why traders who use trading robots do not let them work unsupervised. Additionally, practical actions depend on the resources and character of the situation, which cannot be specified in advance (we cannot predict which specific moves of a basketball player will be mock passes and which ones will be real passes). Even in chess, perhaps the ultimate strategy game, a fully formed strategy is not possible (Fine 2015, 60–61). Therefore, we cannot talk about applying a plan or a strategy except in some figurative sense.

Where do traders stand between these two extremes? Existing ethnographies of trading tell us that strategies of professional traders fall mostly within three categories: a "bazaar of rationality" mixing calculations with experience-based tacit knowledge; disciplinary techniques that separate trading from traders' lives outside trading, so that judgment is not based on emotions; and interaction techniques grounded in aggressiveness and assertiveness (Zaloom 2012, 176, 178–179). Strategies, then, are action, expression, and disposition techniques: professional traders draw upon calculations and tacit knowledge in their actions; they express themselves aggressively and assertively; and they train their inner dispositions, enabling them to enter such modes of action and expression. So then, should we expect retail traders, the necessary "noise" in the markets, to try to replicate such techniques, perhaps in a paler fashion? When compared with professional traders, retail traders are usually viewed as a "lesser" category; should their strategies then be like the ones of professionals, only less well formed? Or are their strategies something entirely different?

At least some tropes of the merchandising discourse seem to treat strategies as akin to military plans. There are plenty of exhortations not to trade without a strategy, to be like a military commander. All attendees at trading shows will encounter strategy presentations at some point, and speakers make liberal use of the term. A sense of accomplishment as a trader can only come from a well thought, successful strategy. Yet, practical actions—including online trading—cannot be mere applications of preset strategies. If they were, they would be foreseeable, and therefore ineffective. One way to avoid this problem would be to conceal one's strategy, but then the mere work of concealing a strategy would be a strategy in itself and could be ultimately guessed by opponents. The puzzle is augmented by the fact that strategies seem, indeed, to occupy a prominent role on online platforms, while at the same time, a closer look at concrete sequences of actual trading reveal little, if anything, by way of recognizable, preset strategies that are applied step by step. How are we to square the traders' constant preoccupation with strategies with the apparent lack of strategies during trading sequences?[2]

When I did my bouts of demo trading, I was straddling two worlds, that of trading and that of professional ethnographers. I was only learning how to trade. Surely other, more experienced traders must have strategies, and I could learn from them. I discovered, however, that the situation is not so simple. Of course, traders use a series of tools and routines that can be associated with "strategies": this does not mean, however, that the use of tools is automatically part of a strategy, or that the use of strategy is unquestioned by the community. Some strategies are seen by traders as basic, yet are not automatically used by all: take the stop loss, a series of easily programmable commands to liquidate positions when prices reach certain limits.[3] This was easily understandable even for somebody like me, a total novice. Or maybe it was understandable exactly because I was a novice, and then it was a false easiness. A discussion in the trader community I was part of revealed that not all members used stop losses. Some stated that they were using "mental stop losses" but not "hard" ones (i.e., not the command embedded in the trading software), or that they had "habits" that prevented the use of stop losses. Others said it was better to use expert advisers (robots that scan trades in multiple timeframes) than to use stop losses. Still others said that exit strategies were better than stop losses, to which other traders replied that a stop loss is the ultimate trading strategy. Moreover, some exit strategies were proprietary and could not be revealed. But neither could some stop loss commands, the use of which depended on proprietary charts. Those who urged the use of stop losses invoked the metaphor of war: markets are a war. No, replied others, markets are like a game of chess: that is why you must use stop losses, not because markets are like a war. I began to doubt myself more and more: so, stop losses are a strategy, not a tool? And there are softer mental stop losses, as well as harder ones. But if each trader has his own mind, how can we make a mental stop loss into a strategy, or into a tool, for that matter? And the right metaphor is chess, not war? But some traders are not in the habit of using them. Hmm . . . then the junction of the diverse practical actions that constitute trading is perhaps more fragile than I thought. And sometimes it takes a polling question from within the community to reveal this fragility.

On a different occasion, I asked a trader about the strategies she used. Nadia had switched from being a nonproprietary (or execution) trader to being a retail trader. She had left the world of institutional trading and had enrolled in graduate school, in a statistics and finance program. So I asked her whether she now had a trading strategy, perhaps one learned in graduate school:

> NADIA: Well, I'm taking a portfolio management class here, as part of my program and for a long time I didn't, I knew . . . it is very theoretical, so there is a lot of theoretical maths involved in it and I, for the longest time I was trying to figure out how I was gonna like fit this in with my own personal investing, and I still, like, haven't really, I mean there is, we learn about a couple of models, but we really only learn theoretical math part of it, and so the biggest thing that I learned was basically that everything, all of those . . . all of those models are just linear functions with weights, so it's like a weight attached to this, so the various different models like might have weights that are, that differ depending on your personal beliefs, like the analyst beliefs and your portfolio managers beliefs, but at the end of the day it's just a linear function of different securities or different, you know, different securities and like different weights.

What is a strategy, then? A linear function with beliefs attached to it? I asked Nadia what a strategy was for her when she was an execution trader. Execution traders execute the orders of (usually) a fund manager, who will give them targets for a specific portfolio (e.g., achieve a return of 5% on trading a given set or assemblage of securities, within a given time frame).[4] In her former position, Nadia had to worry first and foremost about which brokers she was working with, and whether those brokers would respect her authority by executing trading orders. This created problems sometimes:

NADIA: We had a position in an insurance company, and my boss told me to buy 350,000 more shares [. . .] and so I am sitting here trying to buy shares and the stock like at the time that I got the order had already dropped seven dollars, ok? In the span of like not even two hours, ok, so I'm buying shares and I'm not going to buy 350,000 shares all at one time when the stocks dropped seven dollars right? So I gave, I directed the order out, like, a portion of the order out to a broker, and then I was working some myself in the system and then I was also giving it out to other brokers at other times of the day, but at like this particular time I was working with one broker and also trading it myself, and this guy, I think I sent him like 30,000 shares. He bought them all at one time. He had no idea that I wanted to buy 350,000 shares. For all he knew all I wanted to buy was 30,000 shares and he bought them all at one time, and I got really angry and I picked up the phone and I called him and I was like . . . "what the hell was that, why did you buy them all at one time? Can you see that the stock's falling, it's falling at seven dollars?" and by the time he had finished his order the stock had dropped even further, maybe like a dollar or something and I was really angry, and then he, this guy was so much older . . . he tried to lecture me and he was like, "well when a stock drops seven dollars in a session you don't get [cute?]," umm and so that was, his experience was, this time that we are experiencing was a complete anomaly and it . . . didn't fit any of the patterns he knew and he was trying to fit it to one of the patterns that he knew, but for me all that I knew was that I had seen . . . I had seen banks drop like 20 dollars you know and so, seven dollars is nothing, so in that case like, not, *having no patterns* and *having like no fear* and just believing that anything is possible in that case like that helped me out. [my italics—AP]

In this account, Nadia's conflict with the broker is centered around applying prescriptions for execution versus adapting execution to what happens on the screen. Yet, these prescriptions, of one sort or another, are related to experience. In the end, it is about the patterns the broker had seen in the past and about what Nadia had seen in the past. This clash of experiences is translated as a conflict of "strategies" and of authority between an older male broker and a younger female trader, a conflict that arises within the strategic relationship between Nadia and her broker. (She hadn't told her broker how many shares she intended to buy, nor that she had employed more than one broker. Nor had the broker informed Nadia about how he wanted to execute the order.)

What is relevant in this account is that strategy isn't accounted for as a plan to be applied in a particular situation. It is accounted for in terms of personal experiences (the patterns one has seen in the past shape one's judgment of situations) and in terms of a strategic relationship that frames the action at hand. In other words, the strategy of buying 30,000 shares (how we want to buy these shares without signaling others what our intentions are and without reducing potential profits) depends on the relationship between Nadia and her broker. And what is relevant in this relationship is that experiences are different, judgments are different, intentions are withheld, and there is a clash of authority related to gender and age.

Viewed from this angle, the strategies of professional traders link the execution of an action (I have to buy 350,000 shares of X) to sequencing it and distributing the components across their business ties. The ties are then managed in such a way that interaction among sequences is controlled. Only then can the completion of sequences be judged as satisfactory. There is no preset plan, except perhaps for a general prescription (do not buy everything at once). Multiple business ties have to be monitored and managed as the action sequences unfold. This requires personal, sometimes conflictual communication.

These elements of professional trading strategies—action sequencing, mobilization of relevant ties, sequence control—fit the techniques identified by Caitlin Zaloom as pertaining to professional trading. However, they are not encountered in retail trading. Here, in many situations (though not always), traders will go into the open with their strategies, posting prescriptions for action, as well as histories of past actions, for other traders to see.

Strategies on the Front Stage

Being a member of a trading platform requires providing a face for the benefit of one's audience. In the curiously structured world of online trading, especially among retail traders, there is little, if any, personal, direct knowledge of other members of the group or community. When a name or a face say very little, one of the main ways of saying "I am this person" is by means of strategy. Of course, traders can post biographical snippets, some of which have revelatory character. In addition to them, however, one needs to show who one is with respect to action, that is, to trading. Especially the capacity to act, the agentive side of the self, needs to be made visible as the face of the trader in the community. Biographical snippets do not work very well for this purpose. They may provide a glimpse of motives, of the past, of one's education or job, but cannot show how, say, "dark cloud 66" acts as a trader. In the visual world of trading screens, charts, and tables, this information does not need to be narrated, and doing so would be ineffective. It needs to be made visible. One way for traders to make it visible would be to post on their profile page the strategies they use, together with performance data.[5] One can, of course, choose to present a strategy without performance data, or withhold both. While the second option can add mystery, the first will add suspicion. And there is the third option, posting performance metrics without posting a strategy.

Often, traders will select the trades they post so as to present themselves in a favorable light—that is, as successful. Detective work, examining and interpreting the success statistics of other traders, is an important activity in online communities. Questioning the posted performance of individual traders—and especially of those who display unusual marks of success, that is, unusual returns—is accompanied by ongoing discussions about what constitutes an adequate metric of success, as well as by questioning the strategies associated with particular performance data. At the same time, integrating strategy into one's public profile in the community is a game: one does not need to reveal it, partly or in its entirety. Success is relative and questionable. Loud claims of success will draw attention and questions, as well as the investigation of statistical data. But one can also be successful and "mysterious," by posting high returns, according to the metrics of the community (which is supposed to be standardized and controlled by the platform's operators) but refusing to share a strategy. In this case, mystery will attract attention, in the form of followers. Displaying or hiding one's strategies, while keeping performance data visible, becomes itself a means of attracting attention, a social strategy of offering a face to the community.

Traders have to put their strategies and performance on display if they want to be ranked on a social trading platform. About a year into its existence, and with membership growing steadily, the platform I was observing launched a leadership program, in which rankings of the most successful traders (according to a common metric of return and risk) were openly displayed. One could observe the performance of "trade leaders," learn their strategy (if publicly revealed), and, more importantly, become a follower.[6] "Followers," "friends," or "copiers" could search for and identify the most successful traders using a particular type of tool or strategy: who is the best with Fibonacci numbers, with Bollinger bands, or with a fundamental approach. This was not at all an isolated case: other social trading platforms display rankings ranging from "street trader" to "professional," based on strategy and performance.

"Strategy" thus becomes intrinsic to the expression games (Goffman 1969, 10–12) through which traders strive to attain a certain status (with monetary benefits, if successful) while subjecting themselves to the scrutiny of their "friends," some of whom will at least question, sometimes even forcefully contest, the authenticity of what is put on display.[7] In professional trading, strategies are mostly hidden, although some elements might be hinted at or shared in an informal manner among traders (MacKenzie 2017; Abolafia 1996). In retail trading, they are revealed, subjected to examination, contested, replaced, or praised in games of status attainment.

Traders engage in a variety of exchanges and interactions around "live" or "dead," successful or unsuccessful, strategies. What do they look like, though? Broadly speaking, a strategy posted in the community looks less like a minute plan and more like a collection of objects and tools, together (sometimes) with a short definition and a summary specification of routines. A dead strategy will lack statistical data about its performance and will be highlighted in gray, meaning that it hasn't been used in a while. A live strategy will be highlighted in green (if profitable) or red (unprofitable) and will display statistical data about its profitability target, the number of trades conducted using the said strategy, and actual profit or loss over a certain period (usually two or three months). There are strategies for the entire community to see, and there are strategies shared within specific groups. As I learned later, there are also strategies shared by groups outside the community. A strategy is determined by time in manifold ways: not only is its performance measured over time, but it also costs time to assemble it. What is more important, however, a strategy (especially in forex communities) is used for a specific time frame of trading, in relationship to which traders define themselves. There are no universal strategies. Traders, especially in forex, specialize in trading time frames, which in their turn are made visible on the trading interface—the five-minute chart, the one-hour chart, and so on. They do this with a specific assemblage of tools: charts, computer programs (robots, or algos), and visualizations of orders. In this sense, too, a strategy implies a fine tuning of the trader to his or her tools—reciprocal adjustment and attachment at the same time. This is visible not only in the ritual ways strategies are handled sometimes by their producers (as I show below, strategies can be revealed or given as a gift), but also in the ways traders regard strategies as part of their biographies. A strategy takes time to produce and to test. It is not something that can be created quickly.

Strategies have names. The name of a strategy can be the name of the person who devised and posted it, but it can also be a name such as "Thunder Madness" or "the Sacred Mug" (I am not making up these names). Strategies can acquire a quasi-magical force of their own ("The Sacred Mug has done it again!" was once posted by the creator of this particular strategy in a moment of triumph.) Instead of being used by their owner, strategies act on behalf of the owner. Sometimes a strategy, for instance "the Iron Condor," will be offered for sale. There is a market in strategies too. Strategies have descriptions. Sometimes the description is not actually a description at all, but a summons, an invocation, or an exhortation: "I hope this thing works!" or "It is my developed strategy, which combines indicators such as parabolic sar, murrey lines, pivot line, Bollinger bands and moving average 9,30 plus broken trend. Simply we have to begin with a small amount and, after studying, increase this amount when the direction is confirmed."

Seen in this light, strategies appear more like votive objects placed by traders at the shrine of the market, meant to express identity and to articulate personal desires. But they are also a means of finding other traders with similar issues, hopes, and experiences—in short, they are expressions of identity and relationality tools at the same time.

Strategies have domains of application, being used with specific securities or currency pairs. They have indicators: Bollinger bands, Ichimoku clouds, moving averages, and so on. They have a performance target: per day or per week. "Thunder Madness," for instance, had a target of 2% per day. A strategy will be accompanied by metrics of performance, risk, and behavior. The behavioral metrics concern the average leverage used by the trader over, say, a month (which can, in this particular case, go above 20:1) and the time length of a trade (which can be something like a day).[8] At the time of this writing, there were more than 750 strategies posted on the social trading platform I was part of. Many are little more than a name and an author: no statistical data or description is made available for them. They are like burned-down candles, grey accretions at the foot of the shrine, depleted of informational content, signs of past unsuccessful tinkering in the community. Many strategies, however, are active, that is, up-to-date metrics, charts, and descriptions are available for them, together with indicators of the strategies' recent performance.

Few strategies posted in the community appear to bring profit. The votive candle may be burning bright, but the light of relative, temporary success doesn't obliterate unprofitable strategies. What is burning bright today will flicker away tomorrow and will extinguish completely afterward. In the trading team I was part of, only two of the five strategies posted while I was doing my observations were profitable, and their returns were rather modest. Two were losing money (in relative terms, more money than the winning strategies were bringing in). One was dormant. From this perspective, strategies do not compete against each other; they do not build immutable rankings, with the most profitable at the top. Rather, they are in continuous movement, with older ones becoming extinguished while new ones are lit up.

Not all strategies, and not all their components, will always be made public. The inner code of software programs (or "algos") and of signals as part of one's strategy will be kept for the initiated or may never be revealed.[9] Hiding, revealing, and pretending to reveal a strategy, as well as offering it for sale, are interactions supporting particular kinds of activities, which can be grouped under the following headings: merchandising; gifting and revealing; showing and demonstrating; and expressing autonomy. Each one of them, and all together, reveal a fabric of conflictual moral obligations that traders are subjected to, as well as a continuous effort to assert and maintain a hierarchical social system, without which, perhaps, noise would not be what it is.

Selling Strategies

Strategies, especially their algorithmic and signal components, can be bought and sold, sometimes for considerable sums. Subscribing to a signal provider can cost hundreds of dollars monthly, and an algorithm can easily go into the thousands. The place to start such a relationship, the first date, so to speak, can be not only online advertisements on financial sites, but also the trading fairs, which regularly take place in the world's big cities, at road shows, in face-to-face courses, and in many webinars. Once interest is expressed, it will be followed by many e-mails and phone calls, and, as I can tell you, these are very difficult to stop. Lack of interest in the said strategy is hardly a plausible excuse in the eyes of the salespeople involved: "You want to trade, don't you?" Strategies are not only presented as *the way* to successful trading but are also often intertwined with a "boring organizational existence to market success" story of their creators. While the old rags-to-riches story may work elsewhere, here it's the individual independence story that counts: from boring work in an anonymous industry sector to market excitement.

This, however, does not mean that traders will accept commercial strategies (together with the accompanying stories of redemption from organizational hell) just because of an admittedly appealing rhetoric. A lot of online conversations are dedicated to checking the "unique" strategies of such entrepreneurs. If having the right strategy is the key to the prized autonomy, then it cannot be expressed in pecuniary terms. In other words, even in financial online markets, not everything can be sold. One can buy and sell frozen orange juice, but not something like a strategy, because the strategy *is* the trader (Zaloom 2006, 136). Having spent considerable time in online courses, webinars, and at road shows, I was once contacted by a very nice, albeit extremely insistent salesperson (three phone calls a day, day after day), who wanted to sell me a subscription to a signal service with a minimum deposit of $15,000. The author of let's call it the "Golden Dragon" (not so far from its real name) was an entrepreneur who, by perfecting the dragon, had found salvation from the hell of organizational work and had become independent. But salvation is individual. Will it work for me? And sure enough, there were demonstrations and arguments in the forums explaining how it could not really work.

The rhetoric of salvation from organized work appears regularly in the sales pitches with which commercial providers of strategies try to attract customers. Many of the commercial providers I encountered had had earlier careers in finance and now needed to become entrepreneurial in the wake of institutional and technological transformations in markets. Others, especially some I encountered in eastern Europe, were hoping that local stock exchanges would kickstart additional markets in strategies and educational services. Apparently, something like a strategy could not be offered simply as a tool (which might work or not) but had to be reframed as an individual salvation. Seen from the traders' point of view, strategies appear as votive objects, as offerings expressing the hopes and identities of their users. Seen from the point of view of those who peddle them for money, strategies are promises of salvation and are often accompanied by personal stories of salvation, meant to lend them more credibility. The religious undertones are hard to ignore here, yet they are not easily embraced by traders, even though many traders explicitly yearn to be free from organized work.

The problem with the argument of salvation is one recognized by Max Weber ([1921] 1972, 142, 269; see also Biggart 1989) a long time ago (maybe salespeople should read him more often): charismatic authority (together with the associated attributes and artifacts) is grounded in a personal relationship, which cannot be easily transformed into an economic one. The power of the noneconomic does not lend itself to buying and selling without further ado. Hence, objects or tools to help one find salvation, to achieve success, cannot genuinely be offered as merchandise, on the grounds of their charismatic character. Two possibilities remain, nonetheless: to gift or to reveal these tools. In the first case, one builds a noneconomic relationship, a master-pupil bond (Weber [1921] 1972, 271) whereby the pupil inherits the master's strategy and keeps the group thus created around it. In the second case, a strategy is revealed as a means of transforming, in a chiastic fashion, the personal bond into an economic one. These two ways are those of the closed group and of the open, live trading webinar, respectively.

The Miracle of Strategy

I have previously discussed fabricated observations, during which the audience is summoned to see through the eyes of a "master" or a "queen." In this process, audiences are also subjected to demonstrations of masterful uses of strategies, which make profit appear when it is least expected. Yet, miraculous demonstrations of strategies are not easy to perform, even when the trader confronting chance is a master.

Audiences (of up to 300 or 400) must be shown, within a given time frame, that a commercial robot, an algo, an "emotions detector," a signal, a method (e.g., Fibonacci), or a tool (e.g., a "spike scalping tool") is working, not only in the purely technical sense, but also that it produces winning trades.[10] The software will not be opened (no codes revealed here). It befalls the powers of queens and masters, who have summoned the audience to see the screen through their eyes, to fend off chance and, using the tool at hand, conjure up profit.

The problem with enacting or demonstrating strategies in live trading is not so much that the strategy in question might not work. Triumphs— that is, moments when strategies work—are rare, and they cannot be otherwise, since the master's force of attraction will not be devalued by being regularly exercised. The audience will accept that strategies do not always work: uncertainty plays too big a role here. Since triumphs of a strategy are rare, they are very precious too. When a "catch" happens, when a strategy makes pips, or profits, in a webinar, it is celebrated, and it is recounted several times, just as a successful football pass, a baseball home run, or a soccer goal is replayed on TV several times for the enjoyment of the audiences.

Live enactments or demonstrations of strategies are confronted with at least two types of situational repairs, which constantly threaten to undermine the charismatic character of the presenter. The first kind of repair is provided by technology glitches; the second, perhaps more serious, is the lack of market activity during the live trading period. Many of the contingencies with which ordinary traders are usually confronted have been carefully set aside: master traders will use an account with enough money in it, for instance (usually an account set up for this kind of demonstrations), so that they are not subjected to margin calls in front of a live audience. Also, master traders will have excellent broadband connections, so that the screen does not freeze in the middle of a demonstration and so that the all-important data feed does not slow down.

Even master traders are subjected to technological glitches, for instance, when they forget to replace the batteries in their wireless mouse devices and suddenly, unexplainably, cannot move the cursor on the screen anymore. A functional mouse device is crucial for online trading: transactions are conducted by placing the cursor on a cell in the transaction grid or on the chart and clicking the left or right button. In a live trading session, a nonworking mouse device simply means not being able to trade. When a master trader discovers why the cursor does not move (this can take some time), he will tell the audience to stay put while he finds some unused batteries in a drawer. Instead of focusing on creating a charismatic situation and a rapport with the audience, the task is a double one now: while the moderator keeps the audience online by repeating bits of general information or advice about trading, the master trader will have to repair screen mobility and restart the incantations. Such unexpected repairs can ruin any presentation plan. They require careful coordination of each planned step with the on-screen situation, and since the latter changes from second to second, having to find spare batteries means forgetting about the plan—especially if one trades a one-minute or a five-minute chart.

The second kind of happening that can undermine the charismatic character of a live strategy demonstration is actually a nonhappening. Nothing, but nothing at all, happens on the screen for minutes at a time. Usually, live demonstrations are carefully planned for days when action is expected, perhaps when end-of-month or end-of-quarter announcements are made.[11] Planning, however, cannot guarantee that markets will move in the wake of an announcement. Such announcements can be anticipated and hence already discounted by traders at the moment when they occur. For movements to take place, announcements must build up surprises—and these, as their name tells us, cannot be anticipated. A trading opportunity must pop up in order for the strategy to be demonstrated. This can take a long time. Master traders and their assistants have rationalizations at hand for such situations: "watching the paint dry," "not much happening here," or "market gets quiet and we have to wait, we have no choice" can often be heard, although the situation was very different earlier on, or yesterday. Looking for opportunities that may arise totally unexpectedly, at unforeseeable moments, makes it difficult for traders to devise a multistep plan (or strategy) in which each step corresponds to a situation on the trading screen and steps enchain in a foreseeable sequence. One can wait for a situation that fails to materialize, or an unexpected one may appear but not be followed by a situation scripted in any plan. Nevertheless, situational gaps—such as "watching the paint dry"—provide master traders with slots for inserting rationalizations about the strategies they use, even if such rationalizations are not immediately relevant for the trading situation.

When the opportunity comes, however, it will be celebrated and replayed over and over. Fate rewards the faithful. Strategies finally conjure up profit. The market works! The previous wait, the lack of action, appears in hindsight not only justified, but as the only way to go. In the excerpt below, a live trading session is dedicated to showing the audience how a strategy based on a proprietary emotional indicator works. When the trade is executed, under the careful mention of its being live, success is presented as exemplary:

TRADER [LIVE, IN FRONT OF AN ONLINE AUDIENCE]: We've got a riskless trade here. All of a sudden in just a couple of minutes we got a riskless trade. I don't wanna crowd on this but we don't wanna lose money on this either, so that's exactly where I entered 66,8. So we are 14 pips into this trade and you can see the emotion dying down here, the emotion caution above here flared up above 10. That's a very high reading, so I've got 16 pips into this trade, and at this point I really want to capture this, I've got my hand on my mouse . . . and I'm watching very closely. I'm 19 pips into this trade, just took my profit here and made 19 pips . . . and this was live. [. . .] Ahhh 66 out of 82 didn't make 19 pips. Sorry about that, my feel, a lousy feel up and about 17 pips . . . all about nine minutes into this trade and about 17 pips, but a great example, and the reason why I clicked out is because I came back and I'm touching this 34 ema, which is just exactly as I said. We look for retracements to come and bounce off the 34 ema. . . . I could have held out and watched this trade in several ways. One way I could do it is just mechanically keep and type my stop. Ok, that way would keep the door open for return all the way to the upper target line, which would be at 98. Given the fact that we were in a pretty good downtrend, this was a very nice countertrend trade yielding the better part of 17 to 18 pips in just a few minutes. The key is waiting for something to happen, not hunch trending, not thinking I have seen something, but waiting for the opportunity to happen.

Let's look again at what it means to make a profitable trade, as it is expressed in this account. It is happening unexpectedly. The steady hand is on the mouse. The master is patient. The tool (aka the emotions indicator) is showing where emotion is dying and where it is flaring up. The sight is clear. The market is entered with precision. The ritual of observation is expanded here into one of (miraculous) action. The audience sees the action through the eyes of the master (his trading screen is replicated on their computers) while hearing the master glossing on it. This can be regarded as an almost rarefied case of vicarious engagement, in which the audiences do not simply witness a priest of trading conjuring profit to appear, but actively participate in his actions. His eyes are their eyes, and his cursor is their cursor. His indicator is their indicator.

Small wonder, then, that the master trader refers all the time to "we" as the collective who conjured up profit. Demonstrations such as these are meant to reinforce the sense of a trader's autonomous powers in fending off chance (in addition to helping sell strategies). Yet, at the same time, any sense of such autonomous powers is constantly undermined by the call to surrender one's perceptions and judgment to a "master."

The live enactment of a strategy is the live enactment of success. Whereas sales strategies employed by traveling salespeople, for instance, involve attracting the audience to the game of demonstrating the product (Clark and Pinch 1995), what occurs in such sessions—in a way similar to that of staged competitions—is that gameworthiness is made visible to participants. Waiting—which until a certain point could have been just waiting, now becomes a special kind of waiting, a virtue that ensures success. The profit made in the transaction is used to justify the virtue, not the other way around. And this virtue, coming from a master trader, having been revealed in action to the audience while the audience directly participates in it, is supposed to be intrinsic to charisma. It is, again, a very different type of relationship from the rhetoric of revelation invoked by commercial providers (although master traders are no less commercial). Nonetheless, here it is the person, not the product, who can perform miracles of patience and should be followed in his recommendations.

True Revelations

A strategy can be offered or revealed to chosen followers within a group, away from the scrutiny of larger publics. This technique of revelation requires a personal relationship between a master, or mentor, and an apprentice, as well as a (looser) relationship between the two and their followers. It involves a key element, namely, a robot or an algorithm that will allow members of the group to follow and execute trades according to a principle or rule proprietary to the group. This may imply the discovery of a trading imbalance between two currency or commodity pairs, which can be exploited to the participants' advantage. An "algo" will create a concrete search, observation, and intervention device based on such a rule or principle. In a case like this, the algorithm will not be bought from the market but will be created by the master or mentor and rcvealed to the apprentice—which concretely means revealing the programming code:

> PHIL: It was through like a private group which got formed as like a split off from this forum, then he [the mentor] sort of decided to slowly start giving out more and more advice to this group of people and then he would give out some of his indicators. It's hard to explain his system, so at no point . . . at no point is he, has he asked for anything from us, and now everyone, and slowly people started to get results using his tools and his advice and then slowly as I said I've started to come round to trust him with it, and he's given me access now to his code so that I can see what the stuff is based on, to give me again more of a fundamental trust in it, and some people have had amazing results with it, which is what really encourages me to keep going so far.
>
> AP: Mm-hm, all right, so I understand that this so far, that you being able to see his, getting access to his code was a critical point here?
>
> PHIL: Yeah. It was. I mean I was, I'd always struggled like at first, I obviously have the ability to decompile his code and look at it if I want to, but I was sort of trying because I would really, I would by this point consider him as a friend, and I didn't want to have to go behind his back to get it, so I just . . .

These extraordinary acts on both sides—revealing and abstaining (from decompiling)—anchor a noneconomic relationship (a gift), which, in turn, provides the basis for economic action.[12] In the group in question, this revelation from master to pupil is at the core of the relationships with the other members, who do not have the education and the know-how to decompile software codes:[13]

> PHIL: The whole group has access [to the code] if they really want to but it's quite complex and I'm the only other person who understands, but yeah I don't think he would object if the others did, but they seem to be able to trade without having to understand, so it's . . . each person to their own really.

While in the community at large some bits of programming can be revealed from time to time, community-wide, they concern mostly side aspects of trading (e.g., processing tweets), but not trading software.[14]

I have never seen codes of trading software being revealed to the community at large. Building a master-pupil relationship as the core of the trading group implies exclusion, both within the group and with respect to the wider community. Within the group, other members have access to but cannot understand the code. Within the wider community, really important codes will not be revealed.

When revelations provide the foundation for a charismatic relationship, codes are not sold. They are given as a gift; they are improved. At some point in the future, the pupil will become the master of the group.[15] The rhetoric of revelation may be employed by commercial providers of trading robots. Revelation, however, is crucial in building relationships that form the core of trading groups. Revelation is immediate, and it is one-to-one: any intermission will raise suspicions. From time to time, a member of the community will post a commercial strategy on behalf of a guru, or with the permission of a mentor. This, however, will not be accepted by the community without further ado. A guru or a mentor should not have a pecuniary interest in posting a strategy: other members will start taking the strategy apart or openly questioning the proclaimed disinterestedness of its author. Such ambiguity can trigger debates about whether revelations should be allowed or banned in the community and whether they are not in fact a persuasion trick for pushing merchandise. Retractions, caveats, warnings, and declarations of good intentions follow: what has been initially presented as an infallible strategy becomes fallible.

Strategies of Autonomy

I have argued that strategies are intrinsic to expression games. I have argued that they provide the focal point for interactions and situations where charismatic force is put on display. Such interactions can be specific to small groups or to the rapport between larger audiences and a "master." However, strategies are also discursive devices—stories, summons, protests—with the help of which traders struggle to keep upright their self-understanding as autonomous actors, endowed with their own powers of decision and understanding. The communicational setup of retail trading seems to continuously undermine, as well as encourage, such an understanding. The hierarchies of trade leaders and followers and the charisma of masters do not exactly support the notion that retail traders can realistically have autonomous powers of decision. If they had them, why submit to the power of a master, why surrender one's own trading account to a trade leader? And yet, at the same time, this very same communicational setup encourages the idea that traders can (and should) strive to attain such autonomy. From the viewpoint of traders, then, it becomes necessary to deploy efforts at maintaining and, if necessary, repairing their self-understanding as autonomous participants in the game of trading. Strategies provide welcome tools for this continuous, strenuous work to maintain a self-understanding critical for their presence in the game. At the same time, the work itself is an inherent part of the strategies employed by traders in their activities.

They look upon their past actions and performance and try to understand why things occurred as they did. Their rationalizations of the past combine elements beyond individual control and judgments upon their own deficiencies: a trade has gone wrong because the trader was getting too emotional or was incapable of exiting it. Nevertheless, the search for an ideal attitude is not abandoned: in this search, strategy plays a key role. The fact that traders look for the right strategy to correct perceived deficiencies indicates that they view strategy as a means of attaining, improving, or maintaining autonomy. At the same time, if their autonomy needs maintenance and repair, it reveals itself as fragile and prone to disruptions. The result can be visible response cries (Goffman 1978) to the unfairness of winning trades without a strategy:

> A TRADER IN THE COMMUNITY: [. . .] I am very serious and worry about my very small capital and they are car[e]less, but still my stop loss keep hitting and they are still making money, one trade recommendation I got from them on [date] to buy EURAUD, i did not think even for one second that this trade gonna work but it did and I close the trade for about 270 pips profit in just 4 days. What technical or what fundamentals make some body to buy EURAUD last week I still do not know.

Such a situation can reveal that the carefully maintained junction between trading proper and acting strategically is a fragile one. When the trades of careless people work, exhortations about discipline, about the need for strategy, the value of revelations, or about an underlying, encompassing logic of trading receive a blow.

Strategies are presented as fitting the trader's personality; not only are they part of the trader's trajectory, but they are also part and a result of the trader's personal circumstances. It is not unusual that the public biography of a trading guru, for instance, will include a "moment of revelation," marked by the discovery of a strategy (a discovery that can be serendipitous or the result of years-long tinkering). With this discovery, the previous job (which can be anything ranging from the building industry to health care) is abandoned and the new, market career starts. The discovery of the strategy can thus mark a liminal biographical phase, from which a new stage is entered, that of the market.

Traders will justify their strategies not necessarily as a conscious choice among many options, but with respect to their trajectories and biographies. Nadia, who was introduced earlier, told me that for a long time she was "leaving herself alone," not creating any goals, pursuing any strategies, or creating any allocations. It was only when she began getting a "creative and macroeconomic education," when she started forming her own opinions, that her strategy emerged. After leaving her job with a financial services provider (where she felt she was unfairly treated) and going back to graduate school, she found her own voice and, with that, her strategy: "When you have no control, you try and resort to hope and all sorts of illogical emotions. [. . .] As long as you have some kind of analysis that you can fall back on, that is independent of other people, that is within you, I think it's less emotional, it's more structural." A strategy means not "leaving the self alone" but caring for it. Strategy thus becomes who you are, even if you are not a star:

> GEORGE [ACTIVE SINCE 1959]: I've been around for a long time, so I know
> a lot of companies, and so forth. I try and find, . . . companies. Again, we
> only have limited abilities. I'm not strong in some areas, other areas I am
> strong. We cannot have, you know, you can't be all things in the stock market,
> so you've got to find what your strengths are. Part of my strength is
> technical.

Since there has to be a tight fit between a strategy and the trader's personality, and since a trading strategy is a means of expressing autonomy, a trader cannot have more than one strategy at any given time. Attempting to do so would be foolish. The whole notion of discipline sometimes revolves around finding the appropriate fit and sticking with it:

> AP: Tell me, do people have different trading accounts for different styles,
> or it's just, from what you've seen, or is it just that the trader sticks to one

style? Let me rephrase: do people experiment with different styles from the same accounts? Or is it just one style per person?

TED: No, I would say it's just one style, because it's all to do with psychology from trade, so you can't have two psychologies at the same time, so yeah, no, its just one style I would say. Well I, the only, when I tried to mix different trading styles I screwed up completely and amassed my biggest daily loss, which is about five times, my max loss I set myself. [. . .] Yeah, because when you trade, with you trading style, you are completely immersed in it, it's trying to be two different persons at once. Maybe if you were schizophrenic it would work, I don't know [*laughing*]. I've never met a schizophrenic trader, but yeah, I think it would be quite difficult because, the trading styles is rules, that you have to stick to, no matter what, and different trading styles have different rules, so if you are trying to do both at the same time, your kind of trespassing on the rules of the different styles if you understand what I mean. It's, I don't think it goes together, you either do one and you stick those rules and the strategy and do the other, but not both, maybe sometimes, I think.

As Ted puts it, only a "schizophrenic trader" would have two strategies at a time, because that would mean that the person had two personalities and therefore two identities at a time. One has to stick to one's strategy, understood here as rules, but these are not general rules at all. They are Ted's rules, different from other traders' but again not so different that they become unrecognizable. This search for a unique fit between strategy and personal autonomy resonates well with the rhetoric of quasi-mystical experiences (a strategy is revealed; one has an epiphany about strategy), but also with the rhetoric of spiritual healing that I heard once from a conference speaker, at one of the trading shows I attended in London. Although the topic of the talk was how to spot institutional traders on the screen, the speaker (coming from a brokerage house) didn't dive straight into the matter. Trading, he said, is one of the most vicious and cruel learning curves. Trading is about "master over your self, over your emotions, over your psychological maladies . . . about becoming a better individual. [. . .] It is far more sublime than just making money, almost spiritual." Seen in this light, the cry of unfairness previously discussed becomes even more profound. How can one encounter chance when one doesn't even have a self?

Trading as mastering one's "psychological maladies" would mean, in the end, that a "trading strategy" is nothing but a rekeying of a quest for personal autonomy that goes well beyond the domain of finance. Against this background, we can understand better why traders consider that "habits" can prevent strategies from working (as I showed in the opening of this chapter): habits can prevent achieving this mastery of the self, which is the true strategy at stake.

I follow here Erving Goffman's argument that true action resides in confrontations with chance (as opposed to mere routines) (1967, 181). If retail trading provides (the illusion of) such confrontations, then the (illusion of) being autonomously acting individuals, capable of making their own decisions, is necessary too. Strategies, perhaps paradoxically, play a key role both in undermining and in maintaining this illusion. When traders are asked to follow the strategies of masters and trade leaders, there is little room left for such autonomy. And yet, the traders cannot do what they (think they) are doing without it. Hence, the communication formats of electronic retail trading have to enable both movements at once. These formats strip autonomy away by enabling trade leaders, masters, and queens to try to build a charismatic relationship with followers. Yet, traders find in these very same formats resources, and occasions, for expressing and displaying their self-understanding as autonomous actors.

In Homer's *Odyssey*, Penelope kept her suitors at bay by alternately weaving and unraveling a shroud, so that the day would never come when, having finished the shroud, she would have to make a choice (or so she hoped). In retail trading, one could say, traders are kept in by the simultaneous weaving and unraveling of a necessary self-understanding of themselves as autonomous decision makers. Penelope's weaving and unraveling was a strategy for avoiding a choice she didn't want to make. The weaving and unraveling of the retail traders' self-understandings is a strategy that, at least from a communicational perspective, directly contributes to creating "noise as a necessary structural ingredient of markets": participants supposed to be in need of charismatic masters, yet who cannot participate without a sense of autonomy. This is not only about knowing less than professional traders, or having fewer informational resources. It is about the fact that, by definition, participation in trading activities requires a self-understanding as an autonomous decision maker. If noise traders are to be different from, and ranking lower than, a "better" category of traders, this self-understanding has to be made fragile, incomplete, and subordinated to a superior force. It is made so not merely by declarative sentences, but in elaborate social rituals, in small groups as well as in front of larger audiences.[16] This work of "fragilization" and subordination can be resisted, though, and it is undermined by the necessary quest for autonomy that traders have to relentlessly pursue.

CHAPTER SEVEN

The Lives of Traders

Traders have social and professional lives outside their work with the screen, and apparently unrelated to it: families, friendships, and jobs seem to have little in common with trading. If trading is all relationships, and if the social lives of traders are made of relationships too, to what extent can trading and traders' lives be kept apart? How do traders manage, if at all, to keep the two domains separate? We can well imagine that institutional traders are bound not to disclose at home or to their friends what they do in their trading. Retail traders are not subject to such formal requirements. Does this activity—which is not a professional one, but not a very common one, either—affect how traders see themselves as persons? Are family relationships and friendships affected by it? How do nontraders in the immediate environment of traders react to trading?

Moreover, is trading used to intervene in social relationships that are seen by participants as noneconomic? That is, do traders make use of what they do as an instrument in their kinship, friendships, or any other type of relationships that they otherwise would see as decidedly outside the sphere of monetary transactions? This is nontrivial, as until recently the two domains (market and nonmarket exchanges) have been seen as separate. One either does market transactions or one does other kinds of things (ritual exchanges, gift giving, etc.), but the two are not mixed together. Or when they are, it can become destructive. In recent years, Viviana Zelizer's work on intimate relationships (2011, 203) began to challenge the dogma that market and nonmarket transactions have to be kept separate, or else. Yet, there has been a long, ongoing debate about what kind of relationships and interaction formats constitute market transactions. (Are market transactions just particular assemblages of more general types of relationships?) Conversely, we can ask to what extent market transactions shape noneconomic relationships such as family ties.

Trading and Social Life

The link between transactions and social relationships has been approached from two perspectives, depending on what kind of relationships we are talking about: relationships that might pertain to the sphere of economic activities, or relationships that are decidedly seen by participants as noneconomic (such as intimate ties). In the first case, the debates have revolved around whether transactions are encased within relationships (the embeddedness argument), or whether transactions are social relationships (e.g., Granovetter 1985; White 2003; Krippner and Alvarez 2007; Krippner et al. 2004). Of course, if transactions are social relationships, the question arises whether they are of a specific type. In both cases, we would need to account for possible transformations—for instance, how an economic tie can become noneconomic, and the other way around.

In the second case, three possible approaches have been envisioned: that of "hostile worlds," which should not be in contact with each other (intimate relations degrade when touched by monetary transactions); that of norms or values that, under specific circumstances, allow the transformation of an intimate tie into a monetary transaction; and that of differentiated ties, which allow for monetary transactions as long as the latter are seen as "special" (Zelizer 2000, 818–819). If monetary transactions are allowed into a person's personal, intimate life (provided they are rationalized as "special"), we need to think about how they are used and how they become transformed. We can also reverse the question and ask, How is personal life allowed (or not) to seep into market transactions (and decisions about them)?

Retail trading presents itself as a good starting point for examining this question from both ends, because apparently it is a textbook case of "hostile worlds." The coldness of seemingly entering calculated transactions with distant strangers seems to clash with the closeness of family relationships, friendships, or romantic involvements. On top of all this, trading is often perceived as an esoteric domain, and for that reason we would expect it to be kept apart from the personal lives of traders.

If these worlds were truly hostile, we would not necessarily expect traders to reveal to family and friends what they are doing. Do they see themselves as admired by those close to them, or as envied, or as persons to be emulated? Do they disclose to their immediate circle what they are doing? Does trading become a topic of dinner conversations? Often, public perception of financial markets and trading has been shaped by media portrayals of large-scale speculation, of insider trading, or of large losses incurred by institutional traders. This public perception has been a moral one, being tied to questions of common welfare, wealth (re)distribution, and socialization of losses. Such activities and events are actually far away from ordinary lives, and most of us do not experience them directly. We read about them in newspapers and watch reports on TV. How is it when somebody we know personally is engaged in trading? How do we perceive that person and how does the person perceive us perceiving her or him? One of the interesting aspects of this question is that if we had the answer, we could see whether perceptions of trading based on personal relationships overlap with media representations, and whether trading continues to be seen as a moral issue within the context of personal relationships. If this is the case, then we can investigate whether the decision to take up trading appears as a moral choice made in the context of personal ties. With that, the relationship between economic and intimate worlds would be reversed: it would be the intimate world seeping into the economic world, not merely the adapting of the economic world to the needs of the intimate world.

Trading and Family Choices

Especially for younger traders, and I talked to many of them, relationships with parents, or family experiences, play a significant role in taking up and maintaining trading. Being a trader seems to become a way of asserting one's identity within the family. For many of the traders I talked to, especially the younger ones, there was no family encouragement to take up trading. Quite the contrary: the more business background a family had, the more it discouraged the son's trading. The fathers of Ron and Sam were both traders and advised their sons against it—to no avail:

> SAM: Actually my father is in finance. He does . . . makes products for bank center customers and he's also into trading. He does investments into eq-

uity, into property, but he has never told me what he is actually doing even though he is making money and I wanted to learn but he would never teach me. [. . .] He never . . . I did but he was like you're too young . . . you don't understand. But I decided to do it myself and that's why when I came here I joined the investment club. The £300 that I had to put in for investment club, that's actually not from my parents. I had to put it in myself because my parents wouldn't allow me. [. . .] Yeah. That's actual . . . if the investment club screws up and loses money, it's my money going down. It's not my parents'. But I took the interest because I mean people are not free from the influence of the market. I mean I could lose my job or not get a job because the market is turbulent and everybody's depressed. Confidence . . . consumer confidence is down so that's why I started to take interest in this stocks and investment basically, and my parents they say study well, you concentrate on your academics but also don't do, learn market because it's gonna impact your future, and I do want to do some private trading and personal trading in the future.

Sam made his decision against the wishes of his father, and he emphasizes that the money he put into trading is not from his parents. This appears as the moral choice not to jeopardize family money, but also as a matter of asserting independence, as well as a proof that he can do what he has been advised not to do. Trading is rationalized as an economic necessity (one cannot be free from the influence of the market; economic prospects are not good) *and* as a moral choice (I decided to do it myself). And yet, what Sam rationalizes as economic necessity is also something he was warned against by his parents, so one might legitimately wonder whether the same necessity would have been there if his parents had not warned against trading.

If it happens that Ron's parents accept his trading, in the end, it will be only because they want to see him make some mistakes:

RON: Yeah, my father he had a talk with me later on. That was recently . . . that was last year and he told me way back then he didn't want me to do trading because really thinks I mean it's difficult. It's not an easy thing to do, it's more like everybody cash in to the market and make money. It's like learning a skill, he told me, it's like learning to drive, learn to fly a plane. I mean you know there's a list of things you need to do before you actually start doing it then dad will say learning curve involved, that's what he called it, the learning curve. I mean, what I was doing back then

I wasn't, I didn't have this learning curve before, but I started doing this anyway. I didn't have, I didn't learn anything so but that was why he didn't support me too much, but he told me that last year you know, and the reason he didn't stop me was he wanted me to have some mistakes, to make some mistake that I learn from myself rather than somebody to tell you what to do like you are going to do this anyway. Do you see what I am trying to get at?

In their accounts of parental discouragement, Ron and Sam emphasize several things: first, there is an order for learning (the "learning curve"), and the place of trading in this order is contested. At most, family sees it as a mistake to learn from. Second, academic and practical learning are perceived as mutually exclusive. The debate appears to be about the right skills and the right order of learning and about who has a say about it. Trading becomes a locus of contestation, as well as an activity through which both Ron and Sam assert their identities. Hence the emphasis of many traders that they trade with their own money and not with funds from the family.

In other cases, discussions about whether the sons should trade revolve around moral views of the economy: what does it mean to create economic value? What does it mean to contribute to a stable economic life? What sorts of economic activities and business are good? Toby's parents see traders as damaging economic stability and are against their son's trading, although he does it on a much more modest scale. Toby, however, uses an argument he learned in his economics classes: he doesn't damage stability; he just "provides liquidity to the market" (although one could wonder here how much "liquidity" a retail trader can provide to the market, especially when he is not trading in one). Rick's father, who had taught at one of the top US business schools, believes that economic value is tied to creating valuable objects or ideas, but Rick thinks otherwise:

RICK: My dad is a business professor in [country] at a big school. He worked at [top US business school] as well so no he's more business. He's a, he believes in entrepreneurship you know, like that's why he really liked that I was doing engineering. He was like yeah you can create an idea and then you'll be selling that idea. He doesn't like trading too much because he believes we are making money off nothing. You know, like you're buying and then you're selling at a higher price. But then all of life is like this. Like

even here [in a café], you know, they're buying Coca-Cola and they're selling at a higher price, you know. So what he doesn't like is that we're not
actually creating anything, you know.

Parental advice against trading doesn't seem to be very effective, because the logic at work here is one of freedom from parental constraints.
If one's father has lost money from trading and advises against it, the son
will want to prove that he can do better. If one's father has made money
from trading and advises against it, then one will think he is not considered capable of doing it. This sort of logic makes antitrading advice
a losing proposition from the start. It parallels the one expressed by so
many traders: trading as freedom from organized work, although as a
trader one has to put in at least as many hours of work.

The same logic, however, makes protrading advice a winning proposition. John, for instance, started trading in middle school with the support and encouragement of his family, who allowed him to pick up stocks
for them. Jack, in his turn, sees his parents putting money into pension
funds, the traditional way, and wants to reduce costs by cutting out the
fund manager as a middleman. Tim is encouraged by his father to experiment but is hurt by his friends' attitude when he loses money. He
also reflects upon whether he will ever be able to find time to have a girl-
friend, with his trading and his engineering studies absorbing his days.
(Another significant motive for continuing with trading is proving the
others—family, friends, the market—wrong, or, as Tim puts it, taking re-
venge.) Jim, who is freshly married, does not share his trading stories
with his wife; when he took up trading, his father was encouraging but
his mother was scared and his friends were confused. Matt, too, is reluctant to share trading stories with his female friends, but he feels encouraged by the family. Nadia, who has given up a career as an execution
trader to pursue postgraduate education, is annoyed by her mother's talk
about picking stocks: her mother always thinks she knows best. Nadia
also talks about not sharing trading stories or tips with the young men
she has seen in the past, though the latter had a business background:

NADIA: Well, I trade with my own money so, I mean if I want to tell some-
    one about it I can, if not I don't have to, whatever. Generally whenever
    I tell my parents about like a position that I have, my mom tends to be
    very . . . yeah, kind of disparaging. My mom watches a lot of financial news
    in the US and it's full of like, talking heads, saying things that make very

little sense. Like they tell you to invest in things because there might be an earnings prize or some, like, completely unfundamental reasons for investing in things, so if I mention to her a position that I have randomly, because we are somewhere and like, oh yeah, I have like an allocation in like gold or whatever, then she'll equally say, "Oh those people they say that gold is in a bubble right now" or something and I'm just kind of like, I'm really just not interested in hearing it, you know, because I'm not interested in arguing with someone who, we're not on the same, we're not really coming from the same place, there is no basis, it's a waste of time to have an argument with someone who gets all of their information from financial news and there's, if we came to some resolution it wouldn't help me and it wouldn't help her so, yeah . . . the people who I have seen recently have not been, they've been involved in business but not necessarily in the investing side, so they don't, they would think it's kind of cool you know, but that's about it, you know, it's not, like it hasn't really been a issue.

What Nadia indicates is that unavoidably (talk of) trading becomes enmeshed in personal relationships because both mentioning it and not mentioning it affects the relationships. Talk of trading can lead to family arguments, or it can lead to being perceived by a romantic interest in a particular way. There is always a moral choice implied in talking about trading, simply because it belongs to one's identity, though not necessarily in the same way as one's professional identity would when one talks about it. Not all mothers can express firm opinions about engineering or about heart surgery procedures, but they can do so about the price of gold, because they watch the "talking heads" on TV. The account of how talk of trading is positioned in mother-daughter conversations raises questions of identity, but also of status (one cannot be talked to in a disparaging way). Similarly, a romantic interest might find trading cool, but should it be mentioned? In all these situations, talk of trading appears to be a moral choice, as well as a strategy, because it affects the face we show to the world, and this face in its turn shapes our social lives (Goffman 1971, 252).

The interweaving of trading and personal relationships, including family and intimate relationships, does not stop at telling family members or friends about one's transactions or making judgments about their attitudes. Trading can be actively used to intervene in relationships or to communicate feelings and attitudes to others. What I mean is that trading is used not only as something to tell about, but also as a medium of telling something. Take Janice, for instance, a middle-aged trader from the East Coast who, according to her own account, had a complex relationship with one of her siblings. There was the competitiveness about who went to the better college, and so on, but there were also issues of what kind of life she saw herself living, as compared with her brother, perceived as overly materialistic. So when the brother made an initial public offering (IPO) of his company, Janice shorted it. This narrative of shorting the sibling's stock is set into the broader comments about the schools the two attended and about their overall orientation in life:

> JANICE: [Talking about her sibling]: And then by virtue of that I guess even if you're in a mediocre school you come to people's attention OK and— and then he decided he wanted to be in [US city] and he went to work for [firm] in [US city]. He very quickly became one of the partners in [firm] . . . this was around 1990, the tech bubble. One [client] was . . . had a small hi-tech company that he wanted to take public with an IPO and the other had a large real estate development firm. [. . .] He made the decision that this is the moment to go with the IPO thing. OK, so they brought this little [expletive] [*laughs*] . . . this stupid little [name] . . . he was very upset with me because I eventually . . . I shorted it, I mean it was like [*laughs*] . . . this thing is not real, I mean this is . . . and then I think it hurt his feelings [*laughs*] but . . .
>
> AP: Did he tell you that much?
>
> JANICE: Yeah, no he let me know, I mean I could see that he was . . . that he was irritated that this was . . . that I . . . that there wasn't a vote of confidence in this company.

A key aspect in this account is that Janice shorts her sibling's fresh IPO not as a means of making a profit, but as a means of telling her brother something. The shorting isn't done anonymously: it is disclosed to the family. After all, Janice could have quietly shorted the stock and not mentioned it. She could have ignored the stock; she could have evaluated it on purely economic criteria. The "stupid little" firm, though, belongs to somebody who has been in "mediocre schools." Shorting it is used as a signal of disapproval toward a family member. It is also the expression of Janice's choice to lead a different kind of life. As a means of communication within the web of family relationships, particular trades belong, then, to expression games, designed to express attitudes and judgment, and perhaps to change the dynamic of a relationship as well.

From this perspective, two things need to be highlighted: first, profit isn't necessarily the (ultimate) motive of a trade. One can execute a trade as a means of saying something to a certain public, fully anticipating the reactions of the said public. This puts into question a narrower utilitarian view (traders always want to make money) and explains, partly at least, why some traders could knowingly engage in nonprofitable trades. Karin Knorr Cetina and Urs Bruegger (2002, 927–928) emphasize that professional traders might engage in unprofitable trades when they are summoned to do a favor for a fellow trader. What we have here is the reverse: traders can engage in negative sanctioning by means of trades too.

In Janice's account, trading is rekeyed from action to expression (Goffman 1969, 5) and as such is transferred from one relational domain to a completely different one. If we wonder why people trade, one answer would be because activities can be rekeyed as expressions and transported across social domains, enabling the accomplishment of particular strategic actions and moral choices that apparently have nothing to do with the initial one. One activity becomes the expression of a completely different one.

These do not seem to be "hostile worlds," but rather worlds that, on occasion at least, seamlessly flow into each other. They do not seem to be dominated or determined by any single cultural norm, either, one that would constrain Janice to short her sibling's stock. This act is not merely a reclassification or a distinction, akin to treating a particular category of money as fitting a particular kind of intimate relationship. This is the rekeying of an economic transaction as the expression of a moral choice within close family ties, an expression that in its turn is used to reconfigure those ties. If we wonder what kind of economic relationships market transactions are, we need to focus on how rekeyings of such transactions intervene in noneconomic ties.

Trading can be used not only to communicate within (and rearrange) family relationships, but also to supplement their absence. Samantha, who has been a successful professional, took up trading as a means of coping with a stressful family situation:

SAMANTHA: I was not, I didn't have much to do, I was at the time . . . in a state of some distress because my son had been very ill [. . .] and it had all been very traumatic and although he was back, I hadn't really got in. I left where I was living and I came to live near him to support him and then he was two months in hospital, so I wasn't really in any kind of proper rou-

tine. I wasn't at work or I didn't have a lot of, you know, washing and iron-
ing or anything to do. I was just, I was just working on my website and
the house wasn't getting dirty so, that was it really, a very lazy person . . .
so I would say more than eight hours . . . and, in terms of the numbers of
trades, I desire greatly to be a low frequency trader but I'm afraid I am
still too compulsive. [. . .] So I am still unfortunately a high frequency
trader because I keep trying to . . . this is again I think a fatal error, trying to build my little account up, rather than being the kind of person who
knows how much money to put in, in the first place and preserves their equity and doesn't really think about building and doubling it but just, you
know, putting on their 2% or something. So, I am, I guess sublimely stupid I think to, now I know, but I don't have, I don't have a lot of resources
again my son's illness, and I lost a son, his illness, the two of them just
kind of put me in a place where I don't really want to be in so I thought oh
I can, I can trade my way out of where I am. But that is a very stupid phi-
losophy, you can't . . .

While Samantha ascribes her trading mistakes to her personal situation ("I am the problem"), it is the same situation that brought her to
trading: her aims are to "trade her way out" and "trade her way up,"
and these are almost indistinguishable. She acknowledges that this undertaking is a difficult one: the high frequency of her trades (which she
would like to avoid) is situated in relationship to having to abandon her
professional life, but also to "the house not being very dirty"—hence
leaving her with time that is filled up with trading.

While Samantha's account of her trading can be seen as being filled
with gender-specific markers (taking care of a son who is ill, the house
not needing much cleaning), male traders' accounts of how they get into
trading are no less related to family relationships and to personal circumstances. For Eddie, trading came at a point in life when he and his
partner had to choose between changing their life (going back to grad
school) or using the decades-long savings to other ends. Trading became
a means of supporting the actual choice (graduate school) but is also
part of the initial choice:

EDDIE: And it . . . I mean, here's the funny thing, because . . . we're coming from different perspectives, but . . . it was funny because we sold the
house, and we had all this money, and, and [name] inherited some money,
and I said, you know, my way of thinking was, oh, we're at the pinnacle

of our finances. Let's make some money. Let's use this to make money.
You know what she said? Because we talked about this later . . . she said,
"oh, well, I was thinking, we're at the pinnacle, so now I can do something else." But see, I would've much rather made more money, and then
okay, take a couple years, okay, go . . . here, spend it, you know: I've made
a bunch more. [*laugh*] I mean, when you have strength, use it. And then,
you know, when you get beaten down by all this, it's like, okay, start over.
Then there's trouble with it, there really is. And I don't want to be taking all these chances to try to make up for it. It's stupid. I mean, that's the
problem with my . . . that's the tendency, that's the problem with my trading right now. I just have to say, well, this has been costly, let's get by it
and we'll start over. [*laugh*] With less. We're going to start over with less.
And hopefully she'll get a job at least. [*laugh*] Yeah. [. . .] But anyway, I
mean, that . . . this is basically why I don't see myself making good trades,
I mean . . . Yeah. And that's not the way to make money. I make a lot of
mistakes. And a lot of risks.

Eddie, who hasn't been doing very well with his trading lately, justifies his mistakes with respect to his family situation (in a way similar to what Samantha does) but also sees the initial choice as an ethical
one: what does one use money for? Trading (which he would have preferred) appears as an alternative to other choices, which cannot be his
own alone. These are family choices: trading has to be accommodated to
family relationships, and the latter have to accommodate trading. While
a family situation is used to justify lack of luck in trading, in its turn trading is represented as an attempt to get out of an undesirable family situation. Trading and personal lives become enmeshed, to a point where
the decisions made in one domain appear as decisions made in the other.

These stories of family relationships, as told by men and women of
different ages, point at several aspects: first, trading is a personal matter and cannot be separated from family relationships and friendships.
The worlds are not hostile. The decision to take up trading, and decisions about trading, are personal. They are not shared lightly within
one's broader circle of friends, and there seems to be a gender element
in it as well, in the sense that male traders talk more about the influence
of their fathers, whereas (the admittedly rare) female traders talk more
about the influence of their mothers. In the accounts of how families and
friends react to trading, trading appears to be liminally situated between
ordinary life and problematic activities.

The drive to make money is not the ultimate motivating force in these accounts. Sure enough, when money is made—which does not happen very often and not on a grand scale anyway—it is always seen as a means for attaining something else. It is the notion—or, better said, the ideal—of attaining freedom that is ultimately pursued here, freedom with a small *f*. This is not the freedom of civil liberties or of political engagement, but freedom from what is perceived as the constraints of organized work, such as bosses and hierarchies, or freedom from parental authority. This project of freedom, coming from the traders themselves, combines well with the rhetoric of salvation promoted by brokers and all the industries associated with retail trading. Yet, rhetoric itself cannot explain this engagement. What helps explain it better is that trading can be effectively rekeyed as an expression used in personal relationships, and thus it becomes part of the strategic arsenal with the help of which moral choices are made within these relationships. One not only plays the markets, but in doing this one can also play against parents or friends or others, or with them. This is not simply about reclassifying trading. It is about rekeying it into a nontransaction.

Money, Discipline, Freedom: Trading and Life Projects

Is there a relationship between a trader's life project and trading? While motivations such as "I decided to trade because I need money" may be heard, rare are the cases in which somebody needs money just for the sake of money. And as we know, money is not fungible—that is, it is put into boxes, labeled, and destined for particular uses (Zelizer 1994). When somebody declares that she needs money, it means in most cases that she needs money for something very specific, for a project, which could be a small, mundane one or a life project. Therefore, it is worth asking what traders need money for from trading, to see whether trading relates in any way to their life projects. (The question remains, though, what a life project could be; I will discuss that below.) This is not trivial, because while it could well be argued that many people need money for different things, trading is not the sole way of earning money, and as I argued before, it is not a very common way. Therefore, we can assume that some, at least, will resort to trading because they see a particular link between it and their projects, or they see their projects as being enabled by trading in ways in which perhaps other activities cannot be.[1]

I will start here with the life projects, and I do not mean by that just earning a (good) living or earning money to afford large or luxury purchases. In the case of trading, such earning is anything but guaranteed. A life project is something meant to redirect one's entire life, not just to secure a (more comfortable) level of income. In fact, the connection between economic activities and life projects was long ago identified and analyzed by Max Weber in *The Protestant Ethic and the Spirit of Capitalism* ([1905] 2011), when he noted that at the dawn of the modern era, accumulation of capital emerged as a life project, in relationship to Protestant ethical precepts. Of interest here (whether or not Weber was right about the Protestant ethic) is that economic activities cannot be seen as simply self-sufficient: if they are about making a living, then that—to be sustainable and not just a transient activity—has to be related to how one's life is lived. Making a living is a moral choice too, not merely a material one. Hence, it has to be related to a life project, in the sense of a reflexive account of what is a "good" life. Such an account might be informed by religious principles or not, but in any case it implies laying out a ranking of values one adheres to. We see this in many cases related to career paths in the professions, for instance, where justifications of somebody's choice to become a doctor or a lawyer are provided not solely in terms of income, but in terms of broader social values.

Extending the same logic to trading, we should expect trading not to be disconnected from projections of what a "good" life is and what sort of values characterize such a life. I have argued earlier that trading competitions need to solve moral issues for the participants to engage in them; in a similar way, trading itself is confronted with moral issues, because it is not an uncontested activity in the public sphere: the long-standing association with gambling (Bernstein 1998), the dubious reputation of some brokerage houses (Fabian 1990), and the debates around day traders have made retail trading less than uncontroversial. These, however, are not the only reasons. Trading is not separate from personal lives, and we shouldn't expect it to be separate from life projects either. Therefore, we would expect traders to be concerned with justifications of their activities and with relating trading activities to their own lives in some way or other. I argued in the previous section that it was impossible, at least for the traders I interviewed, to keep trading and social relationships completely apart.

One way to find out what sort of project informs people's decisions to take up trading would be to ask them directly. In this case, the ethnographer is provided with a narrative of the trader's path into this activity, of the circumstances, forces, and motivations that made her or him spend hours in front of a computer screen when the outcome of the effort is so uncertain. Another way to learn what kind of project makes people engage in trading would be to look at how they present themselves not to the ethnographer, but to other traders, in mundane biographies (Pollner 1987, 88) and in places such as online forums and trading communities. What is relevant in the first place is that in such communities, a large number of traders feel compelled to provide not only a biographical sketch but also a motivation, what made them take up trading and what they hope to achieve by trading. In other words, they state a life project, in relation to what they do, for the benefit of their fellow traders. The reciprocal disclosure of life projects (which is entirely voluntary) can be seen not only as an expression of the need to bring trading into relationship with values, but also as contributing to creating at least the appearance of a community of individuals who share similar life goals. The tendency of traders to share in these ways goes against the logic of a competitive individualism, according to which the sole motivation for an economic exchange can be maximizing (or at least increasing) individual utility.

Public representations of life projects can, of course, be idealized. Sometimes they can be sanitized, in the sense of leaving aside things one does not want to see mentioned. When experiences are idealized, they tend to be presented as polar extremes, being either epiphanies or deal breakers. It is perhaps harder to detect the ways in which experiences are sanitized, except that in this case negative elements such as starting with a loss would be left out of the picture. In talking with traders about their experiences and how these contributed to their life projects, I looked both for inclinations to idealize (positively and negatively) and for the tendency to sanitize, by, for example, repeatedly asking the same question in a different form about how they started trading.

While inclinations to idealize and to sanitize were certainly present in stories of first experiences, such inclinations were by no means dominant. There were no epiphanies, and losses were not hidden at all; quite the contrary. As I learned later, experiencing losses is not seen as a bad thing. (Losses are, but experiencing losses is not. The experience of a loss disciplines the trader.) In all these accounts, mundane events and relationships dominated the story line, and family and friends took center stage more than once. What is more, in all the accounts the sense of agency played a significant role. What I mean is that in their own accounts of how they became traders, my conversation partners emphasized how important the awareness of their own agency was; they stressed repeatedly that they did not see themselves delivered to the whims of external forces, and they thought of themselves as capable of intervening in their own lives.

First experiences in trading could be broadly seen along these motivational lines: money, play, and relationships. It might sound very mundane, but when one asks what made people take up trading, this is what they come up with. A closer look, however, reveals a puzzle here. Why do traders bring all these elements together: money, play, and relationships? One could say that it indicates that electronic finance is neither far from nor isolated from everyday lives. But why do traders talk about money and play and not, say, about dreaming to get rich?

When traders talk about first trading experiences, all these questions come to mind: they are not merely confronted with the question of how to use money, but how to make money into capital, how to use capital, and how to use the money made by capital. All these issues become important, and one would expect that they would resonate in the first experiences of trading.

The decision to go into trading can be articulated as a choice or, as traders put it, as taking a position. On the screen, a position consists in placing a particular type of order (long or short) in a particular security. That order puts the trader in a specific (observational) relationship with other traders: with those who place similar orders, as well as with those who place the opposite orders and with those who place completely different orders. Orders are opinions in action: at this given moment, I go with some people in the matter of X and against some other people in the same matter of X, while some other people will not act on X. In other words, taking positions consists in permanently shifting relational choices; this relational shifting becomes itself a strategic game, because at stake is not a contemplative proof of who is right and who is wrong. At stake is making oneself right by making the opponents wrong.

Taking a position within trading is not the only aspect, though: taking up trading is itself taking a position. Making money into capital is taking a position. As Nadia explained to me, one can simply let money be money, or one can make money into capital, and this is nothing but taking a position in life:

NADIA: Yeah, because like when you have money, what are you supposed to do with it, right? You can let it sit there in cash but not like, even if your, even if you like to let sit, if you let money sit in cash you are basically taking a position, right? You are taking a position that there is no better place to put your money except for in cash, so whatever you do if you have money, then you have to, then, by virtue of having money you have to invest, so yeah, like it's kind of, it's not, well I wanted to say it's a burden, but it's like something you have to think about, where to put your money.

Nadia didn't see money as savings, as the result of hard work, or as a sign of being thrifty. Having money forces you to take positions: if it is not a burden, then it is a constraint. The profit one makes is the reward for alertness, or responding to this call of money (see also McCloskey 2006, 485). Leaving money in cash is a statement of your choices, and the mere availability of the money opens the possibility of using it as capital—that is, taking positions with or against other people who use money as capital. In this discussion we are far from the nineteenth-century understanding of capital as having to do with factories and machine tools, and creating durable class relations. Capital, in this understanding, becomes a resource in a strategic game of shifting relationships. It also becomes a disciplinary means, in the sense that in this account money, understood as capital, forces one: one has to take a position; one cannot just let money be money. Capital itself becomes a life project, then, requiring one to take and shift positions continuously.

At the same time, capital can be rekeyed as play capital. When this happens, the use of capital is laid bare as merely a game, which is played for the kicks:

CHRIS: I started with a book, usually with books, articles and then when I finally had a taste in the trading club loved . . .

TERRY: Sweet taste.

CHRIS: Yes.

TERRY: [laughs]

CHRIS: I understood that I have a thrill for the game. I enjoy this, I look at it as a strategy game and . . .

TERRY: A game of chess.

CHRIS: Yes, exactly and with money in the end, of course. So two main reasons. Thrill of the game and then financial reward.

TERRY: For me it's part and parcel. Yeah. It's a 50–50 situation. The money comes with the game, the game comes with the money, so you just have to balance everything together, for me.

Terry was the president of a student trading club at a university that didn't belong to the first tier, and Chris was his anointed successor. They both had started with demo accounts, and they encouraged club members to do the same. When I talked to them, Terry had graduated to trading with real money, while Chris was still trading demo accounts. According to his own comments, Terry had invested a lot of time in boosting club membership (he had taken it from 5 to 85) as a means of boosting his own prospects to get a banking job. He described himself as a "money hungry person." He was not the only one. Jim, for instance, a trader located thousands of miles away from Terry, described himself in a very similar way: at about the same age, he said, he wanted to live lavishly; hence he got into trading. All these statements seemed to instrumentalize trading: the real prize was a good job in a bank, or at least a job in a bank, or a lot of money. Yet, contrary to what they professed, these individuals were sucked into the game, from which the money was hardly separable. They had incurred losses and continued trading. At times it even seemed that playing the game was more important than making money. One could infer here that incurring losses (as the opposite of making money) was part of the game too. It was imaginable that players would accept losses as a necessary part of staying in the game, not as the price they would have to pay for the game, but as what it meant to be in the game.

At least as important as the money were the "kicks" provided by the game: this point stands in stark contrast with Nadia's seriousness about how money constrains you to become active and manage it. Nadia was talking about real money, though. Chris and Terry traded with play money, having started with a demo trading account. For them, the motivation was related to the kick: to the staged (one could say fabricated) freedom of a demo account. The freedom of trading is staged not only when demo accounts are involved; it is staged because the kicks give the illusion of a rejection of the existing normative order, of a kind of sovereignty of will that only fate can set limits to (Laidlaw 2014, 175). In Chris's and Terry's own words, the game is the money and the money is the game. This staged freedom can be extended from the engagement with a demo account to a life goal, as shown by some of the short biographies that traders post online:

1. Currently living in [city, Europe]. Always fond of financial markets, I found out about FX 1 year ago. Since then, I have read, learnt and demo traded as much as possible. Live trading since 5 months ago. My personal goal is to quit my job and trade for a living in 2 years time.
2. I am a retired [profession]. After 26yrs, I decided a change was in order. I love trading the forex market, though sometimes it seems more of a challenge than I can handle! I grew up in [US state], but have now transplanted to [US state] these last 24 yrs. I now work as a full-time forex trader, and have been trading (mostly learning) approx. 5 years, the last 2years, full time.
3. Just an old man trying to learn to trade to quit his job and be home with family. Show me something I can understand and make work is all I ask.
4. I am a former Engineer and Hope to make a living trading Forex. I hope to be profitable within this Year. I have to be more disciplined.

Or take Jim, the engineering graduate who came from a business family where, in his own words, the importance of creating value had been instilled in him. He wanted to be successful but also to have freedom from annual reviews at work, among other things:

> JIM: I think no I actually do attribute trading to broader life goals because I think trading is one of the few businesses where you could really, truly be free to live anywhere, work from anywhere, work at any time, right? And you could be running a very lean business because all you really need is a computer and an Internet connection, and your software, you know, your tools and all those things, but outside of that you don't need inventory, you don't need a warehouse, you don't need employees, you don't need, you know, any of that stuff, so from a retail trader standpoint I think it's [. . .] I haven't seen another business model that could be as lean and, you know, it could be made [clears throat] as stress free and, you know, sort of not be dependent on location or not be tied down by any place, you know, specifically so I think it has a lot of benefits to it, you know, but you have to have the mind-set to make it your own and really adapt to it and then you know have the confidence to execute it. [. . .] We were always sort of growing up educated on the importance of, you know, doing something, creating value and, you know, having your own business, so it was that was

definitely part of it so but even then I think more than that it was just, you know, the freedom . . . the freedom that I would get to earn the amount of money depending on, you know, me, instead of an organization and annual reviews and, you know, those kind of things, so I felt like I had better control going at it that way than, you know, being in a company, working as an employee.

Jim voices the same theme as Rick: being educated about the importance of creating value, and the tension between this norm and the yearning for freedom. While Rick saw entrepreneurial ideas as being disproved by reality (all life was like buying low and selling high), Jim thinks that these very ideas are at odds with the lack of control over one's own life and that a freedom project (with a small *f*, of course) is preferable to the classic entrepreneurial ideal. At the same time, a freedom project is nothing but a new entrepreneurial ideal, not tied in any way to the constraints of the old one. Ultimately, trading appears as a moral choice across values and ideals and is tied to judgments about their grounded character (or not). Do I value the creation of values more than freedom? How can I anchor my choice in reality? Ultimately, then, trading appears not to be about money.

While electronic trading is like any other business, there is no business like the trading business: it is lean, unencumbered by organizational chores, and one gets to be one's own boss. Which is not to say, of course, that trading is easy or that it doesn't involve work. As conversations unfold, it emerges that trading can involve substantially more effort and time than organization-based work, being at the same time bound with many more uncertainties. Yet, motivations to take up trading are rationalized with respect to freedom and becoming one's own master. This resonates with the perception of trading as a strategic game that pitches one against opponents, instead of integrating participants into organizational hierarchies, making them compete for a job, be accountable to a boss, and so forth. Of course, submission to an organization would be justifiable, in the participants' perception, by making large amounts of money. Like Paul, whom I discussed in chapter 2, Jack does not ultimately want to pursue a "career" and does not see trading as leading to one. The reward of power, in the form of a hedge fund, is not excluded from the equation, though. Otherwise the ultimate goal remains freedom from organized work:

JACK: Yeah . . . yeah. . . . no I am gonna do this [continue trading]. I just, un-
less I get a very good job at a hedge fund I don't see because, the freedom
with this is incredible as well. It's much harder because it's not, if you, like,
what all of the students here do is apply for banks, apply for jobs and you
basically taken by the hand and shown what to do and every job, you have
to go there every morning, you know you are going to arrive there, you
know . . . You've got a boss who can tell you this and that. This is much
harder but if you are successful at this, there is no, I don't think there is
a better job in the world, because there is so much freedom, you are your
own boss, you can do what you want. If you've had a good week in the first
week of the month, you can take the other three weeks off, like, I've got
friends who work for banks in the City, they have two weeks holidays per
year, I mean, that's, I don't really want to do that, I don't, I prefer doing
something else than . . . basically it's kind of being a slave for the first five
years probably working in a bank and . . . I don't think I'll be able to handle as well. Psychologically I would just say no. To hell with that. I am not
for this [laughing].

And yet, there is work and there is work. While many see trading as
an idealized escape from an office job, it can also mean an escape from
a less glamorous job at McDonalds, for instance. Here is Ben, coming
from an overseas lower-middle-class, single-bread-winner family. He has
won a sponsor-funded scholarship at a top tier university, which means
that after graduation he will have to go back and fulfill his contractual
obligations by working a set number of years for his sponsor. Nevertheless, in addition to his engineering degree he takes finance courses, in
the hope of being able someday to work for an investment bank. Money
is tight, and trading appears as an attractive alternative to menial jobs
meant to improve his budget. He started by trading a demo account, but
the move to trading real money opened up new perspectives for him:

BEN: I was very intrigued by the idea of financial freedom so that is one way
where I can reach the state of being financially free. Yah so that's how it
all started, and prior to that I was already interested in how to get more
money other than just by working. Yah 'cause I didn't come from very
rich family background, so I wish . . . need to try to think of ways to save
money based on what I was given my allowance so I want to get off this
cycle. 'cause I . . . that's my main motivation.

Others, like Ron, want to break the mold of expectations set for them by family and friends:

> RON: How old? Around 20, 20 years old [when he started trading]. Yeah. I mean, I mean I know there are . . . I got some friends who started trading at same time as me but only a handful of friends. Most friends just do most usual things some 20 years old students do. They just, they want get some money then can see they just go get a part-time job in a supermarket or whatever then they just do some voluntary work even though it's not for money but for experience or they prepare to do a internship, but for me I was different. I wanted to do trading. I didn't know, I mean, like I said, I think I was kind of influenced by the media or some people and that's why I got into trading. I mean but anyways so I thought I was, that was at the time I really convinced myself that was the future for me. That was, that was something worthwhile for me to do at the time. But my parents thought otherwise, they think I should just do what other normal students do, which, you know, is to get a normal job in a supermarket.

Both Ben and Ron want to be different but without being extraordinary. Trading for them is a means of asserting this difference, which doesn't articulate any specific politics. While we think of other kinds of differences—cultural, sexual, or otherwise—as implying a politics (with a small p), understood as a struggle for legitimating distinctions and positions, trading doesn't need to accomplish this. What kinds of freedom do we have here? There is freedom from organized work; there is freedom from bosses; there is freedom from the pressure to create something of value; there is freedom from the conformity of peers; there is freedom from family expectations; there is freedom to reconfigure one's life. All these freedoms with a small f stand in stark contrast with Nadia's statement—which is by far not singular—that capital constrains one to be permanently active, that it is an obligation and not a freedom. This doesn't mean that trading is a path to freedom. Certainly not. But it means that in all these excerpts, trading helps articulate a paradoxical yearning for "ordinary" freedom that few other activities help articulate. This is not the freedom of grand exploits, of living on the fringes of society, of self-sacrifice, or of a Thoreau-like recluse. It is a "bourgeois" freedom, which doesn't want to sever links with ordinariness: being comfortable and free at the same time of all the constraints related to bourgeois comforts (organized jobs, bosses, conformity, etc.).

And yet, the rhetoric of "freedom," while powerful in representing—and rationalizing—trading motivations, is not the only one at work here. It cannot even function alone, and it cannot work as an immediate promise. Freedom cannot be immediate, and it cannot be easily attained. It needs work, effort, sweating, discipline—all qualities that are not necessarily and not immediately associated with "freedom." And it takes a long time. The project of freedom and discipline go hand in hand, because the attainment of freedom is conditional upon becoming mentally and bodily disciplined: one cannot be realized without the other. In the domain of professional trading, a trader's discipline has been understood as involving control over one's own body, as well as over one's emotions, with the goal of attaining synchronicity with the market (Knorr Cetina 2004; Zaloom 2012). There is another aspect to discipline, though, one that is not geared toward synchronicity, but rather toward renunciation of the world. If one were to hear traders, brokers, coaches, and analysts talk about discipline without knowing what specific activity this discipline was tied to, one would believe that a monastic order was in view. Renunciation of worldly passions is the key to discipline, and discipline as a virtue is the key to freedom. The self is transformed in this process, and only those who have gone through such a transformation can truly appreciate its power. The project of freedom becomes thus a quasi-religious one, characterized—paradoxically—by renouncing the world while remaining firmly anchored in a mundane, comfortable, and bourgeois world:

RICK: I think trading asks for a lot of discipline and I think the most important trait in a trader is to have no emotions when you're trading. Just tell yourself that that money's there, it's lost you know already, just trade it, make money, but don't be attached emotionally to what you're doing.

AP: Okay. Try and describe a bit closer this lack of emotions. What does that mean and how do you develop this?

RICK: It's to try and not care, literally like try and not care. When you put your trade through, imagine that you've already lost the money. That's the thing. You know, so that, you lose the money, you don't get too disappointed. That's what I try to work on. Never take positions which are too big, like when you take a position and you put your stop loss, look at how much money you could lose or make and look . . . would you be annoyed, you know, with that and I think yeah something I read which really stuck in my mind was when you're trading try to trade in order to trade another day, so don't trade and tomorrow you won't be able to trade any more, you know, risk 1% of your portfolio so tomorrow you could be making that percent back again, you know. Don't put yourself in positions where you can lose so much that you'd be angry . . . so yeah that's the discipline aspect. Don't put yourself in positions where you might lose so much that you'd be angry.

For anyone who knows how much continuous care trading involves—managing positions, nurturing them, rolling them over, and so forth—this exhortation not to care seems puzzling. Money put into trading has to be imagined as lost money from the start, as given up, renounced. One is reminded of ascetic practices, of a monkish renunciation of the world as the price of enlightenment, except that in trading the world cannot be renounced at all. Neither bourgeois comforts nor ambitions are renounced in this quest for freedom. Nor does one have to engage with fate outside the comfort of one's room, by paragliding or off-piste snowboarding, for instance. Rick's dream was to become head of trading for a large European bank and then start his own hedge fund—a dream he shared with other young retail traders.

If money put into trading has to be imagined as being lost from the start, then making profit cannot be the ultimate reason why so many tens and hundreds of thousands of ordinary people engage in this activity. Losing money is what it takes to continue the quest for freedom—as the president of a trading club put it, to cure one's "psychological maladies." Trading is a freedom project—an illusory one, but a project nonetheless. What makes it unique, perhaps, is that it provides both engagement with fate and comfort at the same time, in the following sense: if we look at other modes of fateful engagement (extreme sports, professions such as firefighting), these modes require participants to get out of their comfort and enter physical territories of danger. The trading pits of old would belong to these modes: they required physical engagement, physical strength, shoving and pushing around, and bodily dominance of other traders. In electronic finance, where participants are spatially dispersed and coordinate mainly along temporal dimensions, it becomes possible to dissociate bodily presence from fateful engagements. The body is kept comfortable (although there certainly is a degree of physical participation) while the spirit engages with fate. Yet this engagement is tied to a project of freedom that requires renunciation of money. Electronic trading thus seems more like a syncretic domain combining mundane religiosity with fateful actions within bourgeois comfort zones. What it does, perhaps like no other domain, is to press tightly together three distinct activities (spiritual quests, fateful actions, and known comforts) to the point where they become indistinguishable. To invoke Erving Goffman again, it is a triumph of lamination.

Bourgeois Freedoms

I announced in the opening line that this book was about noise in electronic finance. In my understanding of noise, I went native and adopted the prevalent view in finance, which makes a fundamental distinction between informed and uninformed traders (aka noise), equating uninformed traders, more often than not, with retail traders. I did not aim at questioning the conceptual grounds of this distinction and its implications—which is not to say that these grounds cannot be questioned. It is a distinction that can be seen as a foundational myth as well—the finance version of Gods and Mortals. In taking it seriously, I wanted to examine a conceptual problem that I believe is crucial for understanding how financial markets work (especially, but not only, in their electronic format): namely, if markets depend, for their ability to function, on a particular category of traders, then we cannot assume that this category arises spontaneously or randomly. Such an assumption would only reinforce the foundational myth of markets. The entire premise of a market system (with the emphasis on *system*) would be undermined by the assumption that noise is produced in a random manner—that is, that one becomes a trader randomly. That assumption would lead to the conclusion that the opposite category—informed traders—is produced in a random manner too. But we know, sociologically speaking, that what are overwhelmingly considered to be informed traders (institutional ones) are recruited, trained, and employed in a nonrandom fashion. If we know that individuals are made into institutional traders in a systematic fashion—that this transformation is a social, not a random one—what reason do we have to think that individuals are made into retail traders in a random fashion?

If the market system needs noise—understood as a social category, not as a value judgment—what reason do we have to think that fulfilling this need is left to randomness? What starts as a finance puzzle ends as a sociological challenge: namely, investigating the institutional setup (including the technology) within which ordinary people become traders, and traders become institutional traders.

Throughout this book, I have argued that the transformation of ordinary people into traders is not left to chance. This transformation occurs within specific arrangements that have a quasi-formal character and provide an interface between market institutions and institutions pertaining to other domains of social life. What is more, the transformation of traders into institutional, or professional, traders is not left to chance either. It occurs in a systematic, organized manner. Many of the existing ethnographies of finance take traders as a given—that is, as being already there at their trading desks or in the pit at the moment when the ethnographer arrives to start her work. Yet, this does not mean that we should not investigate how traders become what they are, asking: What were their trajectories? How did they come to be professional traders? What were their trading careers before becoming professionals?

I have answered at least some of these questions—especially with regard to how ordinary people become traders and how becoming a retail trader is sometimes a necessary step toward a professional career in finance. However, in composing an ethnography of noise traders, I have also addressed, directly or indirectly, a number of other, interwoven issues pertaining to economic sociology and to the study of the interaction order in online market settings. Having arrived at this point, I will recall them one by one.

The Embeddedness of Transactions

First, there is the issue of the social arrangements that morph people into traders. These arrangements are not purely formal ones, but they are not entirely informal either. They are not simply noneconomic institutions replicating the organizational hierarchies of banks. They are mostly quasi-formal groups. I have shown how group activities play a key role in this social transformation and how these groups, while not being part of the financial institutions themselves, have various links with the latter and are used, at least in some cases, as recruitment grounds for finance professionals. Quasi-formal groups provide linkages across institutions from various social domains: finance and education, for instance, and finance and the institutions of social leisure. However, there are informal group activities—which can take place within the more formal setting of a trade show—that are essential not only with respect to recruitment but also to how trading is legitimated for audiences. Trading competitions are a case in point here. We know a lot about how formality works in markets and in finance organizations (e.g., Stinchcombe 2001). Informality in markets has been seen mostly from the viewpoint of circulating information, organizing, local temporary collaborations, or reinforcing social networks (e.g., Burt 2010). My first argument is that there is a role for something that I call quasi-formality. Quasi-formal groups play a role at least in establishing interinstitutional linkages, without which the transformation I have analyzed in this book would be much more difficult to achieve in a regular fashion. These groups are self-organized, although they can retain some of the basic elements of a formal organizational structure.

My second argument is that (informal and quasi-formal) group activities need to be paid due attention. I follow in this respect Gary Alan Fine's argument that social life takes place in groups—market activities take place in groups too. This goes against the standard model of market exchanges as involving atomistic agents, but the real challenge here is to identify the types of groups (online) financial markets are made of, their activities, and how these activities are consequential with respect to the setup of markets and to transactions. This is part of what this book has aimed to do. With respect to the online character of markets, I have shown that markets are not made solely of electronic transactions. Electronic finance, broadly speaking, is a mix of online and face-to-face interactions, with the latter still playing an essential part. On-screen trading could never work if it were not for the face-to-face group activities in which trading robots are built, moral issues raised by market participation are solved, and ordinary people are transformed into traders, to name but a few.

This brings me to the next issue, whether transactions (in electronic finance especially) are embedded in group activities. The issue of embeddedness has been amply debated in economic sociology, and there have been arguments for and against. More recent arguments against embeddedness (e.g., Krippner and Alvarez 2007) consider that if market transactions are embedded in social relationships, then the latter appear as external to the former and as something different from transactions. Therefore, the argument goes, transactions are social relationships, not merely embedded in relationships. The challenge, I think, is to spell out how transactions are relationships and how these can be different from other types of relationships. How is a market transaction different from friendship, or from acquaintanceship? In other words, what makes it specific and acknowledged by participants as different from other kinds of relationships they engage in? As Harold Garfinkel (2008, 128) puts it, "the cake is constituted in the very act of cutting." Markets are constituted in the act of engaging in transactions, but how are these cut as different from other kinds of relationships, yet not so different that they become unrecognizable or impossible to reground? This is the issue the arguments for and against embeddedness still have to deal with.

I have tried to show how market activities and relationships are very specific but at the same time can be transformed into a different kind of relationships. They can be transformed into family relationships, friendships, collaborations, and so on. Seen from this perspective, the issue is not whether market transactions are embedded in other kinds of social relationships, or whether markets are made of other kinds of social relationships. The issue is how transactions can seemingly effortlessly morph into other types of relationships. At any given time, participants take transactions—at least in electronic finance—for what they are, namely a kind of engagement that is different from other relationships they entertain. Yet, they are able to transform them—with little apparent effort or planning—into family relationships, friendships, collaborations, collegiality, and so forth. The transformation happens on the level of the interaction order. I pointed out already that, in electronic finance at least, a great number of very relevant activities, including trading, take place in quasi-formal groups. Regrounding of activities is a crucial interactional device through which market transactions morph into different kinds of social relationships. I will deal with the issues of keying and regrounding below, when I discuss the interaction order of (electronic) markets. If we wonder how transactions are linked to other types of social relationships, or simply are other types of social relationships, I would say that it's neither the one nor the other. On the level of the interaction order, transactions are effortlessly (that is, without a preset plan) and collaboratively transformed into other kinds of social relationships: they are regrounded.

The Illusion of Competition

Transactions can be regrounded, but are they truly competitive? And if yes, what happens to their competitive character in the process of rekeying? Market competition has been hotly debated, especially in relationship to ideological blueprints for making competition a more general mode of social organization, by extending this principle to education, public services, and other contexts. If we take finance as the pinnacle of markets, what kind of competition do we see there?

I have argued that on the level of the interaction order (again!), a whole series of moral issues have to be solved before participants engage in competitions. Competition is neither a universal state, nor a general feature of social behavior, nor a natural one, nor a permanent one. Competitive engagements, at least of the type witnessed in electronic markets, are carefully organized and bounded. They are arranged to solve particular transactional issues, but not as a permanent mode of market existence. Competitions are staged. At the same time, the trading screen is assembled in such a way as to produce the illusion of competition. I have shown that traders do not actually enter transactions with each other, but with their brokers. They do not compete against each other, except perhaps in Simmel's sense of a competition for favors (from the broker, that is). This is only apparently a (pure) case of competition (Simmel 1992, 324): competitions are always judged by the public, not by somebody who is at the same time provider of a service, counterparty, and judge. Seen from this perspective, this transactional arrangement has a real and serious conflict of interests at its core, which is far from being a competitive one.

Is the illusion of competition necessary? The illusion of competition is intrinsic to the world of the market: uncertainties there are not natural, but created. And uncertainties revolve around social attributes and values. What is resilience? What is discipline? How can we see them? How can we see who is resilient or not, and how many are disciplined? These are issues pertaining to engagement in fateful actions, and to the understanding of trading as a kind of fateful action. Therefore, to maintain this understanding, the illusion of competition has to be there. Even though, since late 2010, brokerages, at least in the United States, have had to inform their clients that they (the brokerages) are the counterparties to their own clients' transactions, we have not seen a redesign of the trading screen to reflect this. The screen continues to create the illusion that retail traders compete against each other and that the world of the market is made of competitive engagements.

Freedom Projects

I have discussed the argument that traders engage in transactions to provide liquidity to markets (cause and effect are reversed here) and the argument that they trade to make money (a viewpoint plagued by similar logical problems). When engaging in transactions, traders seek to solve particular moral issues revolving around social values, among which freedom is paramount. What does it mean to be free? In what situations? For how long? What does it mean to be able to decide? To demonstrate agency? The issues about social values are serious moral issues, and they cannot be solved based on general perorations and exhortations. Furthermore, they cannot be solved once and for all. These issues are situationally bound. They rise again and again, and they need to be attended to again and again. Discourse alone cannot provide a solution to these issues, and no solution can be eternal. To expand on Garfinkel's phrase, the cake is constituted in the act of cutting, not in the act of talking about cutting. Moreover, issues such as freedom need to be made visible and accessible to participants via action. That is, particular types of social activities are organized around actions that make freedom into a practical problem, visible to participants. Following Goffman, sports (and in our days perhaps extreme sports more than anything else) make issues of freedom and agency visible, provide temporary solutions, and allow the vicarious participation of the public. Trading is another preeminent domain that, I have argued, allows direct and vicarious engagement with issues of freedom and agency while doing two things at once: (1) it preserves the comfort zone of participants, and (2) it separates, in the engagement with the issue, mind and body. If a sport such as off-piste snowboarding cannot be exercised from the comfort of one's home, trading can. If off-piste snowboarding requires full, long-term engagement of the body (hours and hours of training, travel, etc.) and of the mind (attention, good coordination, good balance), trading doesn't. It separates mind and body and requires different modi operandi of engagement (while the body sits for hours, the mind must be active). This way of separating mind and body is common to many religious experiences, which frame it as a way of attaining freedom. But many religious experiences prescribe retreating from the world; trading remains firmly anchored in it.

All in all, we can distinguish—broadly speaking—at least two domains of action dealing with the practical problem of freedom: sports, which (perhaps with the exception of chess) do not separate body and mind and do engage participants in the world; and religious experiences, which in many cases separate body and mind (in the way they are treated, that is) and require retreating from the world. I would argue here that trading is a combination of the two: it engages participants in the world and with the world, but doesn't take them out of their comfort, and separates body and mind. In other words, trading is a bourgeois mode of handling moral issues of freedom.

The fact that, from the viewpoint of participants, trading isn't primarily about "making money" explains at least three apparently paradoxical facts: First, that traders continue trading even if they know that they are not "making money" and even when they know the statistics revealing how few of them are making a consistent profit. Second, the success of the spiritual-religious rhetoric employed by brokers and commercial providers, who do not promise riches but promise redemption and freedom. Money (when and if it is gained) is a means toward freedom, not a goal in itself. Third, the insistence of so many traders (both retail and professionals) on discipline, an insistence that, in its vocabulary, stresses spiritual and mental aspects such as renunciation of worldly possessions like money (every time a trader puts money into trading, he has to treat it as lost money).

Seen from this perspective, retail trading appears as an industry selling opportunities to participate in collective, temporary solutions to moral issues related to individual freedom. In a manner similar to that of the medieval commerce with absolutions, or to the nineteenth-century emigration industries that brought immigrants to promised lands of freedom, electronic trading sells opportunities to engage in searches for temporary solutions to these issues. While this industry arguably isn't the only one that engages in such selling, it does so in a unique way, in the sense that it sells opportunities that both are "bourgeois" (in the sense of comfortable) and allow direct and vicarious engagement at the same time, in one and the same strip of action.

However, it is also an industry that plays a significant part in the reproduction of the financial market system—to use Fischer Black's term.

It does so in at least three respects. First, it transforms ordinary people into traders, some of whom will become professional traders. If we were to imagine an alternative, how would ordinary people be transformed straight into professional traders? How could this work in a systematic fashion, taking into account that the professional lives of institutional traders span about 10 years, as several have told me? What would be the ratio of transformation time to active time as a trader? How would such a process be repeated in time? The retail trading industry provides a solution to all these problems, which, in its absence, would be much more difficult to solve, if not impossible. Student trading clubs are a major recruiting ground for the trading desks of banks, and such clubs are a significant arrangement through which ordinary young people morph into traders.

Second, the financial services industry is one where jobs are not forever. At the same time, the numbers of professional traders are limited, even though the industry has grown significantly over the past two decades. How can the surplus of professional traders be dealt with? The retail industry integrates at least part of this surplus, and by doing so contributes to the reproduction of the financial system.

Third, retail trading contributes to legitimating finance. It does so not primarily by making arcane activities accessible to particular publics (by disenchanting them); above all, it sells opportunities to participate in quests for freedom. By extension, if retail trading sells such opportunities, which are not only legitimate but also sought after, finance gains practical legitimacy. The paradox here is that a domain of activity so often castigated in the media for its lack of morality gains its legitimacy at least in part by offering opportunities for individual moral quests, no matter how illusory these opportunities may be in the end. So is noise necessary for the financial system, as Fischer Black has argued? Yes, and in more than one respect: Gods depend on Mortals, and not the other way around.

The Interaction Order of Electronic Markets

I have repeatedly argued that online interactions are not quite like face-to-face interactions and that online markets are actually very rich in interactions, both off-line and online. These interactions can be keyed in various modes, including, but not limited to, the "serious" mode of trading. Rekeyings and stagings (or fabrications) occur all the time. The notion of synthetic situation, which attempts to capture specific features of the interaction order in online environments, has to be expanded by taking these aspects into account.

While in physical environments spatial copresence shapes the situation, in electronic environments such as markets, temporal copresence defines the situation. The distinction between the two types of situations raises at least two questions. First, to what types of interactions do synthetic situations conduce? Second, what kinds of relationships (if any) are emerging out of such interactions? This is directly relevant to the issue of embeddedness discussed earlier, not least because more and more transactions are conducted nowadays in electronic format.

If we look at interactions not only from the viewpoint of reciprocal orientation (spatial or temporal), but also from the viewpoint of the mode or format in which they unfold, then the following can be said: the major, "serious" format of action isn't all there is to interactions in synthetic situations. Rekeyings routinely occur, and fabrications can be encountered too. A trading session can be staged as the rekeying of observation in a ritualized format, for instance. Processes of rekeying and fabricating modify some significant components of reciprocal temporal orientation, such as coordination. Participants are not necessarily required to coordinate with each other. They can be summoned to adopt, literally speaking, the vision of a single person. This makes room for raising claims of unequal (cognitive) powers among participants, in contrast to the assumption of equality inherent in the notion of temporal coordination. I say this because online markets are not devoid of inequalities, or of claims to status and power. If we want to understand how these claims are achieved in a medium without a long history or memory, we need to consider all the richness and depth of synthetic interactions.

Erving Goffman saw activities in Western societies as employing six basic keys: the "serious" one, rituals, contests, make-believes, technical redoings, and regroundings. Of them, he considered the last to be "conceptually the most troublesome of the lot" (1974, 48, 74). Regroundings (as a particular mode of rekeying) are transpositions of an activity in terms of a different domain—such as when transactions in markets are used to express attitudes toward family members and reshape family relationships. I would argue that we need to pay close attention to such "troublesome" regroundings, since they seem central to how market transactions connect to social life.

We have a long-established idea in economic sociology that market transactions are made of relationships and that markets are networks of relationships (e.g., Burt 2010; White 1992, 2003). Following this logic, electronic markets, where transactions take place online, would be made of networks of relationships too. This, however, is more difficult to establish empirically, especially in retail trading. We do not seem to have here the kind of networks we encounter in production markets, for instance. One way of getting out of this conundrum would be to argue that finance is a different type of market, an interface market (White 2003). Yet, the issue remains and is a basic one: what kind of relationships do we see in electronic markets? Following in the steps of previous ethnographies, I have shown that electronic finance is not devoid of relationships. However, the relationships we see in electronic finance are not like those known from the old trading floor. In many instances, parties do not know each other very well, in the way traders on the floor did. They do not know their habits, ticks, ways of judgment, and families, and they do not stand under constraints provided by the workplace (aka the floor) or by institutions. Often, traders do not even know other traders' real names. Yet, they enter relationships with each other, for instance when they build groups. (At the same time, the trading screen maintains the appearance of relationality as a fundamental requirement.) These relationships are not close, but they are not necessarily similar to loose face-to-face relationships or acquaintanceship either (what we call weak ties—see Granovetter 1983). What makes them special? The approach I have followed here is to consider relationships from the viewpoint of the interactions within which they are enacted, and examine how the relationships are endowed with particular features by these interactions. Ultimately, any kind of relationship is determined by its interaction formats—by definition, we cannot conceive of relationships without interactions. The characteristics of relationships and the properties of the interaction formats in which they occur are interlinked. This is not to say that the latter strictly determine the former. As we know, face-to-face formats produce more than one type of relationships. Yet, when physical copresence is excised from the interaction format of markets, what elements of this format produce relationships? And more importantly, what do relationships achieve with respect to the primary activity of participants, namely trading?

Hence, instead of trying to categorize relationships according to strength metrics, I have analyzed them through the prism of their relevance with respect to trading—that is, of their consequentiality. I have also analyzed them through the prism of their main vehicle—namely, interactions. Relationships are created, maintained, and reproduced in interaction. I have distinguished throughout the book between relationality and relationships. While I understand relationality as an orientation to other market participants, relationships occur when engagement signals are sent and reciprocated by participants, irrespective of the frequency and duration of such signals. Relationships are shaped in and through communication. The difference between relationality and relationships is as follows: relationality requires response presence—that is, the capability, attunement, and readiness to send and receive signals. Relationships require not only response presence, but actual responses—that is, signs that activity-relevant ties are acknowledged as such and reciprocated by participants. While relationality is diffuse, relationships are concrete, in the sense that participants acknowledge each other's coparticipation through signals that are intrinsic to the tie and relevant for the activity at hand.

In face-to-face situations, relationality is anchored in physical copresence and reciprocal orientation supported by "readiness" signals, which can be positive or negative (Goffman 1966, 83–84). These signals preselect coparticipants in relationships—at a party, for instance, we signal through glances and smiles the individuals we would like to engage in a conversation with, while we avoid making eye contact with other people. At a party, tie-making is one of the main activities, if not the main activity. In markets, it is trading. Electronic markets are a mix of face-to-face and synthetic situations. These situations can overlap or succeed each other. They can be encased into one another (see also Luff et al. 2003). A bout of screen trading can be encased in a trading competition in front of a live audience. A face-to-face debate about how to code a robot can be encased in a bout of on-screen trading. Encasement designates here the link between concurrent and overlapping situations, with respect to the ultimate goal of the activity at hand. Encasement can facilitate rekeying of the relevant activity, or it can provide a substantial ingredient for that rekeying (such as the audience of the trading show). Encasement is not mere lamination (Goffman 1974, 182) but implies an order of relevance as well.

One consequence of this is that relationality and relationships can coexist in encased situations, in the same strip of trading. At a party, for instance, once we have entered a tie, we send around signals of unavailability for other possibly concurrent ties. We do not concomitantly have two independent conversations, and we can easily imagine how, at a party, concomitantly flirting with two or more different persons would be received. Active relationships restrict relationality. In electronic finance, having an ongoing chat about on-screen observations (a relationship with other traders) does not restrict relationality, understood as the attunement and the readiness to enter transactions. Relationships orient relationality but do not restrict it.

At parties, making ties is one of the main relevant activities. In trading, making ties is subordinated to a trading-relevant activity, whether it is building pools of experience or monitoring trading reputations. Yet, such trading-relevant activities are neither unspecified (like "doing business with each other") nor transactional. They are trading-relevant social activities. Relationships in electronic trading are there not to directly support or to enable transactions (along the lines of "I know you, you know me, hence we trade with each other"). They are there to organize social activities without which transactions could not take place. Take away common pools of experience organized around group relationships. Now imagine transactions taking place without them.

In trading pits, relationships were organized in networks, and transactions were conducted along ties. In electronic finance, relationships are organized in groups. This difference in organization is due to the social, not the economic nature of the ties. In electronic finance, a tie is not a pipe. In electronic finance, a tie is not a scope through which we observe other players and their ties (Podolny 2001). In electronic finance, ties organize the social activities out of which transactions are made. I have argued above that trading, at least in the retail sector, can be seen as searches for collective answers to issues relevant to individual freedom. Ties organize these searches.

If we are to compare the kind of ties present in face-to-face markets with those of electronic finance, the following come to the fore: (1) multiple keyings and fabrications are present here too; (2) in electronic markets, ties are a mix of often encased face-to-face and synthetic interactions; (3) in electronic markets, relationships do not restrict relationality; (4) relationships organize the social activities out of which trading is constituted; (5) relationships form groups rather than networks; (6) relationships are neither pipes nor scopes. If I were to add to the metaphorical toolbox presented here (coming from plumbing and optics, respectively), I would say that relationships are beams. They cast the cone of light within which participants search for solutions to their issues of freedom. Of course, the solutions they (temporarily) might find depend on how this cone of light is cast, and various beams of light might reveal various solutions.

I started with the sociological translation of a finance puzzle. Admittedly, I have taken something that can be read as a foundation myth in finance and reworked it into a puzzle. I have analyzed the interactional arrangements that support electronic markets and have suggested that some answers to the question "How are market transactions social relationships?" can be found by paying close attention to the interaction order of markets. In this process, I have relied heavily on insights from Erving Goffman, and I have tried to bring some of his notions a step further. More often than not, sociological analyses of markets tend to fall into one of two categories, broadly speaking: (1) investigations of how market institutions and transactions are enabled or made out of social relationships or processes and (2) investigations of how market transactions are actually something else—another kind of social activity made to unfold in the form of a transaction. In the first case, the distinction between the social and the economic is maintained—market transactions remain allocation processes influenced or shaped by social elements (power, relationships, beliefs, and the like). We can call this the structuralist approach, since transactions are supported by a social structure around them. In the second case, market transactions are not necessarily taken prima facie. Their allocative character is not taken for granted (and decidedly not taken for granted as the ultimate aim of this activity), even though they involve, of course, the exchange of money. At the same time, we need to go beyond a position such as "market transactions are allocations, as well as something else." First we need to specify what this "something else" is. Second, we need to specify the relationship between the two. Are allocations as outcomes of transactions a means of expressing something else? An unintended outcome, but not an expression of this something else? An (un)desirable outcome? We can call this a culturalist approach, since it involves expressing a social activity as another type of activity—in a word, rekeying it.

This book falls into the second category: I have argued that market transactions, at least in the retail sector of finance, are not mere allocations. They are—paradoxically, perhaps—collective searches related to specific moral issues. In capitalist societies, such searches are privatized and taken over by particular industries (sports, finance, and gambling are perhaps the most prominent, but not necessarily the only ones), which extract a price for providing search opportunities. Within finance, there are desirable additional effects, such as recruitment of professional traders or absorption of redundant traders. Ultimately, though, what we face here are necessary cultural explorations (necessary from the viewpoint of the human condition) regimented into an industry of hope.

Acknowledgments

A t the closing of this book, after having put my arguments and evidence before the judgment of readers, I will resort to what is a central convention of academic writing and yet much more than that: acknowledging my debt to the individuals and institutions who have offered support, in intellectual, moral, and material forms.

Acknowledgments are rarely seen in works of fiction, where the writer asserts creative force. We could think the creative voice is rarely subject to outside forces and constraints. We know, of course, that this is not true; still, the frequent absence of this convention from fiction writing contributes to positioning the author toward her audiences as concerned exclusively with the story she has to tell, not with how the story came to take shape.

Acknowledgments cannot tell the entire story of how a book came into being. They are not a book about the writing of a particular book. They have to present in condensed form the cast of the main characters who took part in the laborious process of conducting, presenting, discussing, and shaping research into the form of a book. Acknowledgments are not mere recountings of past help but thickened dramas about writing an academic book. In saying this, I am developing one more time on insights gained from Erving Goffman's work (1974, 508), namely that accounts of past processes can be seen as dramas rather than as stories.

It is perhaps the case that fiction writing so often lacks acknowledgments because fiction authors have to focus on the drama they wish to tell. To do this, they abstain from dramatic tellings of how they came to tell a particular drama. Dramatic, even if shortened, tellings of how an ethnographic book comes into being can be seen as having a certain paraethnographic quality: they point to the fact that what is often seen as the individualized enterprise of the ethnographer is actually much more than that. It is a web of relationships, both institutional and individual.

My own ethnographic enterprise would not have been possible without the funding support of the Economic and Social Research Council UK (Technology, Action, and Cognition in Online Anonymous Markets, RES 062-23-1204) and the European Research Council (Evaluation Practices in Financial Management, 291733). I have greatly benefited from the encouragement and the support of my colleagues and friends in the Department of Sociology at the University of Edinburgh and the Department of Management at King's College London.

During an extended stay in the Department of Sociology at the University of Chicago in the fall of 2009, I expanded the scope of my research in a way that ultimately led to this book. I finished work on the copyedited manuscript during a second extended stay, in the winter of 2016. I have thoroughly enjoyed the peerless resources of that department and the university, exchanges with many colleagues, friends, and students at both the University of Chicago and Northwestern University, and being in a city I love.

Karin Knorr Cetina and Donald MacKenzie are wonderful friends and colleagues. I have been in their intellectual and moral debt for many, many years. Not only that: their unwavering support and encouragement, interest in my research, and trust are, in no small measure, echoed in this book too.

Since I joined King's College London, Christian Heath has solidly supported my ethnographic enterprise. The meetings of the Work, Interactions and Technology group and the discussions with Jon Hindmarsh, Paul Luff, and Dirk vom Lehn have been occasions of great intellectual and personal satisfaction.

A special thank you to Charles Smith, who has talked to me about trading on several occasions and has helped me with my research in manifold ways. A special thank you to Steven Kahl, too, who has helped with my field access.

Karin Knorr Cetina, Donald MacKenzie, Gary Alan Fine, John Levi Martin, Christian Heath, Hendrik Vollmer, Juan Pablo Pardo-Guerra, Leon Wansleben, Aaron Pitluck, and Christian Borch have carefully, critically, and challengingly read and commented upon many chapters of this book. I have tried to answer their intellectual summons as well as I can. My heartfelt thanks to all of them.

I am particularly grateful to all the participants in the "Money, Markets, and Governance" and the "Social Theory and Evidence" workshops in the Department of Sociology at the University of Chicago, and in the "Ethnography Workshop" in the Department of Sociology at Northwestern University, who have critically and productively engaged with several chapters of the book.

Many times, I have discussed the travails of ethnographic writing with my friends Zsuzsanna Vargha, Hendrik Vollmer, Jens Lachmund, Juan Pablo Pardo-Guerra, Leon Wansleben, and Christian Borch. More often than not, they had to put up with my sometimes obsessive insistence on writing. Most probably, this is not going to stop.

I had quite a few productive debates about the mechanics and profitability of trading with my students Roland Gemayel and Demetrios Zamboglou. Their comments and insights have significantly helped advance my ideas.

Doug Mitchell, my editor at the University of Chicago Press, has been, one more time, of invaluable help and support. Doug has the most impressive editorial eye I have ever seen, impressive skills at finding and enlisting extraordinarily knowledgeable reviewers, and the sharpest sense of what makes an ethnography. It is not for nothing that the attribute "legendary" is regularly associated with his name.

This being said, my deep gratitude goes to the two anonymous reviewers who provided precise, significant criticism and comments. I hope that I have been able to respond adequately.

Over the years, I have presented aspects of my research to various academic audiences, in the United States, the United Kingdom, and Continental Europe. The comments I have received from them have helped shape arguments in this book in more than one way.

Last, but by far not least, I could not have written this book without the readiness of traders, brokers, software programmers, salespersons, and analysts to talk to me about their activities in electronic finance and to let me observe what they are doing. I thank them all for their support. I have to single out some, though. Donna and EJ started it all: thank you. Thank you to Andrea, David, and Joan. Thank you, in memoriam, to Freddie Schada.

Notes

Introduction

1. Informed traders are also defined in finance as "those whose actions show that they hold valuable short term price information" (Fishe and Smith 2012, 330), or those who possess "signal." Some questions arise: Isn't such a definition a circular one? What actions are implied, and what do these actions show? Empirically, studies take an informed trader to be one who makes profitable trades more than 50% of the time. However, traders can make small profits 50% of the time or more and then engage in one disastrous trade that wipes out their capital. I discuss such situations in this book. Behavioral finance studies dealing with retail traders consider that "being informed" is affected by cognitive biases that in the end would neutralize or even affect negatively any ability to predict prices (e.g., Barber and Odean 2008, 2000; Odean 1999, 1998a, 1998b).

2. As one would expect, finance is not the only area of the (social) sciences where the notion of noise plays a significant conceptual role. In the applied sciences, domains such as signal engineering approach noise either as being random and unpredictable occurrences, or as unwanted modifications of a signal. Sound studies, as a subdomain of science and technology studies, investigate noise as the opposite (and the complement) of sonority—that is, as apparently unorganized auditory perceptions (e.g., Mattern and Salmon 2008, 139). Sonority, by opposition, is organized materially, socially, and culturally. In some instances, however, the notion of noise is contrasted not only with sonority, but with silence as well, based on the premise that all auditory perceptions are organized, while the format of this organization differs (e.g., Pinch and Bijsterveld 2004, 636; Attali 1985, 24). The cultural distinctions including noise are thus multiple: it is contrasted with information, signal, sonority, and silence, to name but a few. In the present context, I focus on a single particular meaning of noise, which relates directly to finance: namely, being less informed, less skilled, less knowledgeable as a trader.

3. More recently, the distinction between informed and noise traders has been refined by including a further category, uninformed traders. These are traders who lose money in trading, whereas noise traders are those who "trade completely at random" (Fishe and Smith 2012, 336). The consistency of such a typology is questionable, since one category is defined according to action outcomes, while the other is defined according to lack of patterns in action. The view of human behavior as being completely random raises issues in itself as well. The purely formal distinction between informed, uninformed, and noise traders is encountered in explanations of financial contagion: uninformed traders imitate the informed ones, and noise traders imitate the uninformed traders (Bloomfield, O'Hara, and Saar 2009). See also, for instance, Froot, Scharfstein, and Stein 1992, 1464; Kalay and Wohl 2009, 30; Nishide 2009, 298.

4. I am grateful to John Levi Martin for pointing this out to me.

5. See, for instance, the work done by scholars such as Christena Nippert-Eng (1996) and Arlie Hochschild (1997) on the relationship between work and social life.

6. For more than 15 years now, the behavioral finance literature has provided empirical evidence that retail traders are not consistently making any money (e.g., Barber and Odean 2000, 2004; Odean 1998b; Chen et al. 2007). Letters and documents sent to the Securities and Exchange Commission provide evidence as well, stating that on average "100% of a retail customer's investment is lost in less than 12 months" in forex retail (Philadelphia Financial Management 2011, 1). A study conducted by the North American Securities Administrators Association in 1997 on a sample of 8,000 trades concluded that 70% of the analyzed retail traders' accounts were not profitable (McEachern 1999, 74). Official documents in Europe acknowledge that a majority of retail forex traders lose money (Maitra 2014, 9). Discussion forums among retail traders document awareness of this situation. A study conducted on the transactions of a population of more than 95,000 foreign exchange retail traders between January 2010 and June 2012 found that the median trade loss was $5.56 each active day (Hayley and Marsh 2015, 10). The average daily loss for traders active for between 10 and 25 days is $11.43 over the first 10 days, but it rises to an average of $32.81 for trades between the eleventh day and the final day of the period studied (21). A trader with 100 days of active trading experience is only 5.8% less likely to have a winning month than a complete novice, a fact suggesting that experience does not improve the trading record (7). Finally, together with two PhD students, I took a closer look at data from two trading platforms as well. One platform had more than 77,000 active traders (Gemayel 2016). The other platform had more than 17,000 traders (Zamboglou 2016). In the first population, only 1.31% of traders were making profit on at least 50% of their trades (Gemayel 2016, 165). In the other trading population, only 21.72% of the traders had winning trades. The daily average loss per trader was $241.87. The probability that a trader would be

profitable in one day was only 14.19% (Zamboglou 2016). While forex traders cannot be taken as representative for all kinds of markets (e.g., stocks, exchange traded funds [ETFs], derivatives), consistent results across these populations indicate that at least in foreign exchange—the most liquid markets in the world— the proportion of traders who win consistently is very low. There is little reason to believe that the ratio is higher in other types of markets.

7. It is interesting to note here that in other areas of economics, the concepts of signal and information are not introduced in opposition to noise, but in opposition to deception (e.g., Spence 1976; Akerloff 1970). In the vocabulary of broker dealers, signal is understood as an action prescription deemed to influence the decisions of traders (e.g., "buy $EUR@1.3583$"), a prescription that can take the form either of a previous trade or of an explicit recommendation. Noise consists in utterances or displays of trading activity considered to be lacking the capacity to influence the decisions of other traders. This of course raises the immediate question, Where does that capacity come from?

8. Besides the pioneering studies of Terrance Odean and Brad Barber (Odean 1998a, 1998b, 1999; Barber and Odean 2000, 2004, 2008), see also Nolte and Nolte 2012; Nolte and Voev 2011; Neumann, Paul, and Doering 2014; Pan, Altshuler, and Pentland 2012; Merli and Roger 2013.

9. See, for instance, Lo and Repin 2002; Lo, Repin, and Steenbarger 2005; Abreu and Mendes 2012; Adam et al. 2011; Füllbrunn, Rau, and Weitzel 2013; Chang, Solomon, and Westerfield 2016.

10. E.g., Heath, Luff, and Jirotka 1994; Beunza and Stark 2004; Zaloom 2005; MacKenzie 2011; Ho 2009; Knorr Cetina and Bruegger 2002, Lépinay 2011.

11. I use the concept of affordance to designate the match between the opportunities for action offered by trading technologies, financial institutions, and instruments, on the one hand, and the actors' possibilities of taking up such opportunities, on the other hand. For instance, if friends offer me the first option to buy their house, this is an opportunity. However, I also need to be able to take up the opportunity—for instance, I need to have enough funds, obtain a mortgage, and so forth. The match between opportunity and possibility is an affordance. Thus I depart in the use of the concept from its established meaning in science and technology studies, where it designates the enabling as well as the constraining features of technologies in relationship to their users (Hutchby 2001, 450). In this latter perspective, technologies are not empty vessels filled with social interpretations, but rather constraints and enablers with respect to a range of possible actions. The notion of affordance attempts thus to provide a middle ground between determinism and constructivism (Hutchby 2003, 581). In the way I use the notion of affordance, I focus more on access to action: how can particular types of actors take up opportunities for action, given what they can do? Conversely, how are such opportunities tailored to fit existing possibilities?

12. I interviewed 62 retail traders, the majority of whom were located in the

United States and the United Kingdom. Only 2 traders were located in eastern Europe. Their ages were (at the time of the interviews) between 20 and 70. The majority of them were male; only 4 were women. The gender ratio is a bit lower than that of the trading populations, from the quantitative data sets I had access to, where 8% are women. All the interviewed persons had college degrees. I interviewed seven brokers, based in London, New York, and Chicago. I attended seven trade shows in the United Kingdom and the United States and seven professional conferences of the trading industry in the United Kingdom and the United States. I did 60 hours of direct observation and recording of trading. I spent one year observing a student trading club in the United Kingdom and three months each with two other student clubs. I spent three months observing another (nonstudent) trading club, in the United Kingdom as well. I traded myself on two different platforms: once over a three-month period, and once over a two-week period. Over one year, I observed and participated in the chats of a trading group based across the Midwest and central Canada. I also participated for more than one year in the communications on a social trading platform that at that time had grown to 22,000 participants, of whom more than 6,700 were active traders (that is, they executed at least one transaction per week).

13. See, among others, Sade-Beck 2004; Wilson and Peterson 2002; Boellstorff et al. 2012; Kozinets 2009.

Chapter One

1. See, for instance, the *Toronto Star*, September 19, 2009, U04; February 11, 2009, B04; August 2, 2008, B01; *Investors Chronicle* (London), March 7, 2008, sec. 0261-3115; the *West Australian* (Perth), July 11, 2009, G04; the *Daily Telegraph* (London), July 18, 2009, 3; the *Straights Times* (Singapore), May 8, 2008; the *Sun Herald* (Sydney, Australia), July 24, 2008; the *Africa News*, March 8, 2008. The fact that newspapers from different parts of the world have devoted space (repeatedly sometimes) to this issue points not only toward the globalization of the media, but also to a phenomenon that was not an isolated one. Most of the stories cited were about local residents.

2. *Affordances*, in the sense in which I use the term, are defined in note 11 to the introduction.

3. US Department of Commerce, Current Population Reports Series P-60 No. 35, January 5, 1961, 1.

4. Discount brokerages (with varying reputations) have existed at least since the 1880s, when they were known as bucket shops (see Hochfelder 2006; Fabian 1990). They offered lower commission rates, had few or no advisory services, and targeted a less well-to-do clientele.

5. Odd lots had been traded on the American Stock Exchange since at least the 1920s. Established exchanges such as the New York Stock Exchange did not accept odd lots, making trading more expensive and out of reach for investors of smaller means.

6. Globex is the first electronic trading futures platform, introduced in 1992 by the Chicago Mercantile Exchange.

7. An alternative organizational format that discount brokers experimented with in the late 1990s was to open retail trading offices, where customers could come in and trade from the brokerage's own terminals ("ProTrader Targets Buy Side" 2001, 60). A disadvantage was that customers had to come in daily and spend most of the day there.

8. In the early years of the 2000s, some online brokers advertised their retail trading technology as better than that available to institutional traders ("Pro-Trader Targets Buy Side" 2001, 60).

9. Contracts for difference and spread betting are not available in the United States.

10. Investment Company Institute, https://www.ici.org/research/stats/etf/etfs_01_16, accessed March 15, 2016.

11. The definition of income derived from spread betting as tax free has not received any attention at all, although the notion that income derived from chance should not be taxed is worthy of analysis.

12. The types of registrable—and hence legitimate—counterparties has multiplied to include retail foreign exchange dealers, futures commission merchants, introducing brokers, commodity trading advisers, and commodity pool operators. This development is indicative of the differentiation and complexity of the institutional structure catering to retail traders within foreign exchange.

13. The organization of retail brokerages is a complex matter. Some are licensed to operate in regulated jurisdictions and some are not. Brokerages can be incorporated in a tax jurisdiction different from the one where the offices are based, with a workforce distributed around the world (programmers and administration workers can be in totally different locations), and with the technology (aka servers) in a location different from that of the offices. Brokerages that operate in regulated jurisdictions have business ties with those that operate in non-regulated jurisdictions simply because they trade with one another as well. As a rule, brokerages trade among themselves to offset the risk of their clients.

14. This number was arrived at by using the Business Premier and EconLit databases.

15. In Chinese financial markets, though, individual participation in trading is substantial. Data from the Shanghai Stock Exchange indicate that in 2013 there were 114,440,000 trading accounts, but only 111 registered brokerages (Shanghai Stock Exchange 2014, 232, 240).

Chapter Two

1. There is a growing number of graduate programs in mathematical finance, statistics, or asset pricing, for instance, from which traders and trading-related analysts are recruited. Traders, however, are not exclusively recruited from such programs. Becoming a professional trader means on-the-job training and certification. In the United States, this means passing a series of exams (among others, the 55, 56, 57 series exams) leading to a Financial Industry Regulatory Authority (FINRA) license. In the United Kingdom, the process is very similar, including examinations with the Chartered Institute for Securities and Investment (CISI), the Chartered Financial Analysts (CFA) Society and registration with the Financial Conduct Authority (FCA). These examinations are required for traders operating with fiduciary funds (that is, belonging to third parties), but not for traders operating with their own funds.

2. I am following here Erving Goffman's concept of key as "a set of conventions by which a given activity, one already meaningful in terms of some primary framework, is transformed into something patterned on this activity but seen by participants to be something quite else" (1974, 43–44). Goffman's analogy with music is explicit: in the same way in which a melodic line can be written in a major or in a minor key (or mode), an activity can be deployed by participants in a major key ("seriously, now") or a minor one ("we are only pretending"). Social activities can be transposed across keys, and when the transposition concerns the activity as a whole, it has to be carefully bounded (a dress rehearsal is made explicit by participants, for instance). However, social activities can contain contiguous strips of action that are keyed differently from each other. Throughout this book, I emphasize that trading in electronic markets can be deployed simultaneously in different keys and that one aspect of this deployment is that the boundaries between keys can be blurred.

3. ISAs, or individual savings accounts (in the United Kingdom), are tax free up to a specific amount. They can include cash, as well as shares.

Chapter Three

1. The concept of competition can be seen as encompassing several formats, including rivalries, contests, and scrambles (see also Werron 2015, 191). I examine in this chapter only contests, understood as public displays of concurrent practical crafts (of trading, in this case) subjected to joint evaluations by participants.

2. In economic theory, competition is defined in behavioral terms, as "rivalry between individuals, or groups, or nations" (Vickers 1995, 3). Real competition

is thus a process of rivalry, while perfect competition is a "state of equilibrium in which well informed agents treat prices parametrically" (7). One could argue that the definition of "real competition" requires sociological specification, since rivalry itself is a social process.

3. For Erving Goffman, contests are one of the "basic keys employed in our society" (1974, 48, 56–57). Yet, contests themselves can be keyed differently, and my argument here is that the transposition of competitive engagements across different keys is a significant arrangement for solving the moral issues related to competitions. The latter appear neither as natural nor as self-evident to participants. They appear to involve serious issues that need to be solved before engagement is deemed acceptable. Rekeying is a major way of solving such issues.

4. For an overview of how the concept of competition has evolved within economic thought, see Morgan 1993.

5. Clifford Geertz makes a similar argument about contests, saying they produce both social values and glosses thereupon (1977, 449).

Chapter Four

1. In some trading pits at least, transactions are conducted in both modes simultaneously. While some traders still shout out bids and offers at each other, others, adjacent to them, conduct transactions on portable electronic devices.

2. I mean here the following: first, that the basic key of "seriously doing trading" can be and is rekeyed in the very act of trading. This rekeying is critical with respect to the activity of trading itself. When, for instance, rituals of joint observation, revelations of software codes, or live demonstrations of trading strategies are organized, particular types of social relationships are created. These, in turn, support specific trading activities. Not only that: the basic key of "seriously doing trading" can be subjected to fabrications too: that is, to intentionally managed displays of activity supporting specific claims made by the main character who manages the display in question. Thus, in addition to rekeyings of the "serious mode of trading," we need to pay attention to fabrications of this mode as well.

3. See also Philadelphia Financial Management 2011, 7–8; White 2015; Maitra 2014; O'Hara 2015, 260–261, and *Conflicts of Interest, Investor Loss of Confidence, and High Speed Trading in U.S. Stock Markets: Hearing before the Subcommittee on Homeland Security and Governmental Affairs*, 113th Cong., 2nd sess. (2014).

4. Even institutional traders will not trade large orders, to avoid signaling their intentions to other market actors.

5. An example in this sense is provided by the forex retail brokerage crisis of

January 2015, when the unexpected decision of the Swiss National Bank to abandon upper limits in the exchange rate of the Swiss Franc to the Euro left retail brokers exposed to heavy losses of their clients.

6. A board is a window of securities that traders will monitor during the day. Several windows can be assembled on a trading interface, and traders need to familiarize themselves with the trading interfaces built up by their electronic brokers. As I had initially started with the spread betting interface of a UK broker, when I started using the interface of a US broker, I had to familiarize myself again with its assemblage of boxes and commands, even though the two interfaces contained similar data. The visual arrangement of data on the interface plays a significant role with respect to how traders react to it, a fact software developers are aware of.

7. The notion of microworld is used by Yuval Yonay and Daniel Breslau (Breslau and Yonay 1999; Yonay and Breslau 2006) to characterize formal economic models, which usually include simplified, sketchy, yet standardized objects: for instance, there are only two actors, or only one commodity in a formal economic model. In some models, time plays a restricted role, or none whatsoever, and the sole purpose of the actors in the model is to exchange with each other. The actors are standardized: they have no lives, only preferences; no past, only utilities. Analogously, an on-screen trading board can be seen as a microworld assembled by traders: there are only a few objects there (yet all standardized), and the sole purpose of their being there is to be traded.

8. A pip is a one-unit change in the last digit of a currency's price (as expressed in a different currency). Making pips, in the vocabulary of currency traders, is making profits on transactions.

9. There are also actions "for the screen," which more often than not are undertaken in preparation for actions with the screen. Actions "for the screen" can be the construction of a trading robot, or of a quantitative model, or of a strategy.

10. Traders usually liquidate their portfolios when they go on holidays and are without an Internet connection.

11. It is not only beginners or ethnographers-cum-apprentice-traders who have this problem. The preservation of capital and the ability to trade depend upon this constraint—staying within margin. Traders are all aware of this. A sign of such awareness is that they become active when regulators threaten to lower leveraging (as the CFTC, the US Commodities and Futures Trading Commission, did in February 2010). Since leverage regulations affect the size of the margin deposit, a lower leverage ratio increases margin requirements and hence the ability to trade.

12. The trading screen offers an array of tools for producing such accounts, the most important of which are the "news" and the "analysts." Both are just a click away, and when a trader does indeed click "news," for instance, a table of

one-liner statements appears. Here's an excerpt from the day when I was assembling my trading boards (9:39 a.m., September 18, 2009): "Treasuries. Bonds ease as issuance concerns fill data void." Clicking on the one liner made a more detailed story pop up, about how $112 billion of Treasury bonds would be coming on the market the week after and how, in spite of solid demand, "traders are worried." It had the name, phone number and e-mail address of its author at a global news agency. In theory, I could have verified it at any given time or I could have called the author to ask for details, causes, or the reason why traders should be worried if demand was solid. There was no time for this, though. It took about two minutes to read that piece of news, and a lot can happen in two minutes. From what I had observed with other traders, news headlines are checked regularly during the day. News stories are read when there isn't much going on. Analysts' statements are somewhat different, in the sense that an explicit judgment is made on a particular entity, as in these cases from the same day: "Analyst James Neale upgraded Chevron," or "Piper Jaffray's Nicole Miller Regan said a trend of moderate improvement in Starbucks . . ." It goes without saying that both analysts could, in principle, be reached via phone or e-mail. Few retail traders, if any, would contact them. Many traders—and in currency markets, all of them—ignore this kind of analysis. Reading it uses up a few minutes of trading time, and during these few minutes, a lot can happen on the screen. At best, analysts' comments can be read when nothing is going on. Yet they are there, only a click away.

Chapter Five

1. An "algo" is a piece of software programmed to detect particular patterns in price variations or discrepancies in these variations or to execute particular transactions. Once the software is uploaded, it will automatically alert the trader to the said patterns or will execute transactions as specified. Algos do not work completely unsupervised; traders who build algos consider that the algos can "misbehave" (i.e., not always work according to instructions). Ideally, the use of algos should remain undetected by other traders, since detection can lead to successfully guessing the working principles behind the algo. An essential aspect is the code, that is, the way in which the trading robot has been programmed. Traders spend a good deal of time observing the market and trying to detect algorithms that are at work.

2. A trading algorithm can be tested on historical market data, on simulated market data, or on real market data. There are issues arising in all types of tests, and algo builders cannot be sure that if their machine has performed well in tests with historical market data, it will perform well with real market data too.

Chapter Six

1. The game-theoretical notion of strategy, which is dominant in microeconomic theory, sees this as "a choice of an action at any information set assigned to the actor" (Gintis 2009, 31). At a minimum, this information set contains a definition of the actor's situation at a given action moment (or node). Situational definitions are discrete—that is, there is no ambiguity or lack of clarity about this. At any given time, actors playing a game should be able to define unambiguously the situation they are in, and keep a memory of these definitions. This is the minimum for a game strategy. It should be noticed here, however, that not all theories of market equilibrium imply a notion of strategy as a well laid plan. For Leon Walras, for instance, market actors act in a step-by-step process of situation-bound tinkering. With the preeminence of game theory, however, the notion of strategy finds a firm place in the modeling of market actors (see also Julien and Tricou 2005). In economic sociology, the notion of calculative agent, and its correlate, calculative devices (see, for instance, Callon and Muniesa 2005), come perhaps closest to the notion of strategy as we encounter it in microeconomic theory. Generally speaking, any sociological concept of economic action and agency has to deal, sooner or later, with the notion of strategy.

2. Traders are not the only ones looking for rules and strategies. Natasha Dow Schuell (2012, 208) shows that machine gamblers, too, are very preoccupied with finding rules and strategies. This is perhaps unexpected from a domain where randomness of outcomes seems to be built into the technological infrastructure of the activity at stake.

3. These limits can be too low, if the trader is going long, or too high, if the trader is going short.

4. While it can be argued that the strategies of fund managers and of execution traders differ from each other, how a trade is executed is crucial for any fund manager.

5. The community's online platform uses standardized profit and performance metrics, which in principle would make a comparison of traders and their strategies possible. In practice, however, this is not very easy, and the difficulties of comparing different strategies and performances are acknowledged by traders. The performance data used by all traders who chose to disclose were given by annualized return and a proprietary risk metric. Combined together, they formed the trader authority index.

6. Becoming a follower meant joining the respective trader's group of "friends" and being able to observe thus the leader's transactions in real time and to exchange messages exclusive to the group. I could observe that during the first three or four days after the leadership program became operational, the numbers of friends who were following the first-placed traders tripled. More important, though, was the project of allowing traders to imitate in real time the

leaders' transactions; ultimately the goal was to see whether leaders would be entrusted by followers with funds, acting as fund managers under the observation of the community. In this respect, strategy emerges not only as a tool of social rankings within the trading community, but also as an instrument of social control: successful traders, or leaders, are under the scrutiny of the community.

7. For expression games in professional trading, see Pitluck 2016; for expression games in chess, see Fine 2015, 70. In online poker, players attempt to tightly control their expression games and not let opponents infer their hand from behavioral cues, while at the same time keeping statistics on the behavioral features of said opponents (Dow Schuell 2015, 52, 60).

8. Existing regulations allow forex traders to use a leverage of up to 1:50 in the United States. Outside the United States, leveraging can go up to 1:400. This opens the possibility of considerable profits, but also of disastrous losses. Traders will therefore seldom exploit leverage to the full.

9. Generally a signal is understood by traders as a summons for action. The fact that trading actions need to be summoned (Goffman 1978, 1981) indicates that they cannot be conducted without a web of social relationships, a web that is built in the "strategies" of the market. A signal can mean a commercial subscription service sending alerts to one's computer about when to buy or sell specific securities or currency pairs. Such a signal will show up as a short message such as "buy GBP/USD @1.5312!" It can also mean a set of indications or marks that summon traders into action, marks that are built into the trading interface (they will appear on the trading chart) and which are private to the trader. In this latter case, signals are closely guarded and will not be publicly revealed or sold. They can, however, become objects of revelation in the relationship between a mentor and his students, or tokens of trust.

10. The session (which can take up to two hours, of which 60 to 90 minutes will be live trading) will have a moderator and the performer—that is, the master trader—who do not necessarily sit in the same trading room. While the moderator will manage the audience and will have the exclusive right to talk to the trader, the audience will have the right to ask questions in an instant messaging system, which will then be voiced to the performer.

11. In forex markets, for instance, one of the biggest events is the announcement of the nonfarm payroll data at the end of each month by the Federal Reserve Bank of New York. End-of-quarter earnings announcements by large corporations and press conferences (of the European Central Bank, for instance) are other significant events that are followed by traders and when larger market movements are expected.

12. The word *extraordinary* is not an exaggeration here. As this trader reported, the antithesis of such personal bonds is provided by decompiling a strategy offered in an open forum and then selling it. Since property rights are codified only for a small part of what is going on in online financial markets, there

are dangers lurking behind communication, to use here Erving Goffman's (1971) words. This may explain why many of the traders I observed explicitly avoid open forums and prefer to communicate within closed communities.

While Max Weber ([1920] 1988, 544) argues that "the ethics of fraternity" severely limit market transactions (understood as completely individualized actions), in cases such as this one, charismatic relationships anchor groups that participate in transactions. As soon as we move away from a view of market transactions as involving individuals and as a mechanism of individualization, the tension between charisma and markets dissolves.

13. I want to stress here that the members of this group, like other groups in online markets, are dispersed around the globe and meet mostly via Skype. Sometimes, but not very often, they talk. Most of the time, conversations are conducted via instant messaging. In the group in question, master and pupil talked, while instant-messaging to other members of the group.

In the case presented here, the master was considerably older than the pupil. The master had a PhD from a top US university, while the pupil was studying at a top UK university.

14. Processing tweets means here transforming the sequential structure of the messages into a table format, which will allow traders to evaluate better the "sentiment" of other traders. Some traders tweet their trades in near-real time and have many followers. The temporal structure of the messages, however, must be visualized in order to evaluate better what others are doing. In other words, the visualization of trading messages must be coordinated with that of trading sequences on the charts.

15. This was more or less explicitly formulated in interviews and subsequent conversations.

16. Among professional traders, autonomy can also be displayed in elaborate rituals such as after-work socialization, where traders regularly take turns picking up large tabs for the entire party. As one trader explained to me, and several others have confirmed (both in the United Kingdom and the United States), one has to show that one is able to pay a bill of several thousand pounds (or dollars, for that matter) at a bar. Otherwise one will get a reputation of being unsuccessful. Success and self-worth are thus displayed not only with luxury objects, but also in ritual actions that remind one of potlatch ceremonies.

Chapter Seven

1. As Jane Guyer (2004, 78) has noted, money can be converted into many things, including spiritual power. Seen from this perspective, and in a way not dissimilar to that of the Igbo of Ghana, traders convert, or rekey, their activities in front of the screen into projects of "good life."

References

Abolafia, Mitchel. 1996. *Making Markets: Opportunism and Restraint on Wall Street*. Cambridge, MA: Harvard University Press.

Abreu, Margarida, and Victor Mendes. 2012. "Information, Overconfidence and Trading: Do the Sources of Information Matter?" *Journal of Economic Psychology* 33:868–881.

Adam, Marc T. P., Matthias Gamer, Jan Kraemer, and Christof Weinhardt. 2011. "Measuring Emotions in Electronic Markets." Paper presented at the Thirty-Second International Conference on Information Systems, Shanghai.

Akerloff, George. 1970. "The Market for 'Lemons': Quality Uncertainty and the Market Mechanism." *Quarterly Journal of Economics* 84 (3): 488–500.

Armstrong, Elizabeth A., and Laura T. Hamilton. 2013. *Paying for the Party: How College Maintains Inequality*. Cambridge, MA: Harvard University Press.

Attali, Jacques. 1985. *Noise: The Political Economy of Music*. Manchester, UK: Manchester University Press.

Barber, Brad M., and Terrance Odean. 2000. "Trading Is Hazardous to Your Wealth: The Common Stock Investment Performance of Individual Investors." *Journal of Finance* 55 (2): 773–806.

———. 2004. "Are Individual Investors Tax Savvy? Evidence from Retail and Discount Brokerage Accounts." *Journal of Public Economics* 88 (1): 419–442.

———. 2008. "All That Glitters: The Effect of Attention and News on the Buying Behavior of Individual and Institutional Investors." *Review of Financial Studies* 21 (2): 785–818.

Beneito-Montagut, Roser. 2011. "Ethnography Goes Online: Towards a User-Centred Methodology to Research Interpersonal Communication on the Internet." *Qualitative Research* 11 (6): 716–735.

Benzecry, Claudio. 2011. *The Opera Fanatic: Ethnography of an Obsession*. Chicago: University of Chicago Press.

Bernstein, Peter. 1998. *Against the Gods: The Remarkable Story of Risk*. New York: Wiley.

Beunza, Daniel, and David Stark. 2004. "How to Recognise Opportunities: Heterarchical Search in a Trading Room." In *The Sociology of Financial Markets*, edited by K. Knorr Cetina and A. Preda, 84–101. Oxford: Oxford University Press.

———. 2012. "Seeing through the Eyes of Others: Dissonance within and across Trading Rooms." In Knorr Cetina and Preda 2012, 203–220.

Biggart, Nicole Woolsey. 1989. *Charismatic Capitalism: Direct Selling Organizations in America*. Chicago: University of Chicago Press.

Black, Fischer. 1986. "Noise." *Journal of Finance* 41 (3): 529–543.

Bloomfield, Robert, Maureen O'Hara, and Gideon Saar. 2009. "How Noise Trading Affects Markets: An Experimental Analysis." *Review of Financial Studies* 22 (6): 2275–2302.

Bloomfield, Robert J., William B. Taylor, and Flora Zhou. 2009. "Momentum, Reversal, and Uninformed Traders in Laboratory Markets." *Journal of Finance* 64 (6): 2535–2558.

Boellstorff, Tom. 2009. *Coming of Age in Second Life: An Anthropologist Explores the Virtually Human*. Princeton, NJ: Princeton University Press.

Boellstorff, Tom, Bonnie Nardi, Celia Pearce, and T. L. Taylor, eds. 2012. *Ethnography and Virtual Worlds: A Handbook of Method*. Princeton, NJ: Princeton University Press.

Breslau, Daniel, and Yuval Yonay. 1999. "Beyond Metaphor: Mathematical Models in Economics as Empirical Research." *Science in Context* 12 (2): 317–332.

Bröckling, Ulrich. 2007. *Das unternehmerische Selbst* [The entrepreneurial self]. Frankfurt: Suhrkamp.

"Brokers and Others Offer Services to Investors Who Own Computers." 1983. *Wall Street Computer Review* (November–December) 58–59.

Burns, Jennifer. 2009. *Goddess of the Market: Ayn Rand and the American Right*. Oxford: Oxford University Press.

Burt, Ronald. 2010. *Neighbor Networks: Competitive Advantage Local and Personal*. Oxford: Oxford University Press.

Callon, Michel, and Fabian Muniesa. 2005. "Economic Markets as Calculative Collective Devices." *Organization Studies* 26 (8): 1229–1250.

Castronova, Edward. 2005. *Synthetic Worlds: The Business and Culture of Online Games*. Chicago: University of Chicago Press.

Chang, Tom, David H. Solomon, and Mark M. Westerfield. 2016. "Looking for Someone to Blame: Delegation, Cognitive Dissonance, and the Disposition Effect." *Journal of Finance* 71 (1): 267–302.

Chen, Gongmeng, Kenneth A. Kim, John R. Nofsinger, and Oliver M. Rui. 2007. "Trading Performance, Disposition Effect, Overconfidence, Representativeness Bias, and Experience of Emerging Markets Investors." *Journal of Behavioral Decision Making* 20 (4): 425–451.

Clark, Colin, and Trevor Pinch. 1995. *The Hard Sell: The Language and Lessons of Streetwise Marketing*. New York: HarperCollins.

Clifford, James. 1983. "On Ethnographic Authority." *Representations* 1 (2): 118–146.

Clifford, James, and George E. Marcus, eds. 1986. *Writing Culture: The Poetics and Politics of Ethnography*. Berkeley: University of California Press.

Collins, Harry. 2004. *Gravity's Shadow: The Search for Gravitational Waves*. Chicago: University of Chicago Press.

Collins, Randall. 2004. *Interaction Ritual Chains*. Princeton, NJ: Princeton University Press.

Commodities and Futures Trading Commission (CFTC). 2010. "Final Retail Foreign Exchange Rules." 75 Fed. Reg. 55409, September 10.

Copeland, Thomas E. 1976. "A Model of Asset Trading under the Assumption of Sequential Information Arrival." *Journal of Finance* 31 (4): 1149–1168.

Cottingham, Marci. 2014. "Recruiting Men, Constructing Manhood: How Health Care Organizations Mobilize Masculinities as a Nursing Recruitment Strategy." *Gender and Society* 28 (1): 133–156.

DeLong, J. Bradford, Andrei Shleifer, Lawrence H. Summers, and Robert J. Waldmann. 1989. "The Size and Incidence of the Losses from Noise Trading." *Journal of Finance* 44 (3): 681–696.

Dow Schuell, Natasha. 2012. *Addiction by Design: Machine Gambling in Las Vegas*. Princeton, NJ: Princeton University Press.

———. 2015. "The Gaming of Chance: Online Poker Software and the Potentialization of Uncertainty." In *Modes of Uncertainty: Anthropological Cases*, edited by L. Samimian-Daash and P. Rabinow, 46–68. Chicago: University of Chicago Press.

Fabian, Ann. 1990. *Card Sharps, Dream Books, and Bucket Shops: Gambling in 19th Century America*. Ithaca, NY: Cornell University Press.

Falzon, Marc Anthony, ed. 2009. *Multi Sited Ethnography: Theory, Praxis and Locality in Contemporary Research*. Farnham, UK: Ashgate.

Federal Reserve System (FRS). 2012. "Changes in US Family Finances from 2007 to 2010: Evidence from the Survey of Consumer Finances." *Federal Reserve Bulletin* 98 (2): 1–80.

Fine, Gary Alan. 2007. *Authors of the Storm: Meteorologists and the Culture of Prediction*. Chicago: University of Chicago Press.

———. 2012. *Tiny Publics: A Theory of Group Action and Culture*. New York: Russell Sage Foundation.

———. 2015. *Players and Pawns: How Chess Builds Community and Culture*. Chicago: University of Chicago Press.

Fine, Gary Alan, and Brooke Harrington. 2004. "Tiny Publics: Small Groups and Civil Society." *Sociological Theory* 22: 341–356.

Fink, Jason, Kristin E. Fink, and James P. Weston. 2006. "Competition on the Nasdaq and the Growth of Electronic Communication Networks." *Journal of Banking and Finance* 30: 2537–2559.

Fink, Matthew. 2008. *The Rise of Mutual Funds: An Insider's View.* Oxford: Oxford University Press.

Fishe, Raymond P. H., and Aaron D. Smith. 2012. "Identifying Informed Traders in Futures Markets." *Journal of Financial Markets* 15 (3): 329–359.

Fourcade, Marion, and Kieran Healy. 2007. "Moral Views of Market Society." *Annual Review of Sociology* 33: 285–311.

Froot, Kenneth A., David S. Scharfstein, and Jeremy C. Stein. 1992. "Herd on the Street: Information Inefficiencies in a Market with Short Term Speculation." *Journal of Finance* 47 (4): 1461–1484.

Füllbrunn, Sascha, Holger Rau, and Utz Weitzel. 2013. "Do Ambiguity Effects Survive in Experimental Asset Markets?" Social Science Research Network, http://ssrn.com/abstract=2227335.

Fuzhou, Gong, and Hong Liu. 2012. "Public Disclosure and Imperfect Competition." *International Review of Economics and Finance* 24 (1): 200–223.

Garfinkel, Harold. 1967. *Studies in Ethnomethodology.* Englewood Cliffs, NJ: Prentice-Hall.

———. 2008. *Toward a Sociological Theory of Information.* Edited and with an introduction by Ann Warfield Rawls. Boulder, CO: Paradigm.

Geertz, Clifford. 1977. *The Interpretation of Cultures.* New York: Basic Books.

———. 1978. "The Bazaar Economy: Information and Search in Peasant Marketing." *American Economic Review* 68 (2): 28–32.

Geisst, Charles. 1997. *Wall Street: A History.* Oxford: Oxford University Press.

Gemayel, Roland. 2016. "Social Trading: An Analysis of Herding Behavior, the Disposition Effect, and Informed Trading among Traders on Social Trading Platforms." PhD diss., King's College London.

Gibson, David R. 2005. "Taking Turns and Talking Ties: Network Structure and Conversational Sequences." *American Journal of Sociology* 110 (6): 1561–1597

Gintis, Herbert. 2009. *The Bounds of Reason: Game Theory and the Unification of the Behavioral Sciences.* Princeton, NJ: Princeton University Press.

Goffman, Erving. 1966. *Behaviour in Public Places.* New York: Free Press.

———. 1967. *The Interaction Ritual: Essays on Face-to-Face Behavior.* New York: Pantheon.

———. 1969. *Strategic Interaction.* Philadelphia: University of Pennsylvania Press.

———. 1971. *Relations in Public: Microstudies of the Public Order.* Harmondsworth, UK: Penguin.

———. 1974. *Frame Analysis: An Essay on the Organization of Experience*. New York: Harper.

———. 1978. "Response Cries." *Language* 54 (4): 787–815.

———. 1981. *Forms of Talk*. Philadelphia: University of Pennsylvania Press.

———. 1983. "The Interaction Order." *American Sociological Review* 48 (1): 1–17.

Golovchenko, Victor. 2015. "Alpari UK First Major Casualty to CHF, LCG Group Facing up to $2.5 Million Losses." Forexmagnates.com, January 16.

Granovetter, Mark. 1983. "The Strength of Weak Ties: A Network Theory Revisited." *Sociological Theory* 1:201–233.

———. 1985. "Economic Action and Social Structure: The Problem of Embeddedness." *American Journal of Sociology* 91 (3): 481–510.

Greene, Jason, and Scott Smart. 1999. "Liquidity Provision and Noise Trading: Evidence from the 'Investment Dartboard' Column." *Journal of Finance* 54 (5): 1885–1898.

Greeno, James G. 1994. "Gibson's Affordances." *Psychological Review* 101 (2): 336–342.

Grossman, Sanford. 1976. "On the Efficiency of Competitive Stock Markets Where Trades Have Diverse Information." *Journal of Finance* 31 (2): 573–585.

Gulbrandsen, Ib. T., and Sine N. Just. 2011. "The Collaborative Paradigm: Towards an Invitational and Participatory Concept of Online Communication." *Media, Culture & Society* 33 (7): 1095–1108.

Guyer, Jane. 2004. *Marginal Gains: Monetary Transactions in Atlantic Africa*. Chicago: University of Chicago Press.

Harrington, Brooke. 2008. *Pop Finance: Investment Clubs and Stock Market Populism*. Princeton, NJ: Princeton University Press.

———, ed. 2009. *Deception: From Ancient Empires to Internet Dating*. Palo Alto, CA: Stanford University Press.

Hayley, Simon, and Ian W. Marsh. 2015. "Do Retail FX Traders Learn?" Working paper #7, Cass Business School. Available at http://ssrn.com/abstract= 2659293.

Heath, Christian. 2012 *The Dynamics of Auction: Social Interaction and the Sales of Fine Art and Antiques*. Cambridge: Cambridge University Press.

Heath, Christian, Paul Luff, and Marina Jirotka. 1994. "Unpacking Collaboration: The Interactional Organisation of Trading in a City Dealing Room." *Computer Supported Cooperative Work* 3 (2): 147–165.

Heath, Christian, Marcus Sanchez Svensson, Jon Hindmarsh, Paul Luff, and Dirk vom Lehn. 2002. "Configuring Awareness." *Computer Supported Cooperative Work* 11 (3): 317–347.

Hernandez, Javier. 2014. "Financial Services and Social Structures: A Comparative Analysis." PhD diss., University of Edinburgh.

Hindmarsh, Jon. 2010. "Peripherality, Participation, and Communities of Practice: Examining the Patient in Dental Training." In *Organisation, Interaction and Practice*, edited by Nick Llewellyn and Jon Hindmarsh, 218–240. Cambridge: Cambridge University Press.

Ho, Karen. 2009. *Liquidated: An Ethnography of Wall Street*. Durham, NC: Duke University Press.

Hochfelder, David. 2006. "'Where the Common People Could Speculate': The Ticker, Bucket Shops, and the Origins of Popular Participation in Financial Markets, 1880–1920." *Journal of American History* 93: 335–358.

Hochschild, Arlie. 1997. *The Time Bind: When Home Becomes Work and Work Becomes Home*. New York: Metropolitan/Holt.

Hutchby, Ian. 2001. "Technologies, Texts and Affordances." *Sociology* 35 (2): 441–456.

———. 2003. "Affordances and the Analysis of Technologically Mediated Interaction." *Sociology* 37 (3): 581–589.

Hutchins, Edwin. 1995. *Cognition in the Wild*. Cambridge, MA: MIT Press.

"The Island ECN, Inc. History." 2015. Funding Universe, www.fundinguniverse .com/company-histories/the-island-ecn-inc-history/.

Julien, Ludovic A., and Farbrice Tricou. 2005. "Specialized Oligopolies in a Pure Exchange Economy: The Symmetric Cournot-Walras Equilibrium." *Research in Economics* 59 (3): 280–292.

Kalay, Avner, and Avi Wohl. 2009. "Detecting Liquidity Traders." *Journal of Finance and Quantitative Analysis.* 44 (1): 29–54.

Kellard, Neil, Yuval Millo, Jan Simon, and Ofer Engel. 2016. "Close Communication: Hedge Funds, Brokers, and the Emergence of Herding." *British Journal of Management.* doi:10.1111/1467-8551.12158.

Khurana, Rakesh. 2007. *From Higher Aims to Hired Hands: The Social Transformation of American Business Schools and the Unfulfilled Promise of Management as a Profession*. Princeton, NJ: Princeton University Press.

King, M. R., C. Osler, and R. Dagfinn. 2011. "Foreign Exchange Market Structure, Players and Evolution." Norges Bank Research Department, working paper. Available at ideas.repec.org (accessed March 9, 2016).

Knorr Cetina, Karin. 2003. "From Pipes to Scopes: The Flow Architecture of Financial Markets." *Distinktion* 7: 7–30.

———. 2004. "How Are Global Markets Global? The Architecture of a Flow World." In *The Sociology of Financial Markets*, edited by Karin Knorr Cetina and Alex Preda, 38–61. Oxford: Oxford University Press.

———. 2009. "The Synthetic Interaction: Interactionism for a Global World." *Symbolic Interaction* 32 (1): 61–87.

Knorr Cetina, Karin, and Urs Bruegger. 2002. "Global Microstructures: The

Virtual Societies of Financial Markets." *American Journal of Sociology* 107 (4): 905–950.

Knorr Cetina, Karin, and Alex Preda. 2007. "The Temporalization of Markets: From Network to Flow." *Theory, Culture & Society* 24 (7–8): 116–138.

———. 2012. *The Oxford Handbook of the Sociology of Finance.* Oxford: Oxford University Press.

Kozinets, Robert V. 2009. *Netnography: Doing Ethnographic Research Online.* Thousand Oaks, CA: Sage.

Krippner, Greta. 2005. "The Financialization of the American Economy." *Socio-Economic Review* 3 (2): 173–208.

Krippner, Greta, and Anthony Alvarez. 2007. "Embeddedness and the Intellectual Projects of Economic Sociology." *Annual Review of Sociology* 33: 219–240.

Krippner, Greta, Mark Granovetter, Fred Block, Nicole Biggart, Tom Beamish, Youtien Hsing, Gillian Hart, Giovanni Arrighi, Margie Mendel, John Hall, Michael Burawoy, Steve Vogel, and Sean O'Riain. 2004. "Polanyi Symposium: A Conversation on Embeddedness." *Socio-Economic Review* 2: 109–135.

Kynaston, David. 2012. *City of London: The History.* London: Random House.

Laidlaw, James. 2014. *The Subject of Virtue: An Anthropology of Ethics and Freedom.* Cambridge: Cambridge University Press.

Lapavitsas, Costas. 2011. "Theorizing Financialization." *Work, Employment and Society* 25 (4): 611–626.

Latour, Bruno. 1988. *The Pasteurization of France.* Cambridge, MA: Harvard University Press.

Lépinay, Vincent. 2011. *Codes of Finance: Engineering Derivatives in a French Bank.* Princeton, NJ: Princeton University Press.

Linnainmaa, Juhani T. 2003. "The Anatomy of Day Traders." SSRN working paper 472182. Available at http://ssrn.com/abstract=472182 (accessed March 10, 2016).

Lo, Andrew, and Dmitry V. Repin. 2002. "The Psychophysiology of Real Time Financial Risk Processing." *Journal of Cognitive Neuroscience* 14 (3): 323–339.

Lo, Andrew W., Dmitry V. Repin, and Brett N. Steenbarger. 2005. "Fear and Greed in Financial Markets: A Clinical Study of Day Traders." *Cognitive Neuroscientific Foundations of Behavior* 95 (2): 352–359.

Louis, J. C. 1999. "Advances in ECNs." *Wall Street and Technology*, second quarter, 16–17.

Luff, Paul, Christian Heath, Hideaki Kuzuoka, Jon Hindmarsh, Keichi Yamazaki, and Shinye Oyama. 2003. "Fractured Ecologies: Creating Environments for Collaboration." *Journal of Human Computer Interaction* 18 (1): 51–84.

Lynch, Michael. 2014. "Representation in Formation." In *Representation in Sci-*

entific Practice Revisited, edited by Catelijne Coopmans, Janet Vertesi, Michael Lynch, and Steve Woolgar, 323–328. Cambridge, MA: MIT Press.

MacKenzie, Donald. 2011. "The Credit Crisis as a Problem in the Sociology of Knowledge." *American Journal of Sociology* 116 (6): 1778–1841.

———. 2017. "How Algorithms Interact: Goffman's 'Interaction Order' in Automated Trading." *Theory, Culture & Society*, forthcoming.

MacKenzie, Donald, and Yuval Millo. 2003. "Constructing a Market, Performing Theory: The Historical Sociology of a Financial Derivatives Exchange." *American Journal of Sociology* 109 (1): 107–145.

MacKenzie, Donald, and Juan Pablo Pardo-Guerra. 2014. "Insurgent Capitalism: Island, Bricolage and the Re-making of Finance." *Economy and Society* 43 (2): 153–182.

Maitra, Bapi. 2014. "State of the Retail Foreign Exchange Market." European Central Bank, www.ecb.europa.eu/paym/groups/pdf/fxcg/2301/retail_FX.pdf.

Marcus, George E. 1980. "Rhetoric and the Ethnographic Genre in Anthropological Research." *Current Anthropology* 21:507–510.

———. 1995. "Ethnography in/of the World System: The Emergence of Multi-sited Ethnography." *Annual Review of Anthropology* 24:95–117.

Marcus, George E., and Dick Cushman. 1982. "Ethnographies as Texts." *Annual Review of Anthropology* 11:26–59.

Martin, Randy. 2002. *Financialization of Daily Life*. Philadelphia: Temple University Press.

Mattern, Shannon, and Barry Salmon. 2008. "Sound Studies: Framing Noise." *Music, Sound, and the Moving Image* 2 (2): 139–144.

McCloskey, Deirdre. 2006. *The Bourgeois Virtues: Ethics for an Age of Commerce*. Chicago: University of Chicago Press.

McCormick, Lisa. 2014. "Turning In or Turning Off: Performing Emotion and Building Cosmopolitan Solidarity in International Music Competitions." *Ethnic and Racial Studies* 37 (12): 2261–2280.

McEachern, Christina. 1999. "Will Day Trading Face Scrutiny?" *Wall Street and Technology* 17 (10): 74.

Menchik, Daniel A., and Xiaoli Tian. 2008. "Putting Social Context into Text: The Semiotics of E-mail Interaction." *American Journal of Sociology* 114 (2): 332–370.

Merli, Maxime, and Tristan Roger. 2013. "What Drives the Herding Behavior of Individual Investors?" *Finance* 34 (3): 67–104.

Michie, Ranald. 1999. *The London Stock Exchange: A History*. Oxford: Oxford University Press.

Mintel. 2008. *Sharedealing and Online Investing—UK, Finance Intelligence*. London: Mintel International Group.

Mirowski, Philip, ed. 1994. *Natural Images in Economic Thought: "Markets Red in Tooth and Claw."* Cambridge: Cambridge University Press.

Morgan, Mary. 1993. "Competing Notions of 'Competition' in Late Nineteenth-Century American Economics." *History of Political Economy* 25 (4): 563–604.

National Association of Securities Dealers (NASD). 2001. "Day Trading Margin." NASD Notice to Members 01-26, April.

Neumann, Sascha, Stephan Paul, and Philipp Doering. 2014. "A Primer in Social Trading: Remuneration Schemes, Trading Strategies, and Return Characteristics." SSRN paper 2291421. Available at http://ssrn.com/abstract=2291421 (accessed March 10, 2016).

Nippert-Eng, Christena. 1996. *Home and Work: Negotiating Boundaries through Everyday Life.* Chicago: University of Chicago Press.

Nishide, Katsumara. 2009. "Insider Trading with Correlation between Liquidity Trading and a Public Signal." *Quantitative Finance* 9 (3): 297–304.

Nolte, Ingmar, and Sandra Nolte. 2012. "How Do Individual Investors Trade?" *European Journal of Finance* 18 (10): 921–947.

Nolte, Ingmar, and Valeri Voev. 2011. "Trading Dynamics in the Foreign Exchange Market: A Latent Factor Panel Intensity Approach." *Journal of Financial Econometrics* 4 (9): 685–716.

Norman, David James. 2009. *CFDs: The Definitive Guide to Contracts for Difference.* Petersfield, UK: Harriman House Limited.

Odean, Terrance. 1998a. "Are Investors Reluctant to Realize Their Losses?" *Journal of Finance* 53 (5): 1775–1798.

———. 1998b. "Volume, Volatility, Price, and Profit When All Traders Are above Average." *Journal of Finance* 53 (6): 1887–1934.

———. 1999. "Do Investors Trade Too Much?" *American Economic Review* 89:1279–1298.

O'Hara, Maureen. 2015. "High Frequency Market Microstructure." *Journal of Financial Economics* 16:257–270.

"OptionsXpress (R) Introduces Real Time Portfolio Margining." 2007. *Business Wire*, June 5.

Orr, Julian E. 1996. *Talking about Machines: An Ethnography of a Modern Job.* Ithaca, NY: Cornell University Press.

Pan, Wei, Yaniv Altshuler, and Alex Pentland. 2012. "Decoding Social Influence and the Wisdom of the Crowd in Financial Trading Networks." In *2012 International Conference on Privacy, Security, Risk and Trust and 2012 International Conference on Social Computing*, 203–209. Institute of Electrical and Electronics Engineers, 2012, http://dx.doi.org/10.1109/SocialCom-PASSAT.2012.133.

Pardo-Guerra, Juan Pablo. 2010. "Creating Flows of Interpersonal Bits: The

Automation of the London Stock Exchange, c. 1955–90." *Economy and Society* 39 (1): 84–109.

———. 2012. "Financial Automation, Past, Present, and Future." In Knorr Cetina and Preda 2012, 567–586.

———. n.d. "Orders of Finance: Infrastructures, Engineers, and the Automation of Global Finance." Cambridge, MA: MIT Press.

Paz, Javier. 2011. *Retail FX: Market Overview: An ECB Briefing.* Aite Group. Available at ecb.europa.eu (accessed March 9, 2016).

Peres, Joel. 2010. "Product Market Competition, Insider Trading, and Stock Market Efficiency." *Journal of Finance* 65 (1): 1–43.

Philadelphia Financial Management. 2011. Letter to the Securities and Exchange Commission, August 2, Release No. 34-64874, File Number: S7-30-11.

Pinch, Trevor, and Karin Bijsterveld. 2004. "Sound Studies: New Technologies and Music." *Social Studies of Science* 34 (5): 635–648.

Pitluck, Aaron Z. 2016. "Performing Anonymity: Investors, Brokers, and the Malleability of Material Identity Information in Financial Markets." *Research in Economic Anthropology* 36.

Podolny, Joel. 2001. "Networks as the Pipes and Prisms of the Market." *American Journal of Sociology* 107 (1): 33–60.

Pollner, Melvin. 1987. *Mundane Reason: Reality in Everyday and Sociological Discourse.* Cambridge: Cambridge University Press.

"ProTrader Targets Buy Side: Touts ECN Connectivity and Cheaper Costs." 2001. *Wall Street and Technology* 19 (4): 60.

QIR3. 2013. "Quarterly Industry Report Forex Magnates 3rd Quarter 2013." London. Available at financemagnates.com.

Rivera, Lauren. 2011. "Ivies, Extracurriculars, and Exclusion: Elite Employers' Use of Extracurricular Credentials." *Research in Social Stratification and Mobility* 29 (1): 71–90.

———. 2012. "Hiring as Cultural Matching: The Case of Elite Professional Service Firms." *American Sociological Review* 77 (6): 999–1022.

———. 2015. *Pedigree: How Elite Students Get Elite Jobs.* Princeton, NJ: Princeton University Press.

Sade-Beck, Liav. 2004. "Internet Ethnography: Online and Offline." *International Journal of Qualitative Methods* 3 (2): 45–51.

Salvadori, Neri, and Rodolfo Signorino. 2013. "The Classical Notion of Competition Revisited." *History of Political Economy* 45 (1): 149–175.

Santoro, Michael. A. 2013. "Would Better Regulations Have Prevented the London Whale Trades?" *New Yorker*, August 21.

Schutz, Alfred, and Thomas Luckmann. 2003. *Strukturen der Lebenswelt* [Structures of the lifeworld]. Konstanz, Germany: UVK.

Securities and Exchange Commission (SEC). 2001. "Margin Rules for Day Trading." SEC, Washington, DC.

Shanghai Stock Exchange. 2014. *Factbook*. Shanghai: Shanghai Stock Exchange.

Shionoya, Yuichi. 1995. "The Ethics of Competition." *European Journal of Law and Economics* 2 (1): 5–19.

Sicherman, Nachum, George Lowenstein, Duane J. Seppi, and Stephen P. Utkus. 2016. "Financial Attention." *Review of Financial Studies* 29 (4): 863–897.

Simmel, Georg. 1992. *Soziologie*. Edited by Otthein Rammstedt. Frankfurt: Suhrkamp.

Spence, Michael. 1976. "Informational Aspects of Market Structure: An Introduction." *Quarterly Journal of Economics* 90 (4): 591–597.

Stinchcombe, Arthur. 2001. *When Formality Works: Authority and Abstraction in Law and Organizations*. Chicago: University of Chicago Press.

Stucke, Maurice E. 2013. "Is Competition Always Good?" *Journal of Antitrust Enforcement* 1 (1): 162–197.

Suchman, Lucy. 1987. *Plans and Situated Actions: The Problem of Human-Machine Communication*. Cambridge: Cambridge University Press.

Tan, Vaughn. 2015. "Using Negotiated Joining to Construct and Fill Open-Ended Roles in Elite Culinary Groups." *Administrative Science Quarterly* 60 (1): 103–132.

Tomasula, Dean. 1997. "Tighter Security Loosens the Constraints on Electronic Commerce." *Wall Street and Technology* 15 (2): 34–42.

Traflet, Janice M. 2013. *A Nation of Small Shareholders: Marketing Wall Street after World War II*. Baltimore: Johns Hopkins University Press.

Turner, Victor. 1964. "Betwixt and Between: The Liminal Period." In *Rites de Passage: The Proceedings of the American Ethnological Society: Symposium on New Approaches to the Study of Religion*, edited by June Helm, 4–20. Seattle: American Ethnological Society.

Useem, Michael. 1996. *Investor Capitalism: How Money Managers Are Rewriting the Rules of Corporate America*. New York: Basic Books.

Van Landingham, M. H. 1980. "The Day Trader: Some Additional Evidence." *Journal of Financial and Quantitative Analysis* 15 (2): 341–355.

Van Treeck, Til. 2009. "The Political Economy Debate on 'Financialization.' A Macroeconomic Perspective." *Review of International Political Economy* 16 (5): 907–944.

Vargha, Zsuzsanna. 2013. "Realizing Dreams, Providing Thrift: How Product Demonstrations Qualify Financial Objects and Subjects." In *Constructing Quality: The Classification of Goods in Markets*, edited by Jens Beckert and Christine Musselin, 31–57. Oxford: Oxford University Press.

Vickers, John. 1995. "Concepts of Competition." *Oxford Economic Papers* 47 (1): 1–23.

Vives, Xavier. 2008. *Information and Learning in Markets: The Impact of Market Microstructure*. Princeton, NJ: Princeton University Press.

Weber, Max. (1905) 2011. *The Protestant Ethic and the Spirit of Capitalism.* Translated by Steven Kahlberg. New York: Oxford University Press.

———. (1920) 1988. *Gesammelte Aufsaetze zur Religionssoziologie: I* [Collected writings on the sociology of religion: I]. Tuebingen: Mohr.

———. (1921) 1972. *Wirtschaft und Gesellschaft* [Economy and society]. Tübingen: Mohr.

Wells, Thomas O. 2000. "E-sign Law: Opportunities for Online Brokers." *Wall Street and Technology* 18 (9): 66–70.

Welser, Howard T., Eric Gleave, Danyel Fisher, and Marc Smith. 2007. "Visualizing the Signatures of Social Roles in Online Discussion Groups." *Journal of Social Structures* 8 (2), www.cmu.edu/joss/index.html.

Wenhong, Chen. 2013. "Internet Use, Online Communication, and Ties in Americans' Networks." *Social Science Computer Review* 31 (4): 404–423.

Werron, Tobias. 2015. "Why Do We Believe in Competition? A Historical-Sociological View of Competition as an Institutionalized Modern Imaginary." *Distinktion* 16 (2): 186–210.

White, Harrison. 1992. *Identity and Control: A Structural Theory of Social Action.* Princeton, NJ: Princeton University Press.

———. 2003. *Markets from Networks: Socioeconomic Models of Production.* Princeton, NJ: Princeton University Press.

White, Mary Jo. 2014. "Enhancing Our Equity Market Structure." Paper presented at the Sandler O'Neill & Partners, L.P. Global Exchange and Brokerage Conference, New York, June 5.

———. 2015. "Optimizing Our Equity Market Structure." Opening Remarks at the Inaugural Meeting of the Equity Market Structure Advisory Committee, US Securities and Exchange Commission, May 13.

Wilson, Samuel M., and Leighton C. Peterson. 2002. "The Anthropology of Online Communities." *Annual Review of Anthropology* 31: 449–467.

Yenkey, Christopher. 2015. "Mobilizing a Market: Ethnic Segmentation and Investor Recruitment into the Nairobi Securities Exchange." *Administrative Science Quarterly* 60 (4): 561–595.

Yonay, Yuval, and Daniel Breslau. 2006. "Marketing Models: The Culture of Mathematical Economics." *Sociological Forum* 21 (3): 345–386.

Zaloom, Caitlin. 2005. "The Discipline of Speculators." In *Global Assemblages: Technology, Politics, and Ethics as Anthropological Problems*, edited by Aihwa Ong and Stephen Collier, 253–269. New York: Blackwell.

———. 2006. *Out of the Pits: Traders and Technology from Chicago to London.* Chicago: University of Chicago Press.

———. 2012. "Traders and Market Morality." In Knorr Cetina and Preda 2012, 169–186.

Zamboglou, Demetrios. 2016. "Behavioral Clustering in an FX Trading Population." PhD diss., King's College London.

Zelizer, Viviana. 1994. *The Social Meaning of Money: Pin Money, Paychecks, Poor Relief and Other Currencies.* New York: Basic Books.

———. 2000. "The Purchase of Intimacy." *Law and Social Inquiry* 25 (3): 817–848.

———. 2010. "Moralizing Consumption." *Journal of Consumer Culture* 10: 287–291.

———. 2011. *Economic Lives: How Culture Shapes the Economy.* Princeton, NJ: Princeton University Press.

Index